ADMINISTRATIVE THEORIES AND POLITICS

By the same author

THE STATE AND THE FARMER
(with Herbert J. Storing)

CITIES IN FLOOD: THE PROBLEMS
OF URBAN GROWTH

METROPOLITAN PLANNING

ECONOCRATS AND THE POLICY PROCESS

ADMINISTRATIVE THEORIES AND POLITICS

*An Enquiry into the Structure
and Processes of Modern Government*

BY

PETER SELF

*Professor of Public Administration
in the University of London*

London
GEORGE ALLEN & UNWIN
Boston   Sydney

First published in 1972
Fourth impression 1975
Second edition 1977
Second impression 1979

GEORGE ALLEN & UNWIN LTD
40 Museum Street, London WC1A 1LU

© George Allen & Unwin (Publishers) Ltd 1972, 1977

ISBN 0 04 351053 1 Paperback

Printed in Great Britain by
Biddles Ltd, Guildford, Surrey

To my Father
with respect and affection

Contents

Preface   1

Introduction to Second Edition   3

PART ONE   ADMINISTRATIVE ORGANISATION

1 The Development of Administrative Theories   19
   The Scientific Administrators
   Herbert Simon and Rational Decision-Making
   The Policy Process and Governmental Planning
   Conclusion

2 The Organisation of Government   55
   The Allocation of Functions
   Goals, Policies and Organisation
   Work Units and Meaningful Tasks
   Administrative Structure and Functions

3 Administrative Competition and Co-ordination   87
   The Values of Competition and Co-ordination
   Agency 'Philosophy' and Independence
   Functional Duplication and Policy Conflicts
   The Forms of Administrative Conflict
   Administrative Reorganisation

4 Staff and Line in Government   121
   The Functions of the Executive
   Staff Agencies in American Government
   Staff Agencies in Cabinet Systems
   Centralisation and Staff Agencies
   The Functions of the Executive (Continued)

PART TWO   ADMINISTRATIVE BEHAVIOUR

5 Politicians and Administrators   149
   Introduction
   Political and Administrative Roles
   The Structure of Top Management
   The Integrative Role of General Administrators
   Political Control and Administrative Influence

6 Administrative Advice and Appraisal   192
   Introduction
   Administrative Structure and Specialisation
   Controllers and Specialists

CONTENTS

'Bureaupathology' and Technocracy
The Problems of Economic Appraisal
The Qualifications of Administrators

7   Administrative Motivation and Performance   224
Introduction
Open and Closed Career Systems
Administrative Egoism
Administrative Élitism

8   The Dilemmas of Administration   247
Introduction
Administrative Organisation Reconsidered
The Meanings of Administrative Efficiency
Administrative Responsibility
Administrative Professionalism

A Short Note on Further Reading   301

Index   303

PREFACE

This second edition contains a new Introduction. Otherwise the text remains as before except for minor corrections and (where possible) adjustments for recent changes. Since many examples are introduced to illustrate theories or issues, they remain as relevant as before. In so far as I am concerned with analysing administrative changes, it would have been useful to consider recent developments, for example over giant government departments (pp. 82–4) or administrative training (pp. 215–21). However, it seemed to me too early for a proper reappraisal.

Government organisations now change their names and powers with bewildering frequency. I try to indicate from the context whether the reference is historical or contemporary, and in the latter case to use the latest title. However I have not altered the titles of the British Board of Trade and Ministry of Housing and Local Government, both abolished in 1970, because their successor departments do not work in the same way. For reasons of convenience and sentiment, I have also stuck to Bureau of the Budget instead of its successor the Office of Management and Budget which covers a wider range of tasks.

I am grateful to my colleagues, Professor George Jones, Dr David Regan and Dr Vincent Wright, for reading various drafts and making some helpful comments. I am also indebted to Professor Richard Rose for some useful comments on Chapter 5. My thanks go to Miss Valerie Beard and Mrs Helen Mason for their skilful typing of a long manuscript. I am also grateful to the Royal Institute of Public Administration for their Library facilities, and particularly to its Librarian, Mr Ivor Shelley, for his courteous help. My thanks go especially to my wife Elaine for her kindly encouragement of an author who took a long time to write his book.

November 1976

INTRODUCTION TO SECOND EDITION

A second edition provides an author with the opportunity to clarify and update his work Some reviewers who were kind enough to praise parts of this book suggested that it would benefit from a more integrated theoretical framework.

A full response to this suggestion would entail a review of theories relating public administration to its total environment of economic, social, and technological systems. This means another book. This book contents itself with relating administration to its *political* environment, and it is this subject, which may be called administrative politics, that I would like to consider in this Introduction, first by some further elucidation of the subject matter and then by a glance (it can be no more) at some current ideas about increasing the political accountability or 'responsiveness' of the administrative system.

The book is more topical than when it first appeared. In the aftermath of the Watergate scandal in the U.S.A., and in the light of growing criticism everywhere of the performance of public bureaucracies, there is little need to stress the importance of the political environment of administration. There also has been a switch of interest from managerial or technical to political remedies for administrative problems. There is readier acceptance of the idea, spelled out in the last chapter, that government is indeed very different from other organisations in respect of its aims, methods, and tests of achievement. Yet reformers have still to reckon with the complexities of public administration, and academic writers most of all should understand before they prescribe.

The allocation of formal powers and resources to public agencies and officials is regulated by a complex system of laws, rules, and conventions. This formal structure of administration is frequently studied in its own right. Whatever its characteristics – for example whether there is or is not a coherent system of administrative law – politics enters the scene wherever the formal structure is indeterminate or uncertain Politics is also concerned with changing or bending the rules of formal structure.

The scope for administrative politics has grown with the proliferation of government tasks, the allocation of discretionary powers to administrative bodies, and the greater use of professional and specialised staffs. The increased generality and frequent inconsistency of public policies has transferred much of the agenda of specific policy-making to the administrative arena. In all countries the formal structure of administrative authority

3

has been relaxed, not intentionally but as a result of these other developments. The Weberian model of a hierarchical, rule-dominated administration still has some validity for parts of the system, but not for others. Public administration has become a patchwork quilt of complex relationships and numerous decision points, on which new forms of politics are brought to bear.

Administrative politics revolve around the discretionary decisions of administrative agencies or departments. The behaviour of any agency depends upon complex factors, including the nature of its task, its formal powers, and its environment. To some extent its behaviour is governed by a kind of situational logic. Its organisation must be influenced by its task – a research station cannot be run in the same way as a social security office. Its formal powers limit its possible actions. Its environmental relations are partly predetermined – for example a Department of Agriculture in any modern democracy must have a close consultative relation with farmers' unions.

Against this background the interpretation of the agency's task provides variable scope for policy-making. We cannot know *a priori* how much scope there is or how it will be exercised. The Agency's decision-making powers are the target for diverse influences, both external and internal. Thus it may be responding fairly passively to the demands of its clients, or it may be actively interpreting its mission according to the views of its own staff. It may be directed by a powerful personality or influenced by a group of specialists or deadlocked through internal conflicts. It may in practice be closely controlled or guided from another administrative centre, or it may enjoy more effective autonomy than its formal powers suggest.

The concept of 'organisational interest' is useful but necessarily imprecise. It refers partly to the need for any public body to pursue a given task under given conditions; partly to the natural tendency of such a body (whether or not fuelled by personal interests or ambitions) to manipulate or stabilise its environment, and to increase its resources and support; and partly to the policies and practices which become particularly associated with its existence and future. A large agency deploying large resources, performing a well articulated task and possessing a good deal of formal autonomy, will tend to develop a strong organisational interest. For example an Atomic Energy Authority concerned with the construction of nuclear power stations and armed with large public subsidies will appropriate the support of numerous scientists and outside contractors. If other scientists become convinced of the feasibility and greater safety of wind or wave power, they will be hard put to make their case against the entrenched organisational interest of the A.E.A., even though some of its staff may agree with the critics. In such a situation, entrenched

4

organisational power can only be overcome by a very strong movement of political opinion that perhaps can only be activated by some catastrophe.

However, as this book demonstrates, public agencies are often difficult even to identify and classify and are usually very much 'open systems'. A point of decision becomes the target for diverse influences conveyed through different structures. For example an English local education authority is influenced by the views of the Minister of Education, of local councillors, of political parties, and of parents' associations; also by those of central administrators, school inspectors, the local education officer, and the National Union of Teachers. The rôles and interests of these groups cannot be very adequately understood in terms of organisational interests, even though they belong to and work through formal organisations. Group and organisational interests interlock.

The political process deals with the input of demands and the administrative process with the output of services. The former process moves upwards, embracing the claims of successively broader constituencies, while the latter process moves downwards, disaggregating laws and general policies into specific operations. Both processes can be said to have become more 'pluralistic', in the sense that influences and decisions have become more diffused and that (in most Western democracies) more contacts occur between the two processes.

Many American writers see administrative pluralism as simply the necessary counterpart of political pluralism. The growth in the number and influence of political interests groups is paralleled by that of administrative agencies responding to or interpreting their demands. Group politics pervades the administrative process. However, this analysis, while true up to a point (especially in the U.S.A. but much less so elsewhere), underrates the integrating functions performed by both generalised politicians and administrators. This activity is not simply a transmission belt for specific (and supposedly 'objective') group demands, but involves interpretations of broader concepts of interest, including that of the whole nation, in just the same manner in principle as an interest group interprets *its* members' interests.

Group politics in administration takes two forms. First there are the variously co-operative or competitive relations between administrative and political groups; for example the relations between specialists providing some service and their client group, and those between generalist administrators and political leaders. Secondly there are the relationships between different public service groups, particularly in respect of balances of authority, influence, and numbers. Group politics of this second kind occurs as a rule within any public authority, but it often also overlaps and permeates organisational boundaries.

In so far as pluralism is a valid theory at all, administrative pluralism is the obverse of political pluralism. The conditions of the latter are provided by the objective characteristics and situation of social and economic groups, which are reflected in the activities of political organisations. These organisations have a degree of flexibility over the interpretation of group interest, but a limited one. They also have the capacity to establish organisational loyalties ('my party right or wrong'), but the test of their viability remains that of their responsiveness to the perceived interests of those whom they claim to represent. Groups permeate political organisations. Administrative organisations on the other hand are guided by the intrinsic requirements of their allotted tasks. Their internal politics is concerned with the contribution of different work groups to the interpretation and implementation of this task. Their viability and effectiveness depends upon their capacity to organise their work and control their environment sufficiently for 'goal achievement'.

It is to be expected of course that 'producer politics' will differ from 'consumer politics'. Administrative politics does not resemble pressure group politics as conventionally understood, but is governed by the special conditions of the administrative process. These include the many rules of accountability concerned with the exercise of coercive powers, with political oversight and control, and with the possibility of judicial review; and the organisational rules relating to the location, differentiation, and co-ordination of numerous tasks. Administrative politics therefore operates within highly regulated and routinised guidelines when compared with the intrinsic fluidity of the political process. Whilst administrative organisations and groups (sometimes in conjunction) act as well-defined protagonists in some situations, they do not provide satisfactory counters for a general pluralist model of power politics. Organisational and group interests are entwined, diffused, and modified by the interlocking rules and conventions of the whole system.

It is worth remembering that administrative politics is a much more universal phenomenon than the democratic politics of pressure groups and parties. In many societies the dominant if not the only form of politics is that practised by public bureaucracies and organisations (including the military). In Communist countries, the understanding of administrative issues has been handicapped by the Marxist assumption that administrative conflicts are a product of economic (capitalist) ones, and that in a socialist society the administration of men should give way to that of things. Conflict has no place. Yet in fact the conflicts of interests and values discussed in this book are particularly evident in socialist societies, as is to be expected in view of the greater weight of public administration and planning which their economies require. An example is the large swings between forms of centralisation and decentralisation which have occurred in the U.S.S.R. and many countries of Eastern Europe. Russian writers now seem to be trying to study these issues more realistically, although as yet their works are not generally available in English.

Public administration can be explored from a variety of stand-points. For example, a recent Open University course dealt successively with the formal structure of administration, decision-making, incrementalism, history, and law.[1] The section on the formal system of authority (in which law should surely have been included) covers the general framework and rules of the system. That on decision-making deals with the methods and techniques available to an organisation for achieving its goals effectively. That on incrementalism corresponds roughly to the pluralist interplay of pressures briefly discussed above. This switching of perspectives enables one to see, for example, how the formal rules become (for an individual authority) both guidelines and constraints, and how goals rationally pursued by individual organisations produce conflicts which are often solved by piece-meal ('incremental') adjustments of compromises.

This book pays particular attention to the interplay between political and organisational factors in administration. One way of looking at this subject is to compare political and managerial precepts for government organisation. The political approach is concerned with the rules of accountability and the control of administrative power. The managerial approach is concerned with the rules for effective work organisation and task performance. The two approaches meet in a concern with the structure of formal authority, but otherwise cover different ground. Until recently, democratic political theory has largely left the subject of administrative organisation to the theorists of management.

My use in Part One of this book of some familiar concepts of classical organisation theory may be criticised on the grounds that these theories are now intellectually outdated because of their excessive emphasis upon formal structure and their dog-matism. However, formal structure is the best starting-point for understanding the intrinsic tensions or conflicts which arise within administration, such as those between specialisation and in-tegration of tasks, or centralisation and decentralisation of decisions. Changes in formal structure will usually have predict-able effects upon organisation and behaviour, although the extent of these effects certainly depends upon other factors and cannot be known *a priori*. While the dogmatism of the classical theorists is out of date, many management experts who advise governments

1 The Open University, Public Administration, Blocks 1–4 (Open University Press, Milton Keynes, 1974).

today use a somewhat similar approach and assumptions. Thus the classical theories are still interesting, both for their continuing relationship to political aims and beliefs, and for their insight into the tensions of formal structure.

Sometimes traditional political beliefs or myths get reinforced by managerial theories. For example (Chapter 4) the large growth in the staffs of chief executives (Presidents, Prime Ministers, or Ministers) is often explained and justified in terms of the executive's need for enough personal assistance to assert his authority and perform his many tasks systematically. But past a rather restricted size these staffs no longer act, as the theory assumes, as instruments of the President's (or Prime Minister's) 'will', for he cannot really know or control them, but become independent and perhaps capricious forces themselves. The Watergate uproar in the U.S.A. concentrated upon corruption in government, without sufficient attention to the theories which had allowed (and indeed commended) the growth of irresponsible staffs who disrupted the normal workings of American government. This is a case where the political myth of 'Presidential will' joined with managerial theories about staff and line to disguise both political and organisational realities. Lines of authority were not clarified but blurred – the opposite of the intention.

A different example is the managerial belief in paradigms of rational decision-making. This belief is not hostile to political leadership or control, but requires it to be exercised in a systematic way. For example the elected leaders are required to lay down general goals or policies which can then be translated into specific decisions or programmes. Organisations may need to be drastically changed to facilitate these methods, an example being the Maud proposals for streamlining the rôles of councillors and officials in English local government. However, political behaviour and politicians' concepts of their rôles are often at variance with these prescriptions. It does not follow that either managerial or political aims are intrinsically 'wrong', but that the results of such reforms (if introduced) may not accord with expectations, and that it is necessary to explore these conflicts from different perspectives.

It is important to remember the difference between prescription and description. Management theory is generally prescriptive, as in the above example, and purports to serve values of rationality and efficiency; so that if it collides with facts of political behaviour, it is politics which *seems* irrational. Conversely when a political prescription collides with facts of bureaucratic behaviour, it is the latter which seems wrong.

In contrast modern organisation theory aims to be more objective and sociological, although its results are often intended to be helpful to managers. Organisation theory investigates the many variables which influence structure and relationships within and between organisations ('contingency theory'). This approach reveals the variety of organisational situations and dispels dogmatism. A limitation of organisation theory is that it concentrates upon the 'micro' level of individual organisations, not the complex interrelations of the administrative system. This follows from its traditional concern with managerial perspectives and business organisations.

Neither classical organisation theory nor the 'human relations' school paid much attention to politics. Even today organisational studies are dominated by social psychology, economics, and quantitative techniques. In recent years the importance of internal group politics for organisational behaviour has been better recognised, and should be linked with the growing interest of political scientists in the way that public authorities adapt their policies to environmental pressures. However, political analysis of the behaviour of public organisations is still in its infancy, because it is off the beat of the mainline interests of both political scientists and organisation theorists.

Understanding the administrative system requires a better integration of political and organisational theories. The evaluation of administrative change or reform needs to rest upon such knowledge. A more sophisticated treatment of administrative politics will assist the evaluation of administrative change. Because of the neglect of political factors in managerial and organisational theories, it is sound counsel to urge the rediscovery of a 'political theory of administration'. But such a theory will be rather worthless if it consists of dogmatic prescriptions about political control and accountability that support or contradict equally dogmatic managerial prescriptions. It has to dig deeper.

The administrative 'dilemmas' which are analysed in this book are to be seen as interlocking conflicts of interests and values. Part One is primarily concerned with organisational tensions such as those between specialisation and integration of tasks, and between centralisation and decentralisation of decisions, which are linked with such dilemmas as goal effectiveness versus policy co-ordination, and responsiveness to local needs versus technical efficiency. Part Two is concerned with tensions over the distribution of authority between different groups (politicians, administrators, professionals, etc.), which produce such familiar dilemmas as political control versus administrative discretion, and expert knowledge versus lay control. These are dilemmas in the sense that more of one desired aim tends to mean less of another.

Naturally, administrative conflicts are not usually resolved through appeal to abstract values. They involve group and organisational interests. However, the participants justify and evaluate their rôles in terms of desirable principles of organisation or of public policy aims, and these represent the kind of criteria to

9

be appealed to in any attempted objective evaluation of administrative change.

Because these issues are so frequently interlocked, any change tends to have multiple effects upon the relevant criteria. For example, an increase in the powers and resources of local government will tend to (a) shift political authority from central to local levels, (b) strengthen the capacity for both political and bureaucratic innovation in local government, (c) strengthen 'horizontal' service co-ordination within local government at the expense of 'vertical' co-ordination of particular services by central departments, (d) strengthen overhead services provided by a local authority, but weaken specialist services done by a central department. These tendencies could be variously described and related to general evaluations. But of course, however this is done, one is describing only the tendencies of formal adjustments to produce certain effects.

The principles of organisation which are still often appealed to as a way of resolving these dilemmas are themselves linked with interpretations of political interests. For example, as Chapter 2 brings out, the various 'principles' for the allocation of work (purpose, process, client, area) get entangled with the goals of political leaders (purpose), the claims of experts (process), the needs of clients for special treatment (client) and for easy access (area). Considerations of administrative 'efficiency' necessarily refer to the weight to be given to different types of interest. Since all these interests have some legitimacy, every solution involves a different kind of compromise. This circumstance is often lost upon participants and some theoreticians – for example, as already noted, the correct controlling principle of all administrative organisation is sometimes held to be the purposes of political leaders; whereas this is to look at the system from only one perspective which, however important, is also transitory.

The rediscovery of the political aspects of administration is shown particularly in the search for political cures for administrative problems. Welcome as this new approach is, when compared with the naïvety of 'managerial' solutions, it will prove equally naïve if it does not reckon with the complex interactions of the administrative system and the varied criteria by which change should be judged.

Public bureaucracies are today under fire from many quarters. Some of the criticism is essentially a reflection of current social values, which are hostile to the Weberian norms of strong hierarchy, impersonality, and anonymity which are traditional in public administration. These criticisms can and are to some extent being met by modifications in administrative practice, without necessarily changing the basic features of the administrative system. For example it is possible for departments to open their files for inspection (as happens in Sweden), for officials to be named instead of being anonymous, for administrative issues to be publicly explained and discussed, for the relations between superiors and subordinates to be 'humanised' and regulated in a more open and co-operative style, with mutual discussion of problems and objectives. Apart from the inevitable feet-dragging by traditionalists, the main obstacle to these developments lies in the old problem of distinguishing the accountability of the paid official from that of the political head.

Such changes will not solve the deeper difficulties of bureaucracy. In the U.S.A. the move towards open and 'humanised' administration has gone further than in most European countries, at any rate at senior levels, and yet it is in the U.S.A. that one finds the greatest intellectual scepticism about bureaucracy. The 'open government' system in Sweden did not prevent a recent election (September 1976) being fought and won partly on strong criticism of bureaucracy.

American writers of the 'Public Choice' school, such as Downs and Tullock and Niskanen,[1] have developed highly pessimistic theories about bureaucracy, based upon the assumption that officials will always prefer their own self-interest to public interest when these conflict. Hence the inexorable internal tendencies towards bureaucratic growth (which produces more rewards for officials) and the inevitable distortions which arise over transmitting messages and executing orders up and down long hierarchical ladders. These theories of 'administrative egoism' are briefly considered in this book (pp. 234–7), but it may be worth repeating that the theories, however plausible up to a point, are based upon a crude psychologism of narrowly conceived self-interest which rests at the opposite pole from sociological theories of administration. They divorce the behaviour and motivations of the official from social culture and norms. (None the less it may be interesting that Gordon Tullock's familiar theories were one of the very few speeches at the 1976 International Political Science Association conference to get press coverage.)

The crudity of such theories does not eliminate the existence of the problems to which they refer. For example, simply in structural terms long hierarchical chains are conducive to delays and distortions. Again, the traditional norms of bureaucratic behaviour were related to a much smaller public sector, more effectively policed to check waste, and confined to a more limited and less flexible range of tasks. The removal of these constraints, and the introduction of newer and often vaguer public purposes

1 For reference see Chapter 7, note 6. Also William A. Niskanen, Jnr, *Bureaucracy and Representative Government* (Chicago, 1971).

and of a much vaster and less controllable administrative system, most certainly has led to new problems of motivation and morale, which call for sociological and cultural analysis.

It is natural, and in principle quite correct, that political solutions should be canvassed for the problems of swollen and allegedly inefficient bureaucracies. One solution of course would be to reduce the scope of government action, but that involves considerations outside this book's scope. A completely anarchic recipe would be to dismantle the whole system and put nothing in its place, which (as it would destroy this book's subject) need not be considered either. More relevant are theories which seek to tie administration much more closely to the exercise of political choice, and to substitute in effect political for managerial tests of efficiency or effectiveness (see pp. 264-77 for this distinction).

Another American writer, Vincent Ostrom,[1] criticises the 'scientific administration' tradition founded by Woodrow Wilson for believing that political authority should be concentrated at a high enough level to set the goals for an otherwise self-sufficient system of administration which could be operated according to independent principles and techniques of efficiency. Wilson himself saw the ultimate political controller as Congress; his successors substituted the President which fitted better with the administrative theory of hierarchy. Ostrom argues that this notion of internalised efficiency remains the dominant element in administrative thought, despite the hatchet work of Herbert Simon who (it is suggested) largely fell back upon the same tradition.

The alternative, claims Ostrom, is the tradition of 'democratic administration' to be found in the Federalist Papers and in de Tocqueville, which was submerged by the later Wilsonian tradition and now reappears in the writings of the Public Choice school of political economists. This tradition calls not for 'summit' but for 'base' relations (my own words) between politics and administration. On this view the first requirement of administration is that it should respond flexibly and obediently to the demands of any and all groups of citizens who share some degree of interest in the provision of some public service or regulation. The test of administrative performance, in other words, is compliance with effective political demands, not with internalised managerial tests of efficiency.

This theory would certainly open the windows of administration to the political environment. But how is it to be applied? The most logical way would seem to be the creation of separate jurisdictions for each principle service, to allow for its control by

1 Vincent Ostrom, *The Intellectual Crisis in American Public Administration* (University of Alabama, 1973).

representatives of its clients or beneficiaries. This would amount to a proliferation of client-based *ad hoc* agencies with effects further discussed in Chapter 2. In addition to the claimed political advantage of responsiveness to relevant demands, there would be the advantage of adapting organisations closely to specific operational tasks and of dispersing large bureaucracies. But the objections would be formidable:

(a) Extensive public participation would be needed in numerous agencies. Otherwise there would be domination by cliques, minorities with entrenched interests, or corrupt politicians and officials.

(b) Some centralised resource allocation would remain necessary, because obviously some clientele groups could not pay directly for their services.

(c) In those frequent cases where an agency controls some visible group (e.g. of industrialists) on behalf of a latent group (e.g. of consumers), pretty insuperable difficulties would surround its constitution. (The same difficulties arise, and have been tackled none too well, in the case of the 'independent' regulatory commissions in the U.S.A. where, however, the members are not elected but appointed by the President as custodian of the general interest.)

(d) Many public agencies produce, in economists' terms, mutual 'externalities' – for example a highways authority can frustrate the aims of a town planning agency and vice versa. Co-ordinated policies for such services would become much harder, and the 'externalities' would be tackled only on a basis of reciprocal advantages. Coercion of outside groups by any agency would seem difficult.

This extreme form of pluralism would require the adoption of some far-reaching theories about the purpose of government – in particular upon a switch from coercive to voluntaristic methods ('the service state') and upon the replacement of bureaucratic by quasi-market models of administrative structure and relationships.

It is perhaps significant that Ostrom derives his model from the Federalist Papers and de Tocqueville, ideas conceived at a time when the problems of large, diverse, technologically advanced societies and of 'big government' were unknown and unforeseen. It was indeed the very problems and abuses which sprang from the application of an elaborate democratic pluralism to the expanding tasks of government, particularly in the big cities, which led to the reforms introduced by the 'scientific administrators', and their partial insulation of administration from politics, which Ostrom deplores. No doubt, as I myself argue, the pendulum has swung too far in the direction of self-sustaining bureaucracies and corrective action is desirable. But the cure must still reckon with the demands placed upon modern governments, and should surely recognise the values of supplementing democratic control with those of a properly conceived administrative professionalism (see Chapter 8).

Another principal method for relating administration more directly to political choice would be increased devolution of powers to elected regional and/or local bodies. This approach is less radical in that it preserves the framework and characteristics of general-purpose government but seeks to move it 'closer to the people'. (It would, however, be possible to articulate some *combined* strategy of functional and geographic dispersion of power.) This approach to administrative reform is now on the agenda of all Western countries, and in the U.K. is the subject of current proposals for the creation of regional assemblies in Scotland and Wales.

The difficulty over assessing the effects of such reforms is to know how far they would actually change the distribution of powers, or affect the performance of services. Organisation theory is now seeking to unravel the effects of increasing organisational complexity. It is known, for example, that an increase in the specialisation of services (fragmentation) is usually partly balanced or offset by expanded techniques of co-ordination; but the second process does not undo the first, the whole system becomes crisscrossed with more complex patterns. Similarly, increased centralisation in the form of departmental controls over local authority services is likely to be balanced (sooner or later) by steps towards increased horizontal co-ordination of services at the local government level. An increase in the political legitimacy of a locally elected council may serve as a necessary cloak for better horizontal co-ordination.

The effects of any actual devolution of powers would fall somewhere between three possibilities.

(1) Little real increase in regional political power, but strengthened horizontal co-ordination of regionally administered services sufficient to complement and modify (but not to reverse) centralised controls over individual services.

(2) A considerable formal accretion of regional political power, but without any appreciable reduction in the central bureaucratic apparatus. In that case there would be some increased regional input into the policy process, mediated and modified through an extended process of negotiation and interpretation between the two levels of government.

(3) A genuine accretion of regional political power, balanced by an equal diminution of centralised political power and (though this is rather theoretical) an equivalent reduction in the size and activities of the national bureaucracy. This is the model which reformers have in mind, though it is clearly one 'ideal type' of theoretically possible change.

This geographic approach also raises crucial questions about the *level* to which powers are devolved. Clearly if the effectiveness of political choice is related positively to the smallness of the area and negatively to the size of the controlled bureaucracy, then a county council will be more effective than a region and a local council than a county. The reformer's classical problem has been to match the supposed democratic case for small units with the supposed functional or managerial case for larger ones, and the latter case has proved triumphant in almost all states in recent years. Services have been steadily transferred from smaller to larger (often much larger) units, or where not formally transferred (as in the U.S.A.) supplemented by services introduced at higher governmental levels.

Even so societies still respond to this dilemma in very different ways. In Sweden, a prosperous and technically advanced country, many public services (including education up to the age of 16) are operated through communes with an average population of only 14,000 people. In Britain, now a less advanced country, most services (including education) have been handed over to enlarged counties with an average size of about 400,000 people on the basis of very doubtful and certainly unproven arguments about service efficiency (even the district councils, with their meagre powers, are far larger than the Swedish communes). Clearly, if there is any political force in the current critiques of large bureaucracy, one should anticipate a swing back towards smaller governmental units in countries such as Britain.

There is also the issue of the 'accountability' of public servants to political heads. Some contributors to what was called (a few years ago) the 'new public administration' in America[1] stress the right of individuals to self-realisation within an organisational framework. But personal realisation must be balanced against the often equally stressed requirements of accountability to elected leaders. Any reconciliation of these ideas needs to be sought through the re-organisation of work tasks so as to give fuller scope for the 'whole individual', not through a denial of the control implications of democratic government. There seems little virtue in replacing irresponsible bureaucracies with anarchic ones.

A related argument urges the desirability of administrators acting as political partisans, usually in the cause of 'social justice and equality'. This viewpoint is expressed by some British and French academics concerned with public planning, as well as by Americans. Sometimes merely a moderate or 'Fabian' partisanship is suggested,[2] sometimes it is pushed much further. This

1 . F. Marini (ed.), *Towards a New Public Administration* (Scranton, Penn., 1971).

2   D. Eversley, *The Planner in Society* (London, 1973).

15

viewpoint is easily confused with a valid argument that administrators should be more actively concerned with the ethics of their profession. Since they have *de facto* discretion, they should care about the consequences of its use for the welfare and harmony of their society. As a very consequence of their organisational position within modern pluralist societies, it is surely desirable that (in their advice and recommendations) administrators stress longer-run as opposed to shorter-run considerations, and the interests of less organised as opposed to more organised groups. The circumstance that the political environment frequently impels them in an opposite direction (towards the short run and the big, ever-present battalions) justifies as well as impedes these ethical counsels. Such counsels can in any case be no more than directions of concern; modern administrators are not Platonic guardians, and it is always questionable when the 'long view' is socially wise.

Such considerations could hardly justify administrators aligning themselves with the claims of political forces within or without their societies. Whilst 'programme politics' and 'organisational politics' can be practised, up to a point, by administrators, party politics is disruptive of the relations of trust and impartiality between politician and administrator. Still more is this the case if administrators actively espouse doctrines subversive of the political system they purport to be serving. This is not to question the right or duty of administrators to protest or resign about acts that they find ethically repulsive – indeed administrative ethics needs to consider such situations more carefully and specifically. But political partisanship is a dangerous prescription for administrative indifference – at the very least it is likely to boomerang.

If this Introduction, like the book itself, ends upon a somewhat old-fashioned note, my plea must be that the basic problems of administration in democratic societies can neither be dissolved by nostrums, whether political or managerial, nor removed by the surgeon's knife without killing the patient. This is not to deny the possibility or desirability of reform. But while reform may readjust it will not remove the persistence of administrative 'dilemmas'. If many of these dilemmas remain in principle highly familiar, they have now to be understood in relation to a much enlarged, more complex, and more discretionary system of administration. It is as a modest contribution towards the understanding of that system that this book should be read.

Peter Self

November, 1976

PART ONE:
ADMINISTRATIVE ORGANISATION

Chapter 1

THE DEVELOPMENT OF
ADMINISTRATIVE THEORIES

THE SCIENTIFIC ADMINISTRATORS

It is a familiar idea that government is unnecessarily inefficient. Very frequently the failures of extravagance of public authorities are blamed upon defects in the machinery of government. It is natural to inquire whether there are any general principles of administration whose application could remedy these defects and improve the general functioning of government. It is also natural, since private enterprise is often supposed to be more 'efficient' than public authorities, to consider what relevance the methods of business management have for public administration.

During this century, a group of writers, sometimes known as the 'scientific administration' school, have tried to show that there are indeed sound principles of administrative organisation.[1] This school drew some of its inspiration from the writings on industrial management of the American Frederick Taylor, and of industrial psychologists in Europe and America. From these writings have stemmed the techniques of time and motion study, production control, and office organisation and methods. These techniques have been largely concerned with what Herbert Simon calls 'physiological organisation theory', and with what Taylor himself believed to be the 'one best way' (for he assumed that there was always only one) of organising workers to perform some task. The focus of these studies is on routine tasks and operations, and influential as their discoveries have been these have not much relevance to general issues of administrative organisation.

These general issues were first subjected to systematic theorising by the Frenchman Henri Fayol, who considered that his principles applied equally to industrial and public organisations. Theories of public administration were further developed by James Mooney, Luther Gulick, L. F. Urwick, and a number of other writers. This school of thought is not limited to theorising, for its members and disciples have been active practical reformers. This is particularly true in the U.S.A., where a great number of changes in the structure

19

of Federal, State, and local governments have been urged or justified in terms of the ideas and concepts of 'scientific administration'. For example, these concepts played a considerable part in the influential 1937 report of the President's Committee on Administrative Management and in the voluminous post-war reports of the two Hoover Commissions. By contrast, the pragmatic surface of British Administration has been little disturbed by appeals to general principles, except for the rare and unsuccessful report of the Haldane Committee in 1919. However, even in Britain certain notions of administrative efficiency bulk larger in the mental furniture of officials and reformers than they realise.

In their early days the scientific administrators, rather like the nineteenth-century Benthamites, could win successes by hitting easy targets. Government was sometimes palpably incompetent and run according to political methods that had little relevance to the vast tasks of modern administration, so that a very loose framework of principle provided an adequate armoury for mounting the attack. This was again particularly true of America where the spoils system in local government, sustained by a confusing plethora of elective offices, offered the first target. The National Municipal League was formed to press for the 'short ballot' and the professionalisation of many posts which were held by incompetent party hacks or nominees. Later, similar ideas provided the rationale for the council-manager movement, which has succeeded in centralising the administration of many American cities under the control of a professional manager, who alone stands responsible to a small elected council.

The theorists of municipal reform went on to play a notable part in overhauling the structure of Federal and State governments. The whole of this reform movement worked under the impetus of Woodrow Wilson's dictum that it was possible to achieve a self-sufficient 'science' of administrative means, so constructed as to leave administrators perfectly amenable to political leadership (of any type) while remaining free of political considerations in the conduct of their work. Wilson's theories may have been naïve, but they provided an ideological basis for measures which most people approved: namely the curbing of political patronage, the advancement of professional skills, and a tighter framework of internal administrative co-ordination.

In rather similar vein, Henri Fayol was able to expose obvious incompetence in French government. What investigation today (at least in Western countries) could start by listing such obvious defects as Fayol found in his 1920 Report on the Department of Posts, Telegraphs and Telephones?

a) An unstable and incompetent chief at the head of the under-taking.
b) No long-term plan.
c) No budget.

Fayol also found that French ministers, who rotated frequently, were getting no proper information about decisions taken or pending, issues under examination, etc. when they took over a department, and had to rely upon a brief talk with their predecessors in office. Clearly, a minimum need was for proper secretarial and reporting services, in rather the same way as the Cabinet Secretariat had to be set up in Britain to instil some order into Cabinet proceedings.[2]

Of course Fayol and the other theorists did far more than point out obvious defects. One of their contributions was to promote the use of certain management *techniques*, such as reporting, accounting and budgeting, in which public administration was deficient. But they also believed that they could furnish a more comprehensive set of principles for arranging the formal structure of administration. Whilst Fayol, Gulick, Urwick and the others do not closely agree on the definition of these principles, their general approach can be briefly summarised.

a) The central problem is one of co-ordinating an elaborate system in which full opportunity ought to be taken of the advantages of specialisation.
b) To assist effective specialisation, principles must be discovered for breaking down and allocating the tasks of government among different departments or agencies.
c) To ensure effective performance, responsibilities must be defined and clarified and 'unity of command' must be secured. This implies that the whole system will follow a clear hierarchical pattern, whereby subordinates will take orders from only one superior and the 'span of control' will be rationally settled.
d) To assist planning and co-ordination, 'staff services' have to be inserted at appropriate points in the hierarchy, particularly at the top of the structure. These staff services have to be properly defined and located, and reconciled with the principle of unity of command.

Although an inadequate summary, this brings out certain features of 'scientific administration' writers. First, they started from a Weberian view of bureaucracy. They stressed the need for a unified and disciplined system of authority, whereby duties are clearly defined and ambiguities avoided. This requirement (expressed in (c) above) encounters the opposing requirements of the use of specialised skills and knowledge, which tend to complicate and weaken 'the construction of a hierarchical system. Solutions have therefore to be sought by seeking rules of functional specialisation (expressed in (b) above) and developing a staff-and-line theory (expressed in (d) above). In seeking such solutions (particularly for (d) above), these writers also make considerable use of military experience and analogies. The device of military general staff offers a model for combining specialised activities of planning and co-ordination with the hierarchical needs of army discipline.

Stated in this way, the assumptions of these writers take on an old-fashioned look. Traditional management theory was guided by authoritarian and mechanistic assumptions. Its emphasis rested upon formal structure and disciplined organisation, rather than upon organisational adjustment to social and psychological factors whose subtle nature has only recently been recognised. Traditional theorists tended to regard staffs as so many 'hands' or 'brains', who would respond predictably to well-defined rules or to economic incentives. Since economic incentives were weaker in government, the stress on discipline there might need to be greater: but even for private industry, military analogies came quite naturally to writers such as Taylor or Fayol.

In the case of public administration, there was and still is the highly pervasive factor of a public accountability, which is usually thought to require a clear-cut hierarchy so that responsibility for decisions can be fixed. In point of fact, the main implication of public accountability is the keeping of very elaborate files and records, so that decisions and the reasons for them can be quickly traced. On the other hand, formal responsibility is frequently vested in a single political head, and the parts of individual officials over reaching some decision are blurred and obscure. Accountability may militate more against than for the concept of clearly defined division of responsibilities. The aim of a public department is to defend itself collectively against criticism, rather than to clarify the responsibilities of individual officials.

These limitations do not destroy the interest of the scientific administration writers. They exaggerated the importance of formal organisational structure in comparison with that of informal relationships within organisations, and they had a naïve view of individual motivation. Conceding these points, it is still possible to agree that formal structure has importance and to ask whether there are any valid principles of organisation.

Certain theories of scientific administration get some attention later. The allocation of functions is treated in Chapter 2, and staff and line theories as they apply to government machinery in Chapter 4. Here it is useful to explore further the central concern of these writers with formal machinery of co-ordination as the means of resolving tensions between requirements of hierarchy and specialisation.

Specialisation is both cause and consequence of the division of labour. It proceeds through two different though related modes, namely the specialisation of skills and of organisation. The dynamism of the former process is partly professional, revealing itself in a continual sophistication and multiplication of personal skills of which organisations can subsequently take advantage. The dynamism of the latter process is institutional, revealing itself in a continuous growth in the size and complexity of organisations themselves. Specialisation as a 'principle' is somewhat meaningless, as there is no logical limit to these two processes and no necessary reason to assume that it is desirable to push either type of specialisation as far as is technically possible. The problems are rather to accommodate increasing instalments of specialisation (of both kinds) to the requirements of hierarchy, and to relate satisfactorily the two processes to each other.

In respect of specialisation of skills, the 'authority of knowledge' is pitted against the rules of formal hierarchy. The extent to which expert knowledge does or should confer a right to decision-making is considered in Chapter 6. Here it is sufficient to note that the organisational importance of experts, and social recognition of their claims, are sufficient to ensure that this right is conceded to a certain though variable extent. Moreover, the practical problems of co-ordinating many varieties of specialised knowledge through the decisions of line supervisors make it extremely difficult to follow the precept that every worker should take orders from only one superior.

This problem is often tackled by providing that a specialist should exercise authority within the limits of his own expertise, and that to this extent his orders should be treated as a 'command of management'. The difficulty here is to define the kinds and limits of specialised authority which are to be recognised. If the recognition of such authority is substantial and explicit, then a dual system of control by specialist and line supervisors comes into play.[3] In

ADMINISTRATIVE THEORIES AND POLITICS

other cases, the formal authority granted to the specialist may be small, but his effective power (by tacit agreement) is usually greater. In any event, it is usually provided that all cases of doubt or conflict shall be reconciled by the line supervisor. On this basis, some unity of executive authority can be preserved even if separate hierarchies of specialists are feeding in their contributions at different levels of operation. Ultimate control rests with one generalised hierarchy, the line supervisors, who function as the co-ordinators of other divisions, resolvers of disputes, and controllers of communication.

The most complete recognition of specialised authority would occur through the model of functional supervision sketched by Frederick Taylor, but discarded by his successors. Taylor suggested that each worker in a machine shop should be subject to four specialised foremen. This approach enables the authority of the expert to be brought to bear fully upon the operator, without being sieved and co-ordinated by a line authority. As a consequence, unity of command is completely lost.

In practice, most organisations contain some elements from all these models. The full Taylorian model can reasonably be regarded as unworkable. The modified 'unity of command' model is more often accepted in theory, but the co-ordinative and arbitrative power of the line supervisors is often much less than the theory suggests. Unity of command often means no more than the existence of procedures for settling disputes.

Organisations cannot settle for either extreme model, because they all have the same problem of encouraging specialisation and innovation while maintaining co-ordination and authority. On the whole, the larger the inputs of specialised skills, the greater becomes the reliance upon informal organisation. This is not an absolute law; initially the growth of specialised authority is often countered by a strong restatement of the formal powers of the line controller, and an insistence that communications pass through his hands. An example is the effort to bolster the authority of the French prefect; but the prefect's actual ability to control the work of more specialised colleagues from other departments is declining.[4]

Following the study by Burns and Stalker,[5] these organisational differences are now often pictured as a choice between the more 'mechanistic' and more 'organic' types of system. The former type inclines towards the traditional hierarchical pattern, the latter towards flexible and informal methods of teamwork which rest more upon the skills than the status of the various participants. However, if one seeks a yardstick for choosing between these structures, one can only turn to the general character and aims of an organisation. For example, a Ministry of Social Security, concerned with the payment of standardised benefits according to formal rules, is bound to have a much more mechanistic structure than is a government research station concerned with innovation and experiment. A major problem for modern governments is to devise more 'organic' forms of teamwork for tackling innovatory tasks than their traditional structures allow. In this sense, the precepts of the scientific administrators have become out of tune with the times, although they may still answer to the requirements of standardised or closely regulated forms of action.

If an organisation is divided into branches wholly on the basis of skills (the process principle), then the problems of co-ordinating skills and co-ordinating branches are closely related. But more usually an organisation is structured on some other basis. A large organisation frequently contains a mixture of divisions which are producing its final output of goods or services, and divisions which provide various inputs for the work of the organisation as a whole, such as research, marketing, finance, etc. The first type of division may be variously described as line, product or functional; and the second type as staff, specialised or (again) functional. Unfortunately, all labels are confusing. But the latter divisions do not of course have a monopoly of specialists, nor are their organisational activities necessarily correlated at all closely with the possession of any particular skill. The central problem of co-ordination is primarily that of reconciling the contribution of diverse tasks and their associated perspectives.

In tackling this problem of co-ordination, large business corporations frequently disregard the principle of unity of command. Thus the Secretary of Imperial Chemical Industries has stated:

> Within I.C.I. it is the practice to ignore what is said to be a fairly widely accepted principle of organisation – namely, that there must be one clear line of authority running from the top to the bottom of every undertaking, and that functional authority can therefore never be direct, but must always be exercised through the appropriate line of authority.
>
> In I.C.I., for every Division problem there is not one line of authority, but two. There is the line from the Division through the Group Director to the Board, and there is a similar line through a Functional Director.[6]

Mr Lynex went on to explain that the I.C.I. system works because of the very close contacts which exist (of an informal as well as formal kind) between the two types of directors: the group directors who look after the various main products of the company, and the functional directors concerned with development, finance, personnel, research, etc.

It is interesting to compare this description of I.C.I. with the report of the Fleck Committee on the British National Coal Board, since the chairman of this committee was also at the time chairman of I.C.I. The Fleck Report recommended a system of parallel functional hierarchies, dealing with production, marketing, industrial relations, scientific research, personnel and finance. Each of these activities would be headed by a full-time functional member of the Board, under whom would work a headquarters director-general, a divisional director (who was also functional member of the divisional board) and area staff. General co-ordination would be effected through a strengthened system of line control, running from the Board itself to divisional headquarters, then to the area general manager, to the group manager, and finally to the manager of the individual colliery. The Board would contain, besides its six functional members, a full-time chairman and vice-chairman concerned with general policy and four part-time members representative 'of the best industrial thinking'.[7]

Although the proposed composition of the National Coal Board showed some signs of 'I.C.I. thinking', the general approach of the Fleck Report followed traditional management theory. The problem with the nationalised coal industry is that the work of a number of specialised divisions, operating mainly at national and regional levels, has to be integrated with production tasks carried out well down the line by area, group and colliery managers. The solution adopted or attempted was to strengthen the authority of the line co-ordinators at five different levels. The Report proposed a more centralised, stratified and hierarchical organisation for the coal industry than was then in existence, and it also followed very different lines from the almost contemporary Herbert Report upon the nationalised electricity industry, which wanted to bring about a more flexible and decentralised structure for that industry.

It would seem that the same organisational principles did not apply at that time to both I.C.I. and the N.C.B.. Good reasons might be adduced for treating the two organisations very differently. One made a variety of products, the other a single principal product. One had the advantage of successful leadership and well-established 'management philosophy', while the other still had to develop its identity and morale under trying circumstances. But the very persuasiveness of these explanations suggests that organisational principles cannot decide very much. More significant influences upon structure appear to be the character of an organisation and the stage of evolution or development that it has reached.

The most specific of the principles of the 'scientific' school was that the span of direct supervision should be limited, usually to five or at most six subordinates whose work interlocks. Graciunas's attempted mathematical demonstration of this proposition showed the absurdity of purely formal reasoning about administration. Actual spans of control in organisations vary considerably without apparent ill-effects. Indeed many factors are relevant to the desireable span of control including:

a) The time and attention which a supervisor can give to the control of his subordinates (as opposed to his other activities).
b) The technical and personal assistance available to the supervisor.
c) The quality and intelligence of the staff at all levels.
d) The nature of the work being supervised (this is particularly important).
e) Psychological and social judgements about the desirability or otherwise of close supervision.

On the last point fashions have changed. Older theorists stressed the importance of close supervision, newer thinkers give more weight to the greater initiative and sense of personal responsibility which may be generated through a looser framework of supervision.[8]

An important factor to be added is the total size of the organisation. A small span of control increases the number of levels of decision-making, which is an obvious drawback as organisations get larger. This is an example of one structural principle contradicting another.

The 'scientific' theorists seem to have been mistaken on two points. One was their excessive belief in the values of a disciplined hierarchy. Fuller understanding of social behaviour suggests that organisations can generally function at least as effectively, and can provide better personal satisfactions to their members, when structured more flexibly. Other factors besides formal structure hold an organisation together and enable it to work harmoniously, and some of these factors (such as the shared beliefs of managers or administrators) may be more important.

This has already been illustrated in the case of I.C.I., where it was seen that the shared beliefs and informal contacts of the top managers was the crucial factor in achieving co-ordinated action, despite the flouting of traditional principles. The same 'co-ordination by ideas' plays a crucial part in public administration. It is this factor which enables any class of general administrators (in France or Britain, for example) to function as a cohesive group and to transcend, at least partially, departmental and sectional divisions. Such shared values can of course also serve as a barrier to effective co-operation between the group of general administrators and other groups such as scientific experts. In that event, formal methods of co-ordination become more important, since they must carry a larger weight, yet the inadequacy of these methods on their own also becomes more obvious. The only way out of these difficulties is the creation of an adequate 'philosophy' of executive leadership, a task which for various reasons may be easier in business than in government.

Secondly, the theorists held an oversimplified view of organisation, which led them to expect too much of a few 'principles' and to overlook the diversity of factors and circumstances which differentiate organisations and even the same organisation at different points of history. One cannot help reflecting that much management theory seems to be obsessed with a tidy-minded desire to spell out procedures. Who is to say when the advantages of specifying the precise duties of any post exceed the drawbacks? A preference for precision or flexibility is partly a matter of individual temperament, but the search for precision is apt to be an occupational disease of management theorists.

Nonetheless the traditional principles have kept more appeal as prescriptions for government than for business. A looser formal structure may be acceptable in a large private company because:

a) Economic tests can be used to check the performance of the various parts of the organisation. Therefore, direct central control seems less necessary.

b) There is less need for accountability. In a public organisation, individual decisions have to be carefully recorded because of the possibility of political challenge or public complaint.

These are two most familiar differences between a public and a private organisation. However, there are other types of test (such as performance tests) which can be used in both cases as a partial alternative to close supervision, while the weight of accountability can be lightened to the extent that administrative discretion becomes politically acceptable. Differences between public and business administration get fuller attention in the last chapter.

It is not difficult now to make intellectual mincemeat of the principles of scientific administration. Herbert Simon pointed out effectively that many of the criteria used to analyse organisation are vague or confused, and that the so-called principles frequently contradict each other. An example was given above; one cannot *both* limit the span of control to a specified number and also contend that the number of levels in the organisational hierarchy should be minimised. Again, one cannot demand that unity of command should be closely preserved and also take maximum advantage of the development of specialised expertise. Even if one concedes that the theorists tried hard to find ways of reconciling these conflicts, one has also to note that the prescriptions were at a highly generalised level. The 'principles' are like proverbs which often come in pairs, and need a great deal of practical interpretation.[9]

Simon still thought that 'almost everything can be salvaged' from this proverbial wisdom by treating the principles as diagnostic criteria for analysing organisation, and by judging between them according to a guiding criterion of 'overall efficiency'.[10] Whether or not he is right, the precepts of scientific administration have continued to play a significant part in the language of such major efforts at administrative reform as the Hoover Commission and the Fulton Committee. How and why this is so gets attention in the next chapter.

HERBERT SIMON
AND RATIONAL DECISION-MAKING

An important figure in the history of administrative theory is Herbert Simon, whose influential *Administrative Behaviour* first appeared in 1945.[11] After effectively exposing the contradictions of the scientific administration school, Simon sought an alternative approach to administrative efficiency through the design of a rational model of decision-making. In doing so, he moved away from his predecessors' direct concern with matters which, however disputable, are of obvious practical concern to administrators, to go into the byways of logical and psychological theorising. Simon's hope, however, was to find an adequate framework for the extensive use of applied behavioural research and quantitative measurement, and his search and its contradictions have some affinity with the application of modern social science to questions of organisation.

We will first briefly consider Simon's 'behaviour alternative model'. This states that in any situation an administrator ought ideally to examine all possible courses of action open to him, trace through the consequences of each alternative course, and then separately evaluate the benefits and losses of each alternative. He should then choose that course of action which is expected to provide the greatest net satisfaction. Simon contended that this model is superior to the traditional ends-means approach by which most administrative action supposedly proceeds. Under this traditional approach, the initial stipulation of 'ends' forecloses unduly the courses that are considered, and to some extent draws the official's attention away from the actual situation in which he is placed. At the same time, Simon holds that the divorce of ends from means is a false one, since means also entail value judgements or assumptions. By contrast, his model separates the factual consequences of an action from its subsequent evaluation.

In point of fact, Simon's model is not so different from the logic of ends-means analysis, when fully spelt out, as he supposes. Thus it is very rare that there is only *one* relevant value or end to be considered. A full description would require *all* the relevant ends to be specified, either as aims to be pursued or as constraints to be observed. This requires the construction of a 'goals matrix' whereby the relative importance and mutual compatibility of these various goals is first determined. The treatment of means as if they were valuationally neutral is a matter of convenience, not of pure logic. If a suggested choice of means involves some significant policy or ethical issue, then the relevant value ought to be incorporated into either the 'goals matrix' or list of constraints. In other cases, the valuational aspects of means are ignored, not because they are absent, but because they are assumed to be too sufficiently agreed or else too marginal to warrant consideration.

Precisely the same problems enter into Simon's model by a different route. The administrator's exploration of possible courses of action cannot be completely open-ended or his task would be infinite. His search must be structured, overtly or tacitly, by some scheme of relevant values which will serve both as a constraint upon the alternatives considered and as a standard for the evaluation of expected outcomes. Again he cannot trace through *all* the factual consequences of a possible course of action which are literally infinite, but must attend to those that are important for his goals and values. Thus similar elements – ends or satisfactions, means or alternative courses, and constraints – figure in both models of decision-making when these are elaborated.

These two models are really familiar and complementary mental contracts. We can give a homely illustration. If I need to buy a house in London, I can start by specifying the goal, such as type and size of house, and constraints, such as travelling-time to work.

(I can of course reduce the constraints by including them in the goal, or vice versa.) I can then make a search in appropriate districts. Alternatively, I can start by looking at houses in Islington, Dulwich, etc. in a more free-floating way, and give each house marks according to the satisfactions I think it will produce. This approach also involves reference to goals and constraints, which are my standards of judgement, but these have been less clearly specified and are probably more malleable than under the first method. The choice between these methods is a matter of temperament, and it would be quite natural to employ both.

A further point about these models is that all decisions are necessarily made within an assumed framework of values and constraints. The decision-maker turns the spotlight of his attention upon some particular issue, but he cannot explore its relationship to the whole skein of relevant values; in public administration he cannot as a rule include even the full range of potentially relevant public policies. Banfield draws a distinction between the 'active' and the 'contextual' elements surrounding any decision; it is the former which occupy the decision-maker's attention, although what items should be placed in this category is partly a matter of opinion and judgement.[12] Sometimes the decision-maker will be shown subsequently to have cast his net too narrowly. For example, he may ignore some important but tacit constraint, such as the need to consult with an affected interest group, which then takes steps to repair this omission.

Why then should Simon's open-ended model of decision-making have a considerable and even revolutionary appeal when applied to administration? The answer seems to be that it accords with the requirements of modern administration, not as a fully adequate concept but as a corrective to the traditional instrumental ways of viewing administration. Administrators live in a world of increasingly complex and conflicting objectives; they cannot put much faith in the classical 'principles' of administration; and they have the use of a sophisticated battery of techniques, which require choices to be viewed more flexibly than of old. These conditions account for the impact of Simon's thinking in America, and for its increasing relevance to problems of administration in Britain and elsewhere.

However, it is also necessary to note the different approaches to decision-making which seem natural to administrators and to planners. The administrator or executive is under a certain compulsion to simplify his approach to decisions, and to identify the goal (if action must be taken) or constraint (if it need not) which

31

at any one moment seems most urgent and appropriate. This approach was well described by the former official head of the British Civil Service, Lord Bridges, who claimed that:

> However complicated the facts may be, however much your junior may try to persuade you that there are seventeen arguments in favour of one course and fifteen in favour of the exact opposite, believe me, in four cases out of five there is *one* point and one only which is cardinal to the whole situation.[13]

Bridges's remark is not so much an objective evaluation as a witness to the pressures which guide administrative thinking. If enough decisions must me taken, including decisions to do nothing, it is a great help to simplify one's thinking, and failure to do so may disqualify one for top positions. Most modern administrators would take a more flexible view than Bridges, but they would not, indeed could not, entirely eschew his doctrine.

By contrast, the planner may be described as a backroom boy who, freed from the requirements of immediate decisions, is able to elaborate and analyse the factors relevant to some policy choice. The full elaboration and costing of alternatives, if not precisely his job, is at any rate increasingly his ideal. This also represents a broadening of the planner's approach, as well as an increase in the size and importance of his profession (or professions, for planners are of many types). Once the function of a plan was to translate some set of objectives into a single concrete and specific form. Increasingly, the tendency is to offer or at least investigate several alternative plans, offering different combinations of benefits and costs, between which a choice can be made.

One can illustrate this development from British urban planning. Abercrombie's famous 1944 Greater London Plan was a somewhat artistic creation which represented the author's interpretation of the goals of urban planning in that region. No alternative plans were investigated or presented, nor were costs and benefits systematically analysed. The next comparable exercise, the Ministry of Housing's South-East Study of 1962, was widely criticised for its failure to elaborate alternative strategies, as was the South-East Strategy produced by the South-East Regional Economic Planning Council in 1967. These criticisms have been taken to heart. The word 'plan' is increasingly replaced by the more flexible notion of strategy, and the latest regional studies are deliberately setting out to examine and sift alternative strategies for guiding the pattern of development. Another Abercrombie plan seems out of the question.[14]

Simon's description of an administrator is really that of a planner. It postulates a degree of open-mindedness, and a readiness to explore the costs and consequences of alternatives, which cannot realistically be postulated of an executive, whether he be a politician or career official. On the other hand, governmental executives must increasingly concern themselves with a flexible range of options, even if they refer the detailed analysis to a planning staff. In particular, Simon's approach commends itself to the exponents of greater rationality over resource allocation, and over the matching up of goals and resources, whose work can be seen in the development of P.P.B.S. (planning, programming, budgeting systems), and of cost-benefit and cost-effectiveness techniques.

These concepts get further attention in later chapters. Here, however, it is useful to point out the sense in which Simon is the 'father' of these techniques. Herbert Simon was very keen on the analogy between economic man and administrative man, and believed that the latter would only become properly rational when his concepts of efficiency corresponded fairly closely to those of the economist. He gives the following definition of administrative efficiency.

A fundamental principle of administration . . . is that among several alternatives involving the same expenditure the one should always be selected which leads to the greatest accomplishment of administrative objectives; and among several alternatives that lead to the same accomplishment the one should be seleted which involves the least expenditure. Since this 'principle of efficiency' is characteristic of any activity that attempts rationally to maximise the attainment of certain ends with the use of scarce means, it is as characteristic of economic theory as it is of administrative theory. The 'administrative man' takes his place alongside the classical 'economic man'.[15]

The behaviour alternative model is much more compatible with economic analysis than is the ends-means model. Simon's decision-maker should opt for that set of consequences (= bundle of goods) which maximises net satisfaction. The trouble with Simon's administrative man is that he has no easy way to read the prices attached to the consequences he examines. The notion of 'the greatest accomplishment of administrative objectives' (for example the goals matrix) is intrinsically resistant to any precise measurements of satisfaction.

Welfare economics helps out this situation with the concept of maximising consumers' performances. On this basis, it might be said that the final aim of the administrator should not be the realisation of any prescribed objectives, but the maximisation of the net satisfactions (for example total benefits – total costs) of all those persons whom his decision affects. The administrator, or policy-maker, then becomes like a market entrepreneur, choosing between alternative mixes of resource allocation according to his ultimate calculation of the net benefits conferred, not only upon his direct clients but upon all individuals who are significantly affected by his decisions. The administrator's own profit is the salary society pays him for his skill in anticipating and meeting social wants; and the 'goals matrix' or relevant public policies becomes primarily a short-hand guide to those measures which have been found (on the whole) to maximise net consumer satis-factions in the past.

This elaboration of the 'behaviour alternative model' is fairly close to the ideal of rational decision-making held by cost-benefit economists. The theoretical equation of administrative man with economic man is thereby achieved, and the concept of a 'social welfare function' – which Simon realised was necessary for the full rationality of his model – is given at least a notional expression. This statement does not of course imply acceptance of cost-benefit theorising. There are many questions concerning how relevant costs and benefits can be identified and measured, and what range of administrative action can in principle be covered by such methods. Other questions concern the respective claims of the goals matrix and of consumers' net welfare as a basis for decisions. The former concept rests upon the right of a democratically-elected government to establish goals and priorities, while the latter concept implies a populist belief in somehow ascertaining the preference rankings of affected individuals as frequently and directly as possible.

Herbert Simon argued in *Administrative Behaviour* that if com-plete agreement could be reached on relevant facts and values in any situation, there could only be one correct decision. (This is a new version of Taylor's 'one best way'.) He conceded that this is never the case. Therefore, the task of administrative theory is to investigate the causes of 'bounded rationality', that is the reasons why correct decisions are not made.

Simon has to put the meaning of a correct decision within its organisational setting. He considers that human rationality is primarily realised through participation in organisations, which structure and discipline the choices open to the individual. The objectives and values of an organisation guide the decisions of its members, partly through the exercise of authority and the provision of information, but also to a large extent through the 'internalisation' of these values in the psychology of the individual. Simon is clear, as many other writers have been, that this process of identification is essential for organisational efficiency. Indeed a *prima facie* interpretation of efficiency is an action that accords perfectly with the goals and values of the organisation to which the decision-maker belongs.

Simon is also aware, however, that organisational goals are frequently narrow or retrograde in terms of some broader definition of social interest. His concept of rationality drives him to seek some appropriate perspective for the decision-maker which will transcend organisational interests, but the search proves hard going.

Take Simon's illustration of the fire chief.* This official will attend primarily or perhaps exclusively to the problems of preventing and extinguishing fires, and will usually seek funds for improved equipment if such becomes available. But for Simon this is not rational behaviour. The fire chief ought to consider whether his engines cause more harm through road accidents than they do good through getting to fires quickly; and he ought to ask himself whether the money he wants for new equipment would not be better spent upon hospitals or roads. Many would agree with Simon's comments, and would stress, as he does, that officials should strive to broaden their perspectives; but how far should they delve into each other's affairs or internalise each other's values? Simon's advice that 'the administrator, serving a public agency in a democratic state, must give a proper weight to *all* community values that are relevant to his activity'[16] is all very well, but hardly offers a criterion for making correct or rational decisions.

Although he himself tends to identify efficiency with rationality, Simon's thought brings out very nicely the conflict of administrative values which can be associated with these terms. The problems of centralisation illustrate this point. Rationality (in Simon's sense) seems to require that all decisions be made centrally which are interrelated in respect of either their goals or their resources. The most obvious example, which Simon stresses, is public expenditure decisions, since the total value of such decisions can only be maximised through completely integrated planning. Many other examples could be given. Indeed the very notions of maximising the search for alternatives and co-ordinating interrelated values,

* I am indebted to Herbert Storing for his clarification of Simon's reasoning on this and several other points. See Herbert J. Storing (ed.), *Essays on the Scientific Study of Politics* (New York, 1962), pp. 63–151.

which are implicit in Simon's idea of rationality, suggest that a centralised decision will always theoretically be best.

But Simon, as an empirical student of public administration, is also very well aware of the *disadvantages* of centralisation. Indeed he constantly stresses them. At the simplest level, he points out that interpersonal co-ordination can never approach the efficiency with which an individual co-ordinates his own nervous system. He quotes the nice story of the Deputy Quartermaster-General of India who to his surprise found that his work hours actually fell when he was required to take over his superior's duties as well as his own, although both men had been working flat out previously. They had been creating work for each other.[17] He analyses frequently the complexities and difficulties of organisational co-ordination.

When it comes to inter-agency relations, Simon (together with his co-authors of *Public Administration*)[18] becomes a trenchant critic of 'overhead units'. These units are actually set up in the name of technical rationality or policy co-ordination to assist and control the activities of operating agencies; but the controls prove often to be vexatious and time-wasting and thus reduce the 'goal effectiveness' of the agencies carrying out line duties. Centralised controls offend against the principle that where an agency performs a clearly defined social function, its operating efficiency is likely to be maximised if the agency is allowed a high degree of autonomy. The agency best understands its own goals and problems, and is dedicated to their realisation or solution.

Possibly these very contradictions in Simon explain the appeal of his writings. In one mood, officials or administrators see the desirability of comprehensive solutions, and in another mood, they want the 'man on the job' to be left free to get on with it. Herein, if one likes such terms, lies the contradiction between rationality and efficiency. Simon provides theoretical fuel for the first mood and empirical fuel for the second; but the basic contradiction is only increased. In a sense, this is inevitable; a generalised clash of attitudes can only be resolved through specific analysis.

Simon's sociology runs also into the sands. He soon accepted that the idea of the 'maximising' administrator was Utopian, and introduced the notion of 'satisficing'. This simply states that an individual or organisation will go through alternatives until one is found which seems tolerably adequate, and will then look no further though there may be a much better decision waiting to be discovered. Simon's sociology of organisations becomes increasingly pessimistic, as he unearths the impediments and inertia to effective co-ordination and adaptation, and to open-ended decision-making.

Indeed, his picture of an organisation tends to become one of a sluggish and rigid system maintained in a state of equilibrium, which will only change its course under strong pressures, and even then will innovate rather little.[19]

Reflecting on Simon's work, one is inclined to conclude that it would be more profitable to investigate administrative behaviour directly, rather than as departures from some idealised model of decision-making. On the other hand, a study of decision models can be helpful in three other ways. First, it should increase the rationality of decisions themselves. Rationality is a regulative ideal, it can never be fully realised, and its interpretation involves the exercise of judgement. However, a decision becomes more rational to the extent that an actor clarifies his goals or ends, examines the courses open to him within the conditions of the situation, and correlates the two parts of the analysis. One or often both of the logical schema discussed earlier provide frameworks for this exercise. Of course, it may still turn out that the actor would have realised his goals more adequately if he had simply worked by hunch, but this does not destroy the definition of rationality or the reasonable presumption that its exercise will increase on average the prospects of success, remembering however that rationality itself changes tests of success through making goals more considered and explicit.

Secondly, the study of decision models is necessary for the design and appraisal of administrative techniques. Although the models are general and flexible, they at least help to lay bare excessive claims about the rationality or efficiency of techniques.

Thirdly, such models can be fruitfully correlated with sociological studies of administration, so long as it is accepted that the participants do not act consciously according to the chosen model. This feat is well achieved in Meyerson's and Banfield's case study of the Chicago Housing Authority. In the appendix, Banfield sets out an analysis of relevant types of end or goal which are exemplified by the case study.[20] For example, an end may be 'intrinsic-concrete', as when a housing project is wanted for the shelter and other direct benefits which it provides; or it may be 'instrumental-abstract', as when the same project is wanted to advance the cause of public housing; or 'symbolic-ideological', if the project is desired as a symbol of racial equality. Of course the project may be wanted for a mixture of these and other ends, while end conflicts occur within as well as between each category; for example, conflict between the aims of maximising the provision of housing and maximising the extent of racial integration can occur within the

37

intrinsic-concrete category, as well as between those with concrete aims and those with ideological ones. This logical analysis of ends provides a framework for examining administrative behaviour, and conceivably could assist the process of conflict resolution.

THE POLICY PROCESS AND GOVERNMENTAL PLANNING

From the idea of rational decision-making, it is natural to move to consideration of the policy process in government. In recent years a number of writers have tried to analyse how public policies are or should be made, and how their success can be tested. This approach has led some thinkers to attempt the creation of a 'policy science' aimed at prescribing conditions and methods of a general kind that are helpful to policy-making.

Such theories sometimes become very broad and comprehensive, as in the writings of Dror.[21] Thus one can consider rules or principles (if such exist) about the *political* feasibility of policies, which leads into such subjects as political sociology and games theory; and about their *economic* feasibility, which leads to the subject of resource allocation and use. One can investigate the *capacity* of administrative systems to operate specified types of policy, and more broadly still the limits placed by social systems and cultural values upon the feasibility and effectiveness of given policies. These discussions about administrative and cultural limitations upon public action have become the standard fare of many books dealing with economic problems of developing countries.

Again one can attempt, as Dror does, a kind of crude cost-benefit analysis of the resources actually put into policy-making itself. Are sufficient staff employed for this purpose? Do they have the right qualifications? Do they obtain the necessary information? Is there too much reliance upon political 'hunch' in the making of policies? Dror maintains a balanced approach to these questions. He accepts that intuitive or non-rational mental processes, as well as systematic research and analysis, can make valuable contributions to policy tasks.[22]

The major limitation with this type of analysis is that it seems hardly to be operational at all. The theories may correct naïve beliefs about how policies should be made, which can be useful, but reading Dror one gets hardly any insight into how even a complex and well-documented process of decision-making (such as the location of the third London airport) might have been better done.

Our concern here is with the relation between the policy process and the administrative process. The theories of 'incrementalism' that are associated particularly with Charles Lindblom are in complete opposition to Simon's concept of rationality, and provide a starting-point for further analysis of administrative organisation and efficiency.

In *A Strategy of Decision*, Braybrooke and Lindblom argue, as against Simon's ideal, that it is both inevitable *and* desirable that policies should be made within a very narrow spectrum of possible alternatives. Their concept of 'marginal incrementalism' contends that an actor in any situation cannot at best achieve more than a very limited and non-radical change of policy in the direction he prefers. Their other notion of 'partisan mutual adjustment' asserts that the various view-points or interests which ought to be considered in a decision will be better served through the accommodations reached between partisan protagonists, than through the determinations of some supposedly unbiased and comprehensive decision-maker. These authors conclude that policy-making involves no more than limited and mostly unco-ordinated adjustments to an existing situation, with decision-makers responding seriatim to the proposals of other protagonists, or to unforeseen consequences of their decisions ('disjointed incrementalism'). This apparently is as it should be. There is, therefore, no scope or need for the ideal of comprehensive decision-making, which is unworkable in a situation of competing interests and view-points, and would work badly (presumably) in a non-competitive one.[23]

These theories are of course very general. They can be posited of relations within organisations as well as between them, and they clearly assume a democratic pluralist system. Even on this basis, the concepts of 'incrementalism' and partisanship are necessarily very broad, despite attempts by the authors to give them precision. For example, would the Redcliffe-Maud proposals for the reform of English local government come within the limits of 'marginal incrementalism'? One would assume not. They require a drastic break with the existing local government system, and the creation of quite new areas and types of authority.

The theorists of 'marginal incrementalism' might view these very facts as suggesting a probability that the Maud Report will *not* be implemented, as has indeed proved to be the case. What then was the purpose of the Commission in making such implausible proposals? The answer might be that the Commission hoped to bring about *marginal* changes by proposing more drastic ones, although this does not seem to have been their intention since they proposed a comprehensive plan which was very difficult to modify. The Conservative Government's revised proposals (1971) were less radical than the Maud ones, but even so will entail the abolition of most of the substantial powers which large towns (county boroughs) have accumulated in England over several centuries. Is this or is this not marginal incrementalism?[24]

The British army, navy and air departments were highly partisan before they were merged into the Ministry of Defence. Each wished to develop its own specifications of increasingly expensive weapon systems, and 'mutual adjustment' mainly took the form of accepting unwillingly such arbitrations and economies as the Cabinet managed to impose. The creation of an integrated ministry did not remove this partisanship, but it did reduce it. Initially, the central planning staffs of the ministry were swollen by the presence of many representatives from each subordinate department, who stressed the claims of their respective services. Subsequently, the ministry introduced a functional system of organisation, which introduced an intermediate level of organisation concerned with strategic planning; weapon systems; and logistics and personnel; but separate organisations for the services continued at a lower level, although their partisanship was modified gradually through the imposed requirements of co-operation. Thus even thorough-going administrative centralisation does not exclude a good deal of 'partisan mutual adjustment'. More to the point perhaps, it seems very difficult to state *in general terms* how much partisanship is desirable.[25]

The Braybrooke-Lindblom thesis has a certain explanatory appeal to participants in the policy process. It corresponds very much better with the experience of most officials than does the rationalist thesis of Herbert Simon (which is of course anyhow an ideal); and perhaps officials feel comforted and flattered to be told that procedures which they supposed merely unavoidable, are in fact the best possible. Yet the thesis is too broad and loose to be of much use as description, and marginal incrementalism cannot really be bent to cover the sudden increases of public expenditure or switches of public policy which occur from time to time.

As a prescriptive theory, this thesis is as flatly pragmatic as the Simon view is Utopian. Essentially, it amounts to a cautionary tale against comprehensive planning, and a recommendation for as much polycentricity as possible, for example the multiplication of separate points of decision or of effective influence upon eventual decisions. Collective decisions, such as those made by a Cabinet, in principle seem preferable to unitary decisions, for example by a President, because they allow for more partisan mutual adjustment. Decisions which represent the net product of independent, separately articulated contributions are better than decisions made by a single authority from a comprehensive standpoint. The multiplication of organisations is also presumably desirable because it factorises more interests and simplifies their calculation. But while the Braybrooke-Lindblom thesis suggests such general conclusions, it does not say *how far* polycentricity should be pushed and in fact fragmentation of decision-making soon becomes rather absurd; nor in what circumstances *some* of the gains of polycentricity might be worth sacrificing for *some* integrated planning.

To these questions I now briefly turn, examining first the special case of budgeting and then an example of administrative planning. Budgeting gets more attention later, but it must be mentioned here as the supreme illustration of conflict between comprehensive and polycentric decision-making within the administrative process.

The problem with budgeting is to know how the benefits of public expenditure are to be defined, determined and quantified. If one believes, as Herbert Simon does, that the relative benefits of different expenditures can be judged in some objective, non-partisan way, the budget should logically be treated as a set of simultaneous equations to be solved comprehensively. Because all items of public expenditure are logically interchangeable, benefits cannot in theory be maximised unless all possible permutations are compared. This points to the budget being produced by a central reviewing agency which can take an overall view of total costs and benefits. But if budgeting is primarily a political activity, in the sense that allocations depend upon policy judgements and priorities, then all relevant interests ought to be heard. These interests include the spending agencies themselves, their clients, professional bodies, interest groups and agencies specially charged with efficiency and economy; as well as by elected representatives, political parties, and the political heads of government.

According to Lindblom, a polycentric pattern of budgeting, whereby the budget is shaped by bargains struck between multiple decision centres, will enable all relevant interests to be expressed and accommodated in the most satisfactory way; and the American budgetary process as described by Aaron Wildavsky[26] conforms very well with this specification. This polycentricity occurs primarily because the President's Bureau of the Budget does not, as happens in almost every other country, produce a definitive budget which the legislature must accept, but a document which is unstitched and re-assembled by the appropriations committees of the House of Representatives and the Senate. The President's budget is still a very influential document, much of which is usually broadly endorsed, but the actual budget is stitched up according to last-minute bargains reached within and between the two chambers of Congress, and the scope for Congressional revision also causes far stronger and more overt bargaining *within* the executive branch than would otherwise occur.

All participants in the budgetary process perform a useful function, while each adjusts his role from experience of those of the other participants. The spending agencies submit estimates which reflect their priorities. The secretaries of the large departments revise these estimates to give more weight to departmental policy, while not offending the constituent agencies unduly. The Bureau of the Budget reflects the President's policy priorities, where known, as well as searching for economies. The appropriation committees of the House of Representatives typically make economy cuts, while those of the Senate often act as a sort of court of appeal for dissatisfied agencies. Many other interests, for example client groups, appear at several stages of the process, while there is also ample scope for such special view-points as the wish of some Congressional groups to spend money more freely than the relevant department.

The argument is that these 'specialised, incremental, fragmented and sequential budgetary procedures'[27] maximise total satisfactions much better than would a more centralised and comprehensive system of budgeting. Clearly, such broad arguments are difficult to judge, but two points need to be stressed. One is that the satisfactions felt by participants in the budgetary process ought not to be equated with those received by the ultimate public. The system is sensitive enough to prominent Congressmen who want Federal benefits extended to their areas or Federal offices and other facilities located therein; and towards client organisations who will benefit from the expansion of some agency's work; but is less sensitive towards the general interests of consumers and taxpayers in avoiding an uneconomic or inconvenient location of facilities, or a wasteful duplication of services. It is indeed the special duty of the President, whose constituency is nation-wide, to reflect these broader interests, but the price of Congressional support and of harmony within the Executive branch is numerous concessions to special interests. The indispensability of such concessions to the American political system is no argument for saying that they maximise final benefits from public expenditure.

The second point is that while all valuations of public expenditure are in a sense political, political costs and benefits can themselves to some extent be measured objectively. For example, one can analyse the probable effects of various subsidies upon the incomes of different groups of farmers, or the likely effects upon unemployment levels of alternative ways of allocating a given quantum of assistance. Since these factors can be measured according to a variety of methods and assumptions, full objectivity is impossible; but objectivity should at least increase as the view-point becomes more general and less influenced by special interests.

Thus, while effective articulation of numerous interests is one desideratum of the budgetary process, the case for a comprehensive treatment of the budget is also strong. There seems no reason to accept that the American system strikes a particularly meritorious balance between these factors, and its treatment of some aspects of administrative efficiency is extremely weak (see Chapter 3). On the other hand, Braybrooke and Lindblom are on stronger ground in criticising the notion that budget decisions could be systematically made according to some general economic or social yardstick.

This is because there is no yardstick which can comprehend all the values that are relevant to policy decisions. The problem is not only that politicians and others are usually reluctant to make their values explicit, and prefer perhaps necessarily to work with conflicting or ambivalent goals. Additionally, the framework for ordering the values is itself a subject of dispute or uncertainty.

Systematic policy analysis is essential for deciding particular issues but is always played within a context (rarely made explicit) of essentially political definitions of relevant interests, and of a simplified treatment of relevant values. What may therefore be possible for one area of public action becomes progressively more difficult as the range of the action to be examined gets wider. It is not that any new difficulties of principle appear, but that the number of factors which need to be fed into the comprehensive equation steadily increase. In the case of budgeting, these factors are so numerous, covering as they do the entire field of governmental action, that comprehensive policy analysis becomes truly impossible – and yet the paradox exists that a budget, unlike most administrative forms of planning, must be produced.

While economic techniques can hardly supplant the political aspects of budgeting their introduction might make some difference to the decision reached. Here we should make a distinction between 'maximising' and 'optimising' techniques. The former represent ways of achieving the same (or very similar) policy outputs with less effort or at lower cost; the latter are or purport to be aids for the making of better decisions. Maximising techniques do not threaten the policy-maker's prerogatives, but serve goals of economy and efficiency in which he is necessarily interested; but optimising techniques are directly concerned with policies, even though their practitioners may try to be politically neutral.

In using devices such as P.P.B.S. and cost-benefit analysis, the analyst is necessarily drawn into making a whole series of value judgements or assumptions. It is true that these assumptions can be dictated by the policy-maker or vetted by him subsequently; but the process is so technical and complicated, and the implied judgements are often so numerous, that this vetting can be only intermittently done, if at all.

Further, the policy-makers will frequently be unaware of the theoretical basis upon which the analyst proceeds. This basis may *appear* to be much more impressive and coherent than is really the case. For example, some members of the Select Committee on Procedure of Parliament seemed to expect a fantastic amount of certitude from cost-benefit analysis.[28] Of course, just as a politician may find technical demonstration of certitude helpful when he is wrestling with a problem, so he will very likely reject the expert's findings if he does not like them for other reasons. Policy-makers can still exercise their ultimate prerogatives. Nonetheless, any skill which is based upon theoretically false or exaggerated pretensions could exercise some baleful influence upon the policy process. If there is no adequate 'welfare function' upon which optimising techniques can be based, as Braybrooke and Lindblom contend, then this baleful result may occur.

Leaving aside budgeting, issues of polycentricity versus planning permeate the administrative process; but generalisation about the results is necessarily difficult, since if the separate decisions of various organisations are replaced by a single decision made centrally, the content of the decision is itself changed, as is the nature and distribution of consequent costs or benefits. The centralised decision will certainly be more complex and difficult to make than any of the separate decisions, but the intellectual resources available for decision-making may also be improved. In general, the centralised decision seems to offer greater scope for both success and failure.

Let us take an illustration. A public airports authority wants to designate the site for a new airport to serve some large city region. The site chosen needs to be acceptable to the airlines, since the airport authority depends upon their patronage for its revenues and reputation; and the need for satisfactory surface access and transportation necessitates some co-operation with the

44

highway and public transport authorities. Additionally, the airport will have substantial effects upon a wide surrounding area; it will create noise, destroy amenities, attract industrial and residential development, create a need for new public services, and radically change the social structure of its neighbourhood. These environmental effects are not the direct concern of the airports authority, save as they may affect the commercial success of the airport.

Polycentric theory would say that the airports authority should be free to pursue its special task, co-operating with other agencies as far as its purposes require, and leaving other interests to be separately articulated. To the extent that they can foresee their future problems and opportunities, the land use authorities will quite reasonably try to veto certain sites or press for others; but in so far as future effects cannot be adequately foreseen by *any* participant, it is reasonable that adaptive action should be left until later. Certainly, the airports authority (or any other body) may be mistaken or shortsighted over analysing its own interest, but it is no cure for this risk to place a far heavier task of intelligent foresight upon central planners.

Those urging the need for a comprehensive decision will stress that important environmental effects *will* be overlooked, because they occur relatively slowly and do not fall within the purview of the authority initiating action. The polycentric theorists could suggest that if important interests are being overlooked, the proper course is not to centralise the decision but to secure a more effective voice for the missing interests. This could be done in two ways, either of which will depend upon achieving sufficient public and political support.

One method would be to place part at least of the indirect social costs caused by a decision upon the agency responsible; for example, a noise tax could be levied upon the airports authority (and indirectly upon the airlines), which would influence the authority's choice towards less noisy sites and provide funds for compensation. This method has the great advantage of preserving the freedom of organisations to make their own decisions within known financial constraints. Leaving aside difficulties of assessment and implementation, the limitation of this method is that it can cover clear effects of a decision which can be isolated and measured, but not outcomes of a more unique kind or which result only partially or indirectly from the decision; yet these outcomes may be important.

The second method would be to strengthen the powers of those authorities whose influence is considered inadequate, or to introduce an additional authority – for example, a body pledged to the reduction of noise. The limitation of this method is that the multiplication of powers and authorities is inclined to produce deadlocks or prolonged delays. The 'polycentric' model works smoothly, whether or not it works well, when the initiating authority has reasonable freedom of action, subject to the necessity of co-operating with other authorities upon appropriate points, but if other authorities can block a decision which is not their direct responsibility, and whose postponement may for them be a matter of indifference, the system breaks down. One need not hypothesise in this instance, since it has recently proved impossible to find any site for a major airport within about forty miles of New York which is acceptable both to the airports authorities, and to local government and local opinion; and the consequent congestion at the existing New York airports has dislocated air services throughout the world.

If a serious deadlock occurs, the only solution is arbitration by a superior authority (in the case of the New York airport, the special problem arises that there is no one superior authority, jurisdiction being divided between at least two States). It should be stressed, however, that arbitration does not necessarily imply comprehensive decision-making and may also be carried out according to the 'polycentric' concept. This latter result will occur if the arbitrating authority casts its vote wholly on the basis of the information and opinions presented to it, without attempting further research and analysis. In that event, the arbitrator is simply using its political power, according either to political bias or some crude attempt at an impartial judgement (quite possibly both), in order to break the deadlock and let the polycentric type of system at least function.

On the other hand, the arbitrating authority may quite naturally decide to undertake a general review of the case, which may be shallow or deep depending upon the importance of the case and the constitution of the arbitrator. With an intractable issue, successive reviews may occur. For example, in the case of the third London airport, an inter-departmental committee first did a summary review of possible sites and accepted the preference of the airports authority (then the Ministry of Aviation). A critical report from the inspector who conducted a public inquiry into the suitability of the selected site, plus considerable political feeling, led the Government to undertake a second review of the same type in order to examine new arguments presented at the inquiry. Again the site first chosen by Aviation was upheld, but this time the strength of opposition persuaded the Government to abandon its decision and appoint an independent body (the Roskill Commission) to give its advice upon the best site. This time, a very thorough and comprehensive investigation was undertaken, although the final arbitrator remained the British Cabinet, which chose a site rejected by the Commission.

The chief problem over reaching a comprehensive decision is, as already noted, the multitude of factors to be considered, analysed, projected and co-ordinated. In the airport case, these factors include future economic demands for air transport, possible technological developments in air and surface transport, air safety and the control of air space, the relative accessibility of sites, the negative environmental effects of airports (noise, pollution, rural destruction, etc.), and positive environmental benefits (economic growth, spreading the opportunities for air travel, etc.). The view of those who consider that complex issues should be 'factorised', with the various aspects distributed among agencies having the requisite experience, is intelligible enough.

Yet the problem is not really so formidable. First, the experience and views of interested bodies will be available to, indeed thrust upon, the review agency; in this sense, partisan mutual adjustment continues. Secondly, an expert team can be assembled by the review body. Its skills will probably be more numerous than those available to any previous participant, and certainly will be deployed within less partisan and limited terms of reference. The *intellectual* contribution of such a team will certainly assist the reconciliation of *institutional* conflicts.

A difficulty throughout this whole discussion has been that the administrative system is so complex and inter-related that conflicts between 'polycentricity' and 'planning' or between 'autonomy' and 'control' are often subtle questions of degree. In general, the development of modern administration is away from the polycentric and self-regulating model, and towards complex forms of administrative co-ordination and planning. It is not much use offering general support or disapproval for this trend unless the analysis is related to certain typical situations which occur in government. This has been attempted in a limited way in the case of the airport.

Since we have been dealing with only one type of comprehensive decision, it is useful to conclude with a summary of three ways in which such decisions may be brought about.

a) The *ad hoc* resolution of a complex single issue, such as the airport case. In this case, central planning is confined to a single important decision, after which all bodies concerned revert in principle to their previous roles.

b) The imposition of a central policy or plan which binds within its terms all decisions taken by organisations. In this case, the autonomy of participating agencies is permanently limited while the plan remains operative.

c) Full integration of all or many of the organisations concerned into a single agency. In this event, problems of internal co-ordination and planning are substituted for external relation-ships. The legal and organisational scope for comprehensive planning is increased, but the elimination of independent view-points may reduce the quality of decisions.

CONCLUSION

Organisation theory has become enormously more complex since the original verities of scientific administration. At least two prin-cipal schools of thought have made their impact. The human relations school studied individual and group behaviour experimen-tally, and concluded that the social satisfaction of work groups was a vital element in the success of organisations. Put simply, individual responses to economic incentives and to organisational loyalty or public duty were inadequate on their own, and the in-dividual's wish for personal fulfilment and for congenial work relations had also to be met.

Secondly, system theorists have switched attention from principles of organisation to methods of decision-making. Rules of organisa-tion are viewed as no more than flexible devices for producing satisfactory decisions. The essential ingredient for good decision-making is adequate and relevent information both for making the decision itself and for checking and reviewing its outcome. For system theorists, effective communications tends to occupy the central place of honour which effective co-ordination had for the scientific administrators.[29]

Herbert Simon was an influential thinker because he opened up these new horizons of organisation theory. His contention that the decision itself is too gross a unit for analysis, and must be broken down into decision *premises*, opens up examination of all the physiological, psychological and sociological factors, including train-ing and acculturation, which shape the behaviour of individuals taking decisions. At the same time, Simon's partial deflation of the importance of formal rules points towards the *organic* type of organisation, where individuals are able to co-operate on the basis of their simultaneous perception of relevant information. The ultimate ideal of the system theorist's stress upon open-ended

48

information flows is a Leibnizian world of individual monads, each knowing everything that is known to all the others. Leibniz was of course a mathematician, and the grounding of systems theories in mathematical forms of operational research, economics and cybernetics makes a Leibnizian ideal very appropriate for this school of thought.

But Simon cannot have it both ways, and his unresolved dilemma is that also of modern organisation theorists. Is the aim of such theories to *understand* organisations as fully and objectively as possible, or is it to help *construct* a more effective system of purposive management? Doubtless many would reply 'both', but the two masters are not so easily served. The academic study of organisations has shot off into scores of different approaches and perspectives, based either upon some branch or sub-branch of the various social sciences, or else upon some synthesising conceptual system proposed by the investigator.

The results have been some interesting empirical studies throwing a little light upon particular aspects of organisational behaviour, but a complete failure of 'grand theory'. In the end, one is left with a great diversity of partial explanations of organisational behaviour, with no real academic way of synthesising them or choosing between them when they conflict. The most honest position frequently is scepticism, as is nicely illustrated by the last pages of Simon's own book *Organisations* (written with James March), when the authors cannot decide how much truth exists in Adam Smith's old belief in the motive of self-improvement.[30] In this situation, it is not uncommon for a writer to make a shopping-list of *all* the espects of organisation which should be identified for study. But however long the list, it remains somewhat idiosyncratic and yet not comprehensive because the possible modes of analysis are illimitable. Those writers make the mistake of supposing that any distinctions that are intellectually possible may be interesting or useful.[31]

To *be* useful is the other concern of Simon and most other theorists. But the only real basis for a practical science of organisation seems to be the concept of purposive or rational action itself. This notion is relied upon and drawn out by Simon quite as much as by the scientific administrators. Their analysis of the desirable processes of administration was very much a paradigm of purposive action. For example, the famous P.O.S.D.C.O.R.B. (Planning, Organising, Staffing, Directing, Co-ordinating, Reporting, Budgeting) is one possible list of processes which should occur in some systematic relation to each other if an executive (or an organisation) is to take appropriate means to realise specified goals. It may still be useful to spell the processes out, or to suggest that they should be differently defined and related.

Simon's rationalism is basically of the same kind though more complicated, only paradoxically he expects still more of it. By taming the famous principles of organisation into diagnostic criteria, he makes their practical use dependent upon the nature of organisational objectives. Thus a still greater load is placed upon this notion of objectives than occurs to even Gulick or Urwick. Moreover, by flirting with the notion of some comprehensive rationality or efficiency principle for determining correct decisions, Simon contributed to the sort of pangloss, conflictless Utopianism so trenchantly criticised by Charles Lindblom. Yet meanwhile Simon, the behavioural social scientist, was rushing in the opposite direction; for empirical studies of behaviour show how utterly unrealistic is the notion of the members of an organisation sharing agreed decision premises or equal communication flows. On the contrary, the sociological and political barriers to an unbiased collection and distribution of information have been increasingly demonstrated.

The scientific administration, human relations, and systems theories schools share one important general characteristic. Their general concern is with problems of management, and their usual view-point is that of the manager.[32] True, the human relations group may claim to be more humanist, and system theorists more genuinely scientific, than their predecessors, but this does not alter the point. Thus modern management theorists can draw eclectically upon contributions from all three schools without running into inevitable contradictions. Knowledge of human relations can be used to assist the goals of managers, without involving any necessary rejection of some of the older principles of organisation; and prescriptions about decision-making and communication can be added on to prescriptions about organisation and co-ordination of work. It is true that such a synthetic brew becomes rather weak and tasteless, but so long as it provides a loose rationale for the practical work of consultancy, it may be considered by the consultants to have done enough.

For academic theorists, however, such conclusions are not acceptable at all, and it is not surprising that despite the efforts of Herbert Simon academic and practical interests in organisation have moved apart since the days when the scientific administrators acted as both practitioners and academic pundits. The two elements remain joined by the usefulness of some specialised research to managers, and by the pragmatic, Deweyist American belief that the social sciences will 'pay off' ultimately.

These conclusions have not so far differentiated between the worlds of government and business, and organisation theorists are more usually interested in business. Indeed, it was the strong point of the scientific administration school (which may justify this phrase instead of the more usual scientific management) that they were especially interested in the problems of government; but even they were often politically naïve, and most of their successors have been less interested. Two concluding points may be made about the relation of managerial theories to the study of public administration.

The first point is the neglect of political factors by many management theorists. The almost obsessional wish of such theorists to spell out the duties of posts explicitly, and to systematise relations between superiors and subordinates, runs quite contrary to the actual practices found in the higher branches of public administration. For example, R. J. S. Baker, writing from 'well over twenty years active and varied administrative experience' states that:

> In relatively few instances can I recollect my own authority or that of my colleagues – equal, senior or junior – being defined by formal rules. Most of the time it was not precisely defined at all. It was nevertheless implicit and well understood.[33]

This implicit understanding, as Baker explains, depends upon the ability of officials to make variable judgements about the policy implications of cases. Now it may be that this is the result of an undesirable degree of political indeterminancy, but a fully explicit treatment of organisational relations may not be desirable either. In the Report of the Fulton Committee on the British Civil Service, these political factors are treated by the Committee's consultants as a series of barriers to the adoption of management by objectives; it does not occur to the consultants that the 'barriers' may be so large as to vitiate their prescriptions.[34]

Again the possible principles for allocating functions are not at all politically neutral. The priorities made between these principles affect the influence of various groups interested in the administrative process, such as specialists, line administrators, politicians, taxpayers and clients. Thus it is not surprising that scientific administration has occupied a warm place in the hearts of political and administrative reformers who can usually select from the theorists those prescriptions which suit them. This point, however, is not exclusive to government, since various interests are also much affected by the structure selected for any type of organisation.

In a political sense, Herbert Simon and his successors appear less operationally relevant and controversial than their predecessors. Simon can be seen as an emissary for the interests of the quantitative social scientists and systems analysts, whose ideals are a mixture of empirical measurements and idealised mathematical tools of problem-solving.

Secondly, one turns to the interesting switch of view-point introduced by the theories of Braybrooke and Lindblom. Organisations are there judged not for their responsiveness to the goals of managers, but for their congruence with modes of policy-making in a democratic society. The focus shifts from the impact of goals upon organisations (the managerial view) to the policy outcomes of various organisational systems (a political criterion). One need not agree with the theories of marginal incrementalism to appreciate the value for government administration of this second approach.

One can carry the same approach to the study of the internal structure of organisations. Thus Blau and Scott attempt a classification of organisations according to the test of which principal beneficiary each one ought to serve. On this basis, business concerns exist primarily to serve their owners; social science agencies to serve their clients; commonweal organisations (such as army or policy) to serve the public-at-large; and mutual-benefit associations (parties, unions, clubs, sects) to serve their members.[35]

Of course this classification leaves much unanswered. How far and how are other interests besides the chief beneficiary to be accommodated in the organisation's structure? How far is the chief beneficiary to speak for himself or to be interpreted by experts, who claim to have his interests at heart, such as social workers acting for their clients or police chiefs defending the safety of the public? Still, the theory does correspond roughly with conventional wisdom about such questions of organisational control, as how to keep military leaders democratically accountable, how to maintain high standards in service organisations, and how to make companies responsive to their owners.

In the case of public administration, there is the problem that any tests of performance or accountability which might be applied to an individual organisation have also to be related to a view of its place within the administrative system as a whole. Many of the tensions which arise within an organisation run also throughout the entire administrative system. It is to further explorations of the nature of this system that the next chapters turn.

REFERENCES

1 Principal works include: Henri Fayol *The Administrative Theory in the State* (1923) and *General and Industrial Management* (republished London, Pitman, 1949); James D. Mooney, *The Principles of Organisation*, 2nd ed. (New York, 1947); L. F. Urwick, *The Elements of Administration*, 2nd ed. (London, 1947); L. Gulick and L. F. Urwick (eds), *Papers on the Science of Administration* (New York, 1937). The last provides a succinct summary of the theories of principal thinkers of this school. For modern management theory in the same tradition, see E. F. L. Brech, *Organisation, the Framework of Management* (London, 1960).

2 'The Administrative Theory in the State', in Gulick and Urwick, op. cit., pp. 99–114.

3 The concept of dual command was introduced by Arthur W. Mac-Mahon, John D. Millett and Gladys Ogden in *The Administration of Federal Work Relief* (Chicago, 1941).

4 James Fesler, 'Centralisation and Decentralisation', in *International Encyclopedia of the Social Sciences* (1968), p. 375.

5 T. Burns and C. M. Stalker, *The Management of Innovation*, 2nd ed. (London, 1966).

6 In C. E. Milward (ed.), *Large-Scale Organisation* (London, 1950), pp. 158–62.

7 National Coal Board, *Report of the Advisory Committee on Organisation* (1955).

8 See Rosemary Stewart, *The Reality of Management* (London, 1963), pp. 31–5.

9 Herbert A. Simon, *Administrative Behaviour*, 2nd ed. (New York, 1957), Chapter 2; and J. G. March and H. A. Simon, *Organisations* (New York, 1959).

10 Simon, op. cit., pp. 35–6.

11 Simon, op. cit.

12 Martin Meyerson and Edward C. Banfield, *Politics, Planning and the Public Interest* (New York, 1955), p. 317.

13 Lord Bridges, in A. Dunsire (ed.), *The Making of an Administrator* (Manchester University Press, 1956), p. 12.

14 Peter Self, *Metropolitan Planning* (London, 1971), Chap. 6.

15 Simon, op. cit., pp. 38–9.

16 Simon, op. cit., p. 186.

17 This illustration is taken from Sir Ian Hamilton, *The Soul and Body of an Army* (London, 1921), pp. 235–6. Quoted in Simon, op. cit., p. 237.

18 Herbert A. Simon, Donald W. Smithburg and Victor A. Thompson, *Public Administration* (New York, 1950).

19 For development of Simon's thought, see March and Simon, op. cit.

20 Meyerson and Banfield, op. cit., pp. 303–31.

21 Yehezkel Dror, *Public Policymaking Re-Examined* (San Francisco, 1968).

22 Dror, op. cit., Chapter 5 and Part 5.

23 David Braybrooke and Charles Lindblom, *A Strategy of Decision: Policy Evaluation as a Social Process* (New York, 1963). Also Charles Lindblom, *The Intelligence of Democracy* (New York, 1965).

24 Royal Commission on Local Government in England 1966–9, Vol. 1 *(Report)* and Vol. 2 *(Memorandum of Dissent)*, Cmnd. 4040–1 (London, H.M.S.O., 1969). The Conservative Government's reform proposals were published as *Local Government in England*, Cmnd. 4584 (London, H.M.S.O., 1971).

25 Michael Howard, *The Central Organisation of Defence* (London, Royal United Service Institution, 1970).

26 Aaron Wildavsky, *The Politics of the Budgetary Process* (Boston, 1964).

27 Wildavsky, op. cit., p. 145.

28 *Scrutiny of Public Expenditure and Administration*, H.C. 401 (1968–9).

29 For a brief summary of development of organisation theories see R. G. S. Brown, *The Administrative Process in Britain* (London, 1970), Part 2.

30 March and Simon, op. cit., p. 200–1.

31 For an example (there are many) see E. W. Bakke, 'Concept of Social Organisation', in Mason Haire (ed.), *Modern Organisation Theory* (New York, 1959).

32 For the points in common, see V. Subramaniam, 'The Classical Organisation Theory and Its Critics', *Public Administration* (Winter, 1966), Vol. 44, pp. 435–46.

33 R. J. S. Baker, 'Organisation Theory and the Public Sector', *The Journal of Management Studies* (Feb., 1969), p. 29.

34 *The Civil Service*, Vol. 2: Report of a Management Consultancy Group (London, H.M.S.O., 1968), pp. 82–99.

35 P. Blau and W. R. Scott, *Formal Organisations* (London, 1963), pp. 40–58.

Chapter 2

THE ORGANISATION OF GOVERNMENT

THE ALLOCATION OF FUNCTIONS

The purpose of this chapter is to explore some of the factors which
influence government organisation and to settle how functions are
allocated, performed and co-ordinated. The analysis starts with the
general allocation of functions, and proceeds to the tensions between
a goal-oriented and functional-oriented view of administrative
structure. In the last section, the relationship between the treatment
of functions and the structure of the administrative system is further
considered.

Following the astringent criticisms of Herbert Simon, the belief
that the work of government can be allocated according to certain
basic principles is now generally discarded; but, as Simon also
concedes, these principles can survive as 'diagnostic criteria' for
analysing structure, and as such form useful tools of analysis.

The Haldane Report on the Machinery of Government suggested
that the work of government could be distributed according to
either the particular classes of persons to be served or the particular
services to be provided. Luther Gulick, among others, took this
analysis further by identifying four competing principles of organisation: the purpose served, the processes employed, the persons
or things dealt with, and the area covered.[1]

Nobody denies that each of these four factors plays a part in
administrative organisation. Every public agency fulfils some purpose (or purposes), uses skills or methods that are more or less
distinctive, deals with some group of clients, and covers a geographical area. The question which engaged the theorists is whether one
of these factors should dominate the allocation of work at the
highest levels, leaving the other factors to be fitted into the structure
lower down. If this question is raised, there is little difficulty in
showing that three of Gulick's principles cannot be assigned a
dominant status; although familiar ground, we will briefly show
why this is so, taking his factors in reverse order.

To make the *areal principle* dominant would amount to a complete devolution of government work to lower geographical levels, where of course the same set of questions would again arise. The areal principle is reflected in constitutional or legal arrangements for the division of powers between central and State or local governments: but once this framework has been devised (including such special arrangements as the existence of the Scottish Office in Britain), area ceases to be a workable first principle of organisation. Meyer points out that the German and Danish collegia of the eighteenth century split up their activities by area not function, but this approach is quite inconsistent with the uniform treatment and policy co-ordination expected in a modern State.[2]

The *client principle* is clearly unworkable in the extreme form stated by the Haldane Committee, who took it to mean that each department should be more or less exclusively responsible for some section of the population. It receives its fullest expression in the work of those agencies who provide a variety of services for certain dependent or privileged groups. American examples are the Bureau of Indian Affairs, the Veterans' Administration and the Children's Bureau; the transfer of the last-named from the Department of Labour to the Federal Security Agency is also a good example of the partial replacement of the client principle by the function principle.[3] Beyond this, the client principle mainly enters into administrative discussion in terms of the dangers of so organising an agency that it will be closely involved with a single powerful interest group.

The *process principle* refers to the advantages of concentrating specialised skills and techniques in the same place. However, this arrangement necessarily blurs the aims of governmental action, producing difficulties both for clients and for political leaders and critics; and it is also liable to produce the 'insolence of professionalism'. As the scale and complexity of organisation increase, difficulties of co-ordination tend to outweigh the gains of full specialisation. Thus no department in British government is genuinely organised on the process principle, although some sound as if they were. Many local government departments (engineer's, architect's, valuer's, etc.) are so organised, but for the reasons given they are subordinated to a functional structure of committees (housing, planning, education, etc.).

If there has to be one dominant principle of organisation, it is not hard to show by elimination that *major function or purpose* should be the one. It is more intelligible, and conducive to goal effectiveness, to base organisation upon output rather than process, ends rather than means. Unfortunately this principle is also obscure and inadequate. Function in this context means the outputs or services of government, equivalent to the notion of product in industry. However, the services provided by government are very numerous and do not all fall in convenient bundles; many of these can be tied up in bundles of varying shapes and sizes.

The notion of 'major purpose' is meant to solve this problem, but it cannot do so. Purpose is not the same as function. The treatment of particular functions or tasks, and their interrelationships, may depend upon public goals, but these goals are numerous, variable and sometimes conflicting. They do not come in neat, tidy and reasonably durable packets called 'major purposes'. It may still of course be desirable that a government should seek to determine its major objectives, and adjust organisational structure accordingly; but this is a recipe for adjustments to structure (and still poses problems – see later), not an adequate blueprint. Sometimes, it is true, some large goal will hold a dominant place, such as victory in war or (conceivably) economic development or solvency, and then the orderly structuring of goals is facilitated; but this is not the normal situation.

Whatever government departments in fact exist will produce to some extent their own goals. This departmental generation of goals cannot at the same time be used as a criterion of which departments should exist. Sometimes, indeed, a department invents a basic goal for itself, thus justifying its existence. For example, Alfred C. Wolf claims that the activities of the U.S. Department of the Interior are becoming unified, through the emergence of a dominant goal of resource conservation and development.[4] This is not of course how some of the bureaux within the Department viewed their work historically or probably today; nor does it correspond with many people's understanding of the work of the Department. This new unifying goal may be valid, but would it have emerged so easily if a welcoming sponsor did not exist?

However, the notion of *major function* or *functional field* may still seem a plausible basis for demarcating the work of government departments, but only smuggling in some of the other 'principles' of organisation through the back door. What makes education so obviously a major function is that this subject is relatively self-contained in terms of its distinctive purposes, processes and clientele. This containment is only relative, a matter of rough judgement; for example, public goals of economic development impinge increasingly upon education, and many of the processes which education utilises, such as building techniques or data processing, are common to other fields.

The mapping of functional fields changes continuously in accordance with the character of social demands, the development of techniques, and altered views about the interrelation of government tasks; for example, a Ministry of Health often now deals primarily with personal health services, and is more concerned with related welfare, housing, and recreational services, than with drains or sewerage. The environmental health services, which were once central to the health problems of the community, have now reached a stage of technical efficiency such that their relationship to town planning and public works takes administrative priority.

A department may be concerned with a variety of goals which do not relate very closely to each other, although often some of them relate to goals being followed by a different department. Such unity as the department presents is usually provided by the technical field or distinctive clientele with which it deals, a situation which resembles Gulick's elaboration of the 'client' principle. Ministries of Agriculture or Aviation or Transport correspond to some extent with this description. Sometimes an over-riding public purpose for intervention in any of these fields does exist, but more often each department is concerned with a miscellany of tasks of regulation, aid, technical advice and policy co-ordination developed at different times and for different reasons.

Sometimes the basis of a department seems to be balanced between three of Gulick's criteria. The British Ministry of Technology (1964–70) sounded like a process department, and certainly it has brought together a large part of the technological resources available to British government – but by no means all of them. Simultaneously, though, the Ministry of Technology was a client-based department which had responsibility for a group of particular industries, and a purpose-based department which was intended to carry forward the policy goal of technological development.[5]

In any event, functions cannot be assigned to a Platonic model, but have to be fitted into a given governmental framework which has limited capacities for growth and adaptation. Any 'principles' of functional allocation must be squared with requirements of political management. These requirements vary considerably between systems. The large size of U.S. departments is partly a reflection of the problems of span of control implicit in a Presidential system with one man at the top. The basic units of Federal government are the bureaux which are grouped to form a small number of departments. The basic rationale of purpose of a large heterogeneous department may seem vague when compared with that of a compact bureau, with adverse results for the department's effectiveness.

Contemplating his department's 112 operating programmes, at least one Secretary for Health, Education and Welfare found his job too vast and amorphous, and resigned.[6]

Under Cabinet government there are obvious political influences upon the number and work load of ministries. The number of departments must not be too large for political co-ordination, and there are drawbacks to leaving any but the ministers of minor departments outside the Cabinet; but, on the other hand, the workload of each department ought not to be too heavy. Chester and Willson say that 'the ideal size for a ministry is the size that throws up no more business than can flow smoothly across the desks of the minister and his permanent secretary'.[7] The rather slow growth in the number of British departments, when compared with the expansion of government work, represents the compromise struck between these pressures. It emphasises in particular the stress placed upon Cabinet co-ordination, although the erratic omission of some important ministers is a serious blot upon the Cabinet ideal.

Of course the terms of this equation can be altered through introducing changed methods of departmental management, such as the allocation of sub-functions to second-rank ministers and the confinement of the main minister to central co-ordination and control. Some experiments in this direction have occurred in Britain, and these are considered later. However, this development requires the acceptance of a formal hierarchy among ministers – which does of course simplify Cabinet membership – and abandonment of the administrative concept of a reasonably compact department. Similarly, in France some theorists have suggested that there should be only six departments covering all public affairs (interior, exterior, economic, financial, social, cultural). Any such concept encounters not only the difficulties of internal management – a consolidated economic department would be enormous – but also the party, personal, and interest group view-points which tend to reject this degree of rationalisation.

Superficially, the allocation of work between departments looks a bewildering muddle. One main key to its understanding lies in another aspect of political management. British departments vary enormously in size, depending mainly upon how far they engage themselves in direct operations or simply control and co-ordinate the activities of other agencies. The latter type of activity requires as much attention to policy issues as the former, but far less staff. Some relatively small departments are exacting politically, starting with the smallest of the principal departments (the Treasury) which generally now requires the attentions of two Cabinet ministers,

59

and including such traditional departments as Education, Health, Transport, Housing and Local Government, prior to mergers in the late 1960s and in 1970. Of course a redefinition of the scope and tasks of central policy co-ordination over other agencies would affect these workloads considerably.[8]

Some critics attempt to give a final *coup de grace* to theories of departmentalism by demonstrating the arbitrary effects of purely personal factors, and the delaying effects of administrative inertia. Very many examples exist of the ways in which administrative changes have been tailored to suit the prestige or ambitions of political leaders. Many other instances can be given of the power of departmental traditions and of the resistance of officials to changes which they dislike. To give just one example, a logical proposal to transfer the Factory Inspectorate from the Home Office to the newly-created Ministry of Labour during the First World War was successfully opposed by the head of the industrial division of the former department, who was 'prepared to die on the steps of the Home Office rather than yield one iota of its prerogative to any upstart department'. It took the Second World War, and the powerful insistence of Ernest Bevin as Minister of Labour, to effect this transfer.[9]

However, management theories are concerned with prescription rather than description, so that these demonstrations are rather beside the point: if sound theories indeed exist they provide a yardstick for opposing such 'arbitrary' distortions. In addition, it does seem that these personal and departmental factors have mainly a delaying effect, and that the long-term evolution of government machinery does follow rather more objective and logical patterns.

Should we then regard the allocation of functions between government departments as a wholly political issue? In general, this is a fair conclusion, so long as politics is broadly understood as including the views of officials, professional groups, clients, etc. The governmental system and factors of political management determines the general contours of administrative structure; and public policies (which frequently change) settle the importance given to any one service or task and the relationships between them, to the extent that these matters are not settled by administrative tradition and convenience. However, these conclusions do not mean that functional allocation is necessarily random and illogical, and could not be improved.

The evolution of some function of government usually has a certain logic. For example, in Britain civil aviation started as an offshoot of military aviation at the Air Ministry (dependent phase).

THE ORGANISATION OF GOVERNMENT

After the Second World War, a separate Ministry of Civil Aviation
was created to cope with a phase of rapid development (expansion
phase). Subsequently, civil aviation went in 1953 to its most logical
home, the Ministry of Transport. From 1959–67, however, an
enlarged Ministry of Aviation took over civil aviation as well as
responsibility for the heavily subsidised aircraft and electronic
industries. The department was intended to co-ordinate the production and purchasing of British aircraft, but the Ministry's close
involvement with the aircraft industry had in fact a baleful effect
upon its relations with the public airline corporations. (The history
of the Ministry of Aviation illustrates the dangers of the client
principle.) In 1967 civil aviation was passed to the Board of Trade,
not Transport. While this choice seemed less logical, the Board's
responsibility for international trade is helpful for the negotiation
of air landing rights (process principle), and the co-ordination of
civil aviation with inland transport (purpose principle) is less significant than in a larger country. Probably, though, the main reason for
this arrangement was a wish, following experience with the Ministry
of Aviation, to find a detached departmental sponsor for the airline
corporations, a requirement much better met by the Board, through
the nature of its responsibilities and history, than by the Ministry of
Transport which was more interventionist.[10]

The evolution of the economic departments in Britain has pro-
ceeded through successive offshoots of the ancient Board of Trade.
As public aid and regulation became especially significant for some
sector of the economy, a separate department was created – Agriculture in 1889, Transport in 1916, Power in 1942, Aviation in
1959. A different kind of subdivision occurred with the creation
of the Ministry of Labour (1916), largely under trade union pressure
and covering labour relations and manpower. The Board continued
as a residual department for all industrial affairs. The symmetry
of this system was somewhat broken by the creation of the Department of Economic Affairs (1964) for economic planning and development, and of the Ministry of Technology (1964) covering a wide
range of science-based industries and government research and
development activities. Then in 1970 a new giant department
(Trade and Industry) again unified responsibility for all sectors of
the economy except for agriculture, transport and aviation supply.

The allocation of functions often involves three related issues:

a) How important is a function?
b) How should functions be grouped?
c) What type of central control is desirable?

61

To give an example, the Robbins and Trend Committees both favoured the creation of a Minister for the Arts and Sciences who would be responsible for the universities and the scientific research councils in Britain. These seemingly innocent proposals concealed a number of controversial issues. Are these functions important enough to warrant a separate ministry? Are the links of higher education with pure research more or less important than its links with the rest of the education system? Does pure science belong with higher education or with applied research? Is a 'trustee' minister desirable or should these functions be controlled by a normal type of department?

In this case the last question was really the key one for the Robbins and Trend Committees, as also for the then Minister of Science (Mr Quintin Hogg, later Lord Hailsham); their wish was to uphold the full dignity and maximum possible independence of academic and scientific life. But this question was closely tied up with a complex choice over linkages which would influence the reciprocal performance of functions, for example, between school and higher education; and between pure and applied research. In the end, broader educational interests insisted upon the creation of an integrated Department for Education and Science, while the links between pure and applied research were broken, the latter going to the Ministry of Technology.[11] A similar set of linked issues about control and co-ordination arises over the health services, and is discussed under administrative re-organisation.

An important aspect of the politics of functional allocation is the effort of interest groups to shape the machinery of government to their wishes. This is usually viewed as a perversion of the client principle, although pressures may also be exerted by public employees who wish to organise functions according to their ambitions or convenience. Agricultural departments are familiar targets for such pressures. For example, Danish agricultural organisations have always protested at proposals for locating regulatory functions which will affect them in general-purpose agencies, 'and usually their protests have been successful'.[12] In Britain, the 1956 amalgamation of the Ministry of Agriculture with the Ministry of Food was opposed on the grounds that the united department might be too dominated by agricultural interests. On functional grounds, the amalgamation made sense, since the extensive trading and control functions that justified a separate Food Ministry had been largely dismantled and it was desirable to relate agricultural aid to a general food supply policy. However, *The Economist* and others opined that the Ministry of Agriculture's susceptibility to producers' wishes ought to be balanced by a separate Ministry of Food dedicated to the consumer: a view which gave primacy to the clientele factor. In practice, the feared consequences did not occur, since some of the 'consumers' champions' from Food permeated the new Ministry and realigned its policies.[13]

It is naturally at the highest levels that the allocation of functions becomes most political. As one moves down the structure of a department or agency, organisation is much more determined by factors of functional convenience. However, administrative style and tradition play a considerable part as well, for example over the reconciliation of such competing principles as area and service (or product). One solution is to establish parallel units based on different principles. A curious example is the wartime experience of the Special Export Licence Branch of the U.S. Foreign Economic Administration, which controlled the export of scarce commodities to different parts of the world. This organisation set up both a Bureau of Areas specialising in the needs of particular countries, and a Bureau of Supplies specialising in the availability of particular commodities. The not surprising result was that the former Bureau stressed its clients' needs ('specialised in vertical head-nodding'), while the latter Bureau stressed the shortage of supplies ('specialised in horizontal head-shaking'). Probably because of the logic of the situation – supplies *were* very scarce – the Bureau of Supplies gradually gained the upper hand.[14]

A conflict of this kind between two competing bases of organisation can be solved *either* by making one factor dominant, *or* by establishing a dual system (as in the example above), *or* by having a pattern of mixed responsibilities. The first approach has generally been favoured by administrative theorists because it recognises hierarchy and avoids confusion. The second approach ensures full attention to each conflicting need, but it is administratively costly and complicated. The third approach reduces specialisation but facilitates an economical, home-brewed type of co-ordination. So it may not surprise to find this approach used in Britain where one administrator sometimes has responsibility for both a specialised task, and for the whole of his division's dealings with a particular area. Clearly this makes him less specialised and knowledgeable than if he were dealing just with one subject or one region: but given the limitations on administrative manpower (and the fact that he is anyhow a generalist), the arrangement does enable him to 'get the feel' of both these aspects of his department's work.

An analysis of actual administrative evolution provides both check and counterpart to more theoretical treatments. In their authoritative survey of the evolution of British government,[15] D. N. Chester and F.M.G. Willson show the significance of 'administrative convenience' in fitting minor functions into the system. Often new tasks will be simply added on to the existing tasks with which they have the closest apparent affinity. This process will be continued until the introduction of some major new service (the national health service or the national insurance system, for example) causes a fresh integration of scattered elements. A new administrative structure places its seal upon a new view of public purpose.

Administrative analysis plays an essential instrumental role in these developments. If some new public purpose is regarded as especially important, it is necessary to show how its administrative requirements could be satisfied without inflicting damage upon other functional linkages. Views of public purpose dominate the conclusions of many inquiries into administrative machinery. The Haldane Report has its modern parallels in the efforts to secure more comprehensive frameworks for economic or physical planning. Thus competing views about the relative importance of public goals are bound to be reflected in the analysis of administrative machinery, but this need not exclude other factors. The administrative reformer ought to recognise that he is dealing with what are often narrow balances of advantage.

A study such as the Chester-Willson one suggests that administrative systems are controlled by certain governing factors. First may be placed the character and degree of flexibility of the basic political framework. Second comes the influence exerted by changing public purposes as these become politically and administratively clarified. Third and fourth might be put the needs of clients and the economies of specialisation. Other factors are also relevant. At any point in time there will always be a number of unresolved or emergent issues, which offer the frontier posts for administrative analysis. There will also be untidy and awkward elements in any system: for example, some department (in Britain the Home Office) has to serve as a 'dumping-ground' for miscellaneous or untidy tasks. This untidiness can even be deliberate. The Haldane proposal for a Ministry of Justice fell foul of the ancient belief that liberties may sometimes be better served by a confusion of authority.

GOALS, POLICIES AND ORGANISATION

So far this discussion has been couched in terms of the general allocation of functions within government. It is now appropriate to look at the factors which influence or should influence the structure of particular organisations. The usual starting-point for this discussion is the concept of goals. As already noted, the scientific administration school placed considerable stress upon an orderly system of goal-setting as the basis for rational organisation. In doing so, they followed the normal prescriptions of business management theorists and consultants who still stress a clear determination of objectives as the starting-point for the design of formal structure.

Curiously, the critics of 'scientific administration' have frequently adopted a similar approach. Herbert Simon, after effectively repudiating the wisdom of the traditional 'proverbs' of administration, also bases his notion of administrative efficiency upon the definition and measurement of aims. For research to investigate 'the relative desirability of alternative administrative arrangements', it is necessary that 'the objectives of the administrative organisation under study be defined in concrete terms so that results, expressed in terms of these objectives, may be accurately measured'.[16]

There are, however, two ways of conceiving this process of goal-setting and its implications for structure, depending upon whether one starts from the top or the bottom of the organisation. The former approach, which we shall examine first, is that of scientific management. On this view, it is the duty of the leaders of an organisation to set goals and to distribute work so as to achieve them. For example, Chester Barnard views purpose as the controlling principle of organisation, to which the other criteria of process, client, area and product (or service) ought to be subordinated. This is in line with the 'purposive' concept of functional allocation discussed above.

Barnard recognises that the general goals of any large organisation are bound to be general and somewhat imprecise: thus they must be broken down into a series of sub-goals corresponding to more precise and manageable tasks. On this view, organisation ought to be specialised at every level in those ways which will best realise a hierarchy of goals. Of course sub-goals (and even full goals) will be periodically revised so that new techniques can be effectively utilised: but the appropriateness of techniques will always depend upon their relevance to goals.[17]

It was noted earlier that the concepts of scientific management are historically rooted in the assumption of a somewhat rigid formal hierarchy. Authoritative goal-setting is easiest to apply to the organisation of an army or of a disciplined industrial undertaking, but the principle can be modified to allow for participation by workers and others in the process of goal-setting; and on this basis recommended, as it continually is, for adoption by government as well as modern industry.

However, the concept of orderly goal-setting still presents great difficulties in government. In democracies the formal leaders of public organisations are usually elected politicians. Most of these politicians are untrained in managerial methods, but in any case the conditions of politics do not favour systematic goal-setting. The political process provides an input of numerous demands which are frequently contradictory or inconsistent, while political attitudes are often vague and ambivalent. In order to manage conflict and maintain an adequate coalition of support, political leaders must be wary of systematic policy-making and often confine themselves to vague aspirations until specific decisions must be made. The theorists, who recommend an orderly distinction of policy and administration, with politicians settling the broad issues and officials filling in the details, are at odds with the nature of political behaviour which is marked by an intermittently strong interest in detailed cases and frequent vagueness over policy.

A second point is that the requirements of consultation are heavy, and becoming more so, in democratic governments. Goal-setting in a business concern is a relatively simple process. The shareholders' interest is confined to financial returns and the consumers' interest is supposedly covered by market competition. In government, however, the interests of electors and legislators are multiple not simple, and consumers of public services express their demands through political or consultative channels, not the market-place. Because it possesses statutory powers of control and coercion, government is expected to discuss its goals and methods with affected groups in ways which arise much less, or not at all, with private organisations. Finally, public policies are expected to be consistent but present numerous unresolved conflicts, calling for continuous but only partly successful efforts at co-ordination.

A third point is that the higher direction of government is conducted by mixed groups of politicians and career officials. The latter possess considerable discretion or influence over policy formation as well as execution, but their acts are subject to restraints of political control and accountability. The relationship of these groups is explored in a later chapter. However, this third factor also contributes to the complexities, inconsistencies and ambivalence of goal-setting in government.

It may be said that, even if these propositions are true for the governmental process as a whole, they need be less true for the organisation of a particular service such as health or education. This point should certainly be conceded, but orderly goal-setting is still a difficult ideal for any functional branch of government.

Difficulties also arise over the meaning of 'goals'. Words such as goal, objective, task, aim and purpose are often used more or less interchangeably in discussions about organisations. In general, these words convey different degrees of concreteness ('objective' is more specific than 'purpose'), distinctions of view-point (a task is set but an aim is autonomously determined), as well as ethical connotations (purpose is normative in a way that task is not). However, it is sufficient for this discussion to make some distinctions between task, policy and purpose.

Administrative tasks can be stated fairly objectively and specifically. Typical *tasks* of an education service are to teach children certain subjects during certain hours, to set and grade examinations, to provide buildings and equipment of a prescribed standard, and so on. Many of these tasks are specified by law and regulations, while others are filled in through professional or administrative discretion. Educational *policies* represent changing directives as to how these tasks should be interpreted and performed. Typical policies might be to move towards equality of access to educational facilities, to increase the output of scientists, to improve staff-student ratios. These policies must then be translated into specific tasks, although the policy may be changed or modified before the task is achieved. Finally the *purposes* of education refer to a broad spectrum of social values. Typical purposes are to produce good citizens, to develop the cultural life and capacities of the individual, and to produce efficient manpower for economic development. The meanings and relative importance of these purposes are obviously controversial.

Logically goal-setting would proceed from general purposes to particular policies to specific tasks. In practice, the discussion of purposes often occupies a different universe of discourse from that of policies. The former is the realm of general value controversies, the latter of political and administrative conflicts of opinion. Policies assume certain concepts of purpose, but it often seems wiser to the policy-maker not to explore this relationship too closely. Policy-making occupies a middle spectrum of values, and tends to assume some measure of consensus about basic purposes as a matter of practical and political expediency. This is particularly true of a service like education, where even educators find it more expedient to concentrate on policies and particularly on tasks, save in scholarly conferences. If controversy about educational purposes

67

raged too freely, education might enjoy less prestige and secure less resources for development.

Applying these concepts to government organisation, we should concede that policy-making has its own special features and rationale, in terms of the continuous adjustment of contending interests and view-points. As already noted, tasks are reshuffled in accordance with varying views of their importance and inter-relationships, and new agencies are created to handle new tasks. Since politics works largely through marginal adjustments, the impact of changing policies upon organisation will also often be marginal, although sometimes of course much more significant. Politicians are sometimes criticised for failure to adjust structure to their changing policies, but they can just as reasonably be blamed for making too frequent organisational changes, especially at high levels, in an effort to demonstrate the novelty of their goals. Switches of government machinery can also be criticised as too 'political' if they are based excessively upon current policies, and with too little regard to enduring professional or social evaluation of tasks.

A basic prescription of scientific management is the orderly relationship between sub-goals and subdivisions or organisation. This prescription is applied both to the horizontal division of work within a department or agency, and also to its vertical division between headquarters' staff and field or operating agencies. There is no reason for quarrelling with this general prescription, but its application once again poses problems.

An administrative agency or department may comprise a number of blocks of work which have rather little in common save the requirement of general political management. In that event, it becomes artificial or impractical to lay down a logical pattern of sub-goals, since a dominant goal is lacking. Examples might be the Home Office in Britain or the Department of the Interior in the U.S.A. Conversely, a department may be deliberately intended to impose general goals or policies upon a complex field of activity, but no easy or satisfactory way of dividing its work according to sub-goals may be available. In that event, the attempted allocation of work on this basis becomes difficult and perhaps undesirable. An example, further considered later, is the Department of Defence.

According to conventional thinking, the danger to be guarded against is that a subordinate division or agency will emphasise and interpret its limited assignment in ways that are detrimental to the overall goals of the department. This may of course happen; but the converse dysfunction that worthwhile limited tasks will be spoilt by subordination to inappropriate or vague policies can also occur in administration. There are excellent arguments for rationalising the diversity of public tasks, and attention to 'basic objectives' is one usual approach to this work; but the investigation must be thorough, working from the bottom upwards as well as the top downwards, if worthwhile changes are to result. Once again, political behaviour inclines more easily towards the multiplication of goals than their simplification, and attempts to simplify the machinery of government tend to be flimsy affairs, often inspired by an urgent need for economy. The review of government organisation has too high a policy content to be left to management consultants or experts, yet policy-makers are usually too busy to probe organisational structure in any depth.

A further aspect of the goal-organisation problem is the relationship between nominally independent agencies which co-operate in the provision of the same service at different levels of operation. Here one might expect the theoretical division between general policy-making and detailed implementation to prove its worth, but the actual relationship is never so simple. Thus in Britain the Minister of Education does not confine himself to general goals nor are the local education authorities confined to implementation. Local education authorities have initiated important and controversial new policies quite as much as the Minister, for example over comprehensive schools; but conversely the Minister (or rather Ministry) intervenes frequently over questions of detail, such as standards of equipment or even the detailed choice of which schools shall be built. There is little evidence here of a logical structure of goals and sub-goals.[18]

This type of relationship *seems* even more illogical than it is unless we distinguish different concepts of hierarchy and consider their appropriate application. If goals can be clearly and successfully articulated from the top downwards, then a system of 'positive' hierarchy seems desirable, i.e. one where firm instructions move down the line. If meaningful articulation of goals occurs at lower levels and the upper echelons perform only a role of organisational co-ordination, then a 'negative' hierarchy seems desirable, that is one concerned primarily with the arbitration of conflicts. Of course most systems of hierarchy perform both positive and negative functions. However, the bias of the system and its particular procedures can reasonably be adjusted to views of which goals are most meaningful and how they relate to each other.

This theory provides a starting-point for critiques of administrative structure. Thus one can take any piece of the administrative system and ask whether the allocation of duties and the system of control is in fact well-designed for the ends in view. A department of agriculture, for example, may be viewed as a hold-all organisation for carrying out tasks which are largely autonomous, such as various forms of technical aid or regulation, financial assistance, educational and advisory work, etc. In that event, the various field services or divisions should possess considerable freedom to decide their own structure and methods, subject to limited general co-ordination and arbitration. This is how most agriculture departments in fact started. Alternatively, the department can be seen as having overall goals, such as the achievement of a satisfactory level of income for all farmers at minimum public cost, the elimination of inefficient holdings, the conservation of agricultural resources, etc. In that event, the various divisions will need to be so structured and controlled so as to achieve these general goals. This is how agriculture departments have tended to develop.

When a department does not develop as it should, critics allege a failure to give priority to the right goals. This is different from the criticism of defective hierarchy, which may be a quite erroneous one if limited co-ordination is all that is required. For example, the U.S. Secretary of Agriculture and his staff seem unable in practice to change, save within narrow limits, the structure of the various agencies which comprise his department. The main criticism of this situation must be that general goals (including the goal of public economy) are being thwarted through the inflated and over-lapping programmes of various sub-agencies; if this were not so, there would be no obvious need to change the situation. It is worth noting that this situation is not due to the Secretary's lack of formal powers of control, but to the circumstance that he cannot amass enough political power to overcome the wishes of his own agencies without risking the loss of his legislative influence and perhaps his job. There was also resistance in Britain to administrative changes which have subordinated the various agricultural field services to a general pattern of regional offices, but it was not effective.[19]

Those who favour certain overall goals for health or education in Britain will favour a stronger hierarchical pattern for these services, that is fuller powers of control over local authorities and other agencies. It is worth noting that we have here the converse situation to that in the U.S. agriculture department. There is not a formal hierarchy at all (for central and local agencies are legally distinct), but central direction is much stronger than the formal structure suggests. Nonetheless some critics think is insufficient.

70

A proper balance has to be struck between the positive and negative aspects of hierarchy. In theory, this should be regulated by the specification of goals. The more fully the goals can be specified by the controllers of an administrative system, the less will be the burden of adjudication which results from obscurity or ambiguity as to how these goals should be applied. If, however, it is undesirable or impractical to specify goals, then care has to be taken that the arbitrative functions of hierarchy are not over-loaded. Otherwise the controllers will have too much work to do. without the benefit of adequate policy yardsticks for determining their decisions. The proper remedy in such a case is the grant of fuller discretion to make final decisions to the line officials or subordinate agencies; since they in effect (and not the final con-trollers) are making policy, there is little rationale in continuous appeals to higher authorities who do not have the means for reaching adequate decisions.

An example of unbalance in an administrative system is pro-vided by the working of development control under the Town and Country Planning Acts in Britain. The Ministry of Housing and Local Government was statutorily responsible for securing consis-tency and continuity in land use policies, and could guide the work of local authorities (who make the plans and administer the controls) by way of regulations, directions, advisory circulars, call-ins of development applications, and the review and amendment of local plans. The same Ministry was also responsible for deciding appeals against the decisions of local authorities and for settling the not infrequent disagreements among the local authorities them-selves over matters of common concern.

By laying down adequate policies, the Ministry would reduce the volume of appeals or conflicts and simplify their resolution, since the basis for its appeal decisions would be known. However, the Ministry proved unable to elaborate consistent or adequate policies with the result that its appellate tasks became most burdensome and difficult, so that in turn the staff of the Ministry had less time for working on basic policies. This led to a degree of administrative frustration which eventually (1967) caused the Ministry to propose the remedy of allowing local planning authorities to produce the more detailed aspects of their plans without getting its approval, and of allowing most appeals to be settled on the spot by the Ministry's inspectors without recourse to the Department.

One might cite this as a simple case of maladjustment of structure to goals. If land use policies cannot or should not be laid down centrally (as is quite possibly the case), then the Department ought

71

not to try to settle all disputes. If the rights of the citizen need protection (as they do), it would be logical to provide this through independent tribunals or the law courts. The objection to this arrangement is that the tribunals or courts do not know enough about land use issues to make wise decisions; the Ministry is presumed to have this knowledge and to be aloof enough from local interests to have some impartiality. However, it is still the case that the Ministry's role combines inconsistent elements. If the Ministry is really laying down the goals, then it cannot be impartial and its arbitrations must be directed to remedying erroneous applications of its own policies. If the Ministry is not laying down the goals, then arbitrations (whoever handles them) must be based upon some other criteria, presumably of a more limited and judicial nature.[20]

WORK UNITS AND MEANINGFUL TASKS

So far our discussion of organisation has moved from the top downwards in terms of the goals or policies set by leaders. It is now desirable to reverse this approach, and consider structure in terms of the social functions performed by organisations and the changing techniques which they utilise. It is helpful to contrast the goal-oriented theories of Chester Barnard with the more functional notions of John Millett.

Millett contends that a basic work unit always exists which reflects the technical task of the organisation in question. Examples of such units are schools, police precincts, national forests, traffic control units. These units are based upon mixed considerations of area, process, product or programme, and clientele, but whatever its precise form, a basic work unit appears to have a hardness and durability which does not apply to the higher levels of organisation.

On Millett's analysis every organisation contains three further elements besides (i) the basic work units, which are (ii) the managerial hierarchy which co-ordinates the basic work units; (iii) specialised forms of supervision concerned with management, services, and programmes; and (iv) top-level responsibilities for adapting the organisation to its environment (external relations, forward planning, etc.).[21]

Millett's analysis points up very neatly some of the trends in modern administrative systems which are sometimes lumped under the word 'centralisation'. A basic work unit can be more or less self-contained. In simple administrative systems, it is fairly self-contained; one thinks of the working of an old-style borough police force or of a local American school board before these agencies were subjected to a variety of controls and supplementary services provided from higher levels of organisation.

Part of the 'invasion' of the basic work unit occurs through the provision of various specialised services which cannot be offered at the local level; such as (to follow our examples) the services of Scotland Yard's Criminal Investigation Department or the provision of technical educational aids (this corresponds to Millett's third organisational component). Another part of the 'invasion' occurs through the transfer of organisational control and goal-setting from lower to higher levels; as occurs when police or educational policies are partly transferred from local to national levels (Millett's second component). A further erosion of the autonomy of the 'work unit' occurs when its development is subjected to long-term planning and to co-ordination with the goals of other organisations (Millett's fourth component).

It is useful to point out these aspects of centralisation here, although they are further explored later. This description illustrates well, not only the general trends of large organisations, but certain special features of public administration; in particular, the emergence of long decision-making chains and of interacting and conflicting goal systems, causing enormous problems of 'co-ordination' and a tendency for the basic work unit to be buried, so to speak, beneath an elaborate administrative superstructure.

This analysis supports two conclusions. First, it would be wrong to think of administrative structure as being easily malleable according to goals set by headquarters. The organisational elements (ii) to (iv) distinguished by Millett appear to be more malleable through the shifting goals of organisational leaders than does the basic work unit, which has its own type of functional rationale. On the other hand, too much should not be made of the durability of the basic work unit. Its structure changes, in line both with technical developments and with the changing goals laid down at a higher level.

We can illustrate this from the earlier examples. The basic work unit of the police force has shifted from the copper on the beat and the local precinct to the mobile squad and the regional headquarters. This is not primarily because 'purpose' has changed: it is because new techniques, available to both criminals and police, require a larger and more mobile type of work unit for discharging the old function of stopping crime. An example of the impact of changing goals upon the basic work unit is provided by education, where secondary schools must be much larger and more complex in order to satisfy new concepts of equal opportunity.

73

A second conclusion is the need to distinguish between authoritative goals, as settled by formal leaders, and the concepts of social purpose held by the staff of an organisation. Simon, Smithburg and Thompson define a self-contained organisation as one capable of pursuing a socially meaningful task. The enthusiasm and energy with which this task is pursued will tend to be reduced to the extent that the organisation is subject to the control of 'overhead units'. These units are not dedicated to the same view of social task as the operating agency but are concerned with the application of some specialised skill (or pseudo-skill) to a particular service, or with organisational maintenance or policy co-ordination.[22]

The belief that social workers or field workers have a 'meaningful' view of their tasks which is not shared by organisational leaders or controlling specialists is a familiar theme, not without validity. However, there is still the problem of where to cut the administrative cake so as to identify this sentiment. The members of a 'basic work unit' often have a view of their social function which is not shared by their line superiors within the same agency. More broadly, all the members of an operating agency, including its headquarters' staff and specialists, may be oriented towards a 'meaningful task' in ways that are lacking among *external* controllers or specialists. One difficulty is to define the boundaries of 'operating agencies' within public administration. Is the Ministry of Education part of a large operating agency which comprises the national education service, or is it an 'overhead unit' for local operating agencies? Is the *x* county council an operating agency or a holding company, so to speak, for various operating services? These questions about the complexity of administrative structure are discussed in the last chapter.

More fundamentally, one has to ask whether the 'meaningfulness' of a task to its executants is an adequate plea for organisational differentiation and the maximum possible self-containment. Tasks which appear meaningful to executants often appear much less so, or even actually harmful, to outsiders. This is because 'meaningfulness' depends not simply upon the intrinsic nature or general social characteristics of the task, but upon the training and traditions which the staff have imbibed. *Esprit de corps* can invest some tasks with an improbable degree of meaningfulness when viewed by a more objective analyst of social functions.

The U.S. Army Corps of Engineers, for example, possesses considerable *esprit de corps*, but the tasks which to its members are apparently highly meaningful look often to outsiders like a ragbag of jobs derived from a nineteenth-century problem of how to employ military engineers under peacetime conditions. Put in terms of the earlier analysis, this is a process agency which has invented its own purposes. But if it is now subordinated to definitions of goals laid down at the Presidential level, are we to view this as an invasion of a 'meaningful' operating task?

Thus the concept of socially meaningful task proves to be something of a boomerang. It is perfectly true that the operators of some particular service, particularly those who are most directly performing it such as field workers, often have a commitment to the service which it not matched by controllers and co-ordinators. In particular, they may feel resentful and discouraged through the imposition of controls which reflect broader requirements of organisational maintenance and policy co-ordination. To this extent, there is a case for structuring the work of government so as to respect the integrity and autonomy of activities which command this kind of support or allegiance.

On the other hand, the authoritative goals of governmental action emerge from a complex process which often does not respect 'functional' boundaries (however these be defined), and entails a considerable degree of goal interaction and conflict at higher administrative levels. This shifting determination of public goals and priorities has an impact upon administrative structure, which is frequently, although of course not always, in conflict with the tests of social function preferred by those dedicated to some particular end-product of government.

The general contrast between a downward and upward approach to formal organisation is familiar enough. The view from the engine-room is hardly likely to look the same as that from the bridge. However, this analysis has attempted to pursue these contrasting views of organisation in terms of the special conditions of public administration.

The complex and somewhat incoherent methods of goal-setting in public administration have been stressed. By contrast, the notion of 'social function' reflected in a basic work unit seems to be relatively firm and durable. Few would quarrel with the propositions that it is the function of the police to control crime, of town planners to regulate land use, of hospitals to cure patients, and so on. However, descriptions of this kind leave out the explanations about goals and techniques which tell us how these general tasks are viewed and performed. It is the infusion of goals and values, whether by professional participants or authoritative leaders, which breathes life into the system of functional organisation.

In this discussion, the word 'goal' (or its equivalents) has covered a range of policy formulation from the broad and abstract to the narrow and specific. This makes it difficult to envisage goal formulation as a basis for organisation in a very precise way. The notion seems to make sense when applied to a group of executives who are in clear command of limited resources. It might be applied in a similar way to the structure of small administrative units, where the framework of general goals can be taken as given, and it is the specific task which needs giving precision. The notion seems unrealistic when applied more broadly to public administration, because of the complexity of the goal-setting process and the overlapping and controversial nature of the goals themselves.

Nonetheless, discussion of goals does play a critical part in the evolution of administrative structure. Although agencies could not be graded in terms of the 'meaningfulness' of their activities, judgements can be made of the extent to which they are believed to have worthwhile goals by their workers, clients and general public. A high rating in these respects seems a good basis for administrative differentiation. Moreover, review of goals is the indispensable accompaniment for review of structure. It is the view-point from which the critic judges whether an administrative system is excessively or insufficiently hierarchical, too concentrated or too diffused, for the realisation of a desired range of objectives.

Moreover, public administration is unique in the variety of goals it exists to forward, and in the complexity of their interlocking relations. Continuous tensions arise over which goals merit more attention, how these should be defined, and what are their effects upon other accepted goals. In this sense, it is true that arguments about goals are fundamental to the review of administrative structure.

In conclusion, we may refer back to the distinctions between tasks, policies and purposes that were made earlier. Task is itself a neutral notion; it has to be infused with values of some kind. These values may represent the significance placed upon the task by those performing it (for example professional values) or its possible contributions to society as laid down by political and opinion leaders (for example public policies). The realm of purposes represents an appeal to general social values which can be adduced by all participants. Therefore, to insist that administrative organisation should be based upon goals is right in a very broad sense but almost tautologous, the real issue being *whose* evaluation of the meanings of tasks should form the basis for organisation.

ADMINISTRATIVE STRUCTURE AND FUNCTIONS

We can now look at administrative organisation from a fresh perspective which will utilise the previous discussion of the 'principles' of work allocation. The entire administrative system can be viewed as a continuum divided up in two interlocking ways. The system comprises a series of organisations, more or less separately defined, which represent focal points of managerial co-ordination and control; and it handles a complex set of tasks or functions which are separated and combined in diverse ways. Naturally, these two elements are closely interrelated. All functions must be allocated among organisations, and the rationale of every organisation is to perform functions. Nonetheless, the difference of perspective may prove illuminating.

The point becomes clearer, perhaps, if we define organisation in terms of the performance of certain managerial tasks. These tasks consist of the procurement of the basic inputs of administrative action in the form of legal powers, finance and staff; the allocation of these resources to various functions; and subsequent supervision over how the resources thus allocated are deployed. The entire administrative system is bound together through the discharge of these tasks at successive levels. Each organisation performs these tasks in relation to its specific bunch of functions, but, in addition, organisations are linked through a managerial chain, the resource outputs of one being the inputs of another. For example, local authorities and public boards are dependent upon central departments for essential inputs of money and legal authorisation; and the departments in turn must secure parts of their inputs from co-ordinating agencies. Consequently, the managerial chain has a generally hierarchical appearance, although it cannot be known *a priori* as to how far resource control involves policy control.

At the same time, functional organisation raises distinctive issues which cannot be comprehended within an analysis of this general managerial system. As already indicated, functions can be and are defined, divided and reassembled in a great variety of ways and a frontier of controversial issues about these matters always exists. Additionally, the social and technical conditions of functional performance are continually changing. Those concerned with the performance of a particular function or 'functional field' will press for organisational changes which meet their particular needs. Whilst functional claims will to some extent be offset or cancelled by rival interpretations of functional need, they will also in aggregate constitute pressures for change upon the general structure of administrative organisation.

In this section we shall consider two aspects of the interrelationship between functional organisation and general administrative structure. First, we will examine the impact of functional change upon the administrative system, and then reverse the approach to consider the effect of shifts in the general management system upon the performance of functions.

Functional organisation can be pictured as controlled by a blend of the *client* and *process* principles. The client principle often appears to dominate, in the sense that work is subdivided according to increasingly specialised definitions of the needs of clients. For example, welfare services, which once had a generalised character, have been subdivided to cater for a growing list of handicapped or deprived groups in need of public care or assistance. Educational services have been specialised so as to meet the needs of mentally subnormal, partially sighted and maladjusted children. Measures of industrial regulation and assistance have been broken down to meet the varying needs and problems of different sections of industry.

However, the client-oriented specialisation is frequently directed or guided through the development and specialisation of professional skills. Varying with the function in question, administrative 'producers' play a large part in defining the needs of clients and in deciding how these should be met. For example, the development of educational psychology made it possible to offer special assistance to mentally subnormal children, and this service then needed to be organised so as to produce suitable load factors for scarce and fairly expensive specialists. However, organisational tensions easily arise between expert opinions and those expressed by clients themselves, or by politicians or administrators on their behalf. Professional drives towards more specialisation and more elaborate career structures conflict with clients' preferences for more easily available forms of service; and political definitions of client need are offered in ignorance of professional developments.

The multiplication of specialised services for clients leads to counter-efforts to re-establish generalised services at a more sophisticated level. Once again these developments usually turn upon a new definition of 'client need', but are guided, or at least supported, by professional developments. The fragmentation of welfare services led to neglect of family-based social problems, and produced a professional movement in favour of family welfare that was reflected in Britain by the Seebohm Report and by the creation of social service departments in local government.[23] Similarly, town planning in many places is trying to expand its scope so as to conserve local community values which are threatened by population dispersal. In this case, the community, particularly the deprived community, is the intended client, paralleling at a wider level of social structure the situation of the problem family.

These efforts towards functional integration cannot overcome the stronger pressures towards functional specialisation. They may achieve a limited measure of service integration, if they can amass public support for new social goals, and can concretise these goals through the development of appropriate skills and techniques. Functional integration requires stronger political as opposed to professional efforts than does functional specialisation, because it must achieve a broader and less technical type of appeal. These problems are further discussed, in terms of administrative integration, at the end of the next chapter.

This account must be modified by further consideration of the 'process' principle. An increasing use of skills and processes which contribute only indirectly to the final service or output is usually seen as an extension of the process principle. However, some of these skills are closely conditioned by the nature of the final service, while others are applicable to a range of services which can be very wide. For example, teacher training, educational advice and inspection, and educational aids represent specialised skills which are shaped by the requirements of front-line teaching. On the other hand, land conveyance, building construction and the purchase of stores require skills that are relatively detached from the nature of the final service.

The first type of process specialisation is closely influenced by the nature and requirements of the ultimate clientele. The second type is much less influenced, or not at all influenced, in this way. However, the development of 'overhead' specialisations of the second kind does constitute a pressure for organisational enlargement or amalgamation. As the final services to clients become more specialised, there is some countervailing pressure to group the services together so as to achieve the advantages of joint overheads. Functional organisation thus becomes more complex in both its clientele and process aspects.

The 'area principle' enters this discussion mainly as a competing interpretation of the needs of clients to that offered by professional experts. Clients have a general interest in the geographic accessibility of all services and a special interest in relating services to geographic communities (local government) or to distinctive cultures (regionalism). However, these benefits decrease as physical mobility grows and as community ties are weakened, and they must, in any case, be balanced against the advantages of more specialised services operating across larger catchment areas.

The processes of functional specialisation and co-ordination have to be accommodated within the administrative system. This system consists of general-purpose or multi-purpose governments established at central and various local levels, which are flanked and supplemented by a variety of special-purpose agencies. The organisational contours of the system are the result of constitutional and political factors which usually have deep historical roots, and major changes in the general structure of the system tend to be slow and difficult. Adaptation to functional change follows three main lines:

a) A *horizontal* proliferation of departments and agencies at each principal level of government, as a response to functional specialisation. At a later stage the agencies thus created are often recombined into larger departments, for a mixture of functional and managerial reasons (see later). However, these large departments are necessarily complex organisations, containing considerable internal functional specialisation.

b) A *vertical* shift of specialised functions from lower to higher levels of government. Examples are shifts of many functions from the smaller to the larger local authorities, and from local government to central departments. A converse development is an increase in the range of field services provided by central departments or large local authorities so as to reach back to the final consumers.

c) A creation of *semi-detached* agencies or boards to carry out particular tasks. At central government level these agencies are created for a mixture of political and managerial reasons. At local or regional levels, the usual reasons are the inadequacy of local resources to support some major development (for example new town corporations); or the unsuitability of local boundaries for some functional or developmental task (for example various port and transportation authorities; regional hospital boards).

The pressures for functional specialisation push towards some maximum limit of organisational self-containment, involving an appropriate pattern of areas, finance, and accountability. Ideally this means a unique pattern of administrative areas; maximum freedom in the choice of methods and procedures; minimum dependence upon the overhead services of general-purpose governments; maximum financial independence; and lines of accountability directed more to the clients of the service and less to the public at large, often combined with a preference for more professional and less political control. The success of such claims can be seen in the frequent creation of special-purpose authorities, but the limitations of 'functional politics' are also revealed, not only through obstacles to the creation of such authorities but through the very limited autonomy which they achieve if created.

In the first place, the performance of many functions is dependent upon co-operation with related functions, which is an argument against organisational autonomy unless motives for co-operation are mutual and balancing. A special agency may try to meet this problem through incorporating responsibilities for closely related or dependent functions, but this achievement is difficult. There are some kinds of integrating functions, such as town planning, which are vitiated by administrative fragmentation, so that their practitioners will resist this process.

More importantly, pressures for functional autonomy conflict with the requirements of political, financial and administrative oversight exercised through general-purpose government. General-purpose government is usually accepted as the desirable arrangement for democratic and co-ordinative reasons, while specialised structures are usually defended as exceptions introduced for technical reasons. This contrast is a little too simple. One is dealing rather with pairs of opposites: specialised versus generalised concepts of accountability; functional economies versus overhead economies; 'goal effectiveness' versus goal co-ordination; and functional versus organisational forms of co-ordination.

Functions have to be fitted into the managerial requirements of the general administrative system. We can now reverse our approach and reconsider these requirements. We noted earlier the basic importance of political factors in this context. For example, the number of British departments had for long been dependent upon the size and structure of the Cabinet. However, these political factors themselves change and are also influenced, sometimes considerably, by general ideas about administrative or managerial efficiency.

Certain differences between managerial and functional aspects of co-ordination should be noted. Managerial co-ordination proceeds systematically up and down the administrative system following the lines and divisions of organisational structure. It must necessarily be comprehensive, in the sense of equally covering all parts of the system, and it cannot be avoided. Mechanisms must exist for controlling the flow and use of resources, and for settling jurisdictional disputes, whether they involve strong or weak degrees of collective planning.

Functional co-ordination is a more erratic and sporadic phenomenon. It entails variable degrees of policy co-ordination, affecting specific tasks very unevenly. It is less tied to organisational lines. For example, there is often much closer co-ordination between different organisations over the performance of some function, than there is co-ordination of related functions within the same organisation. Despite these limitations, there may often be considerable advantage in organisational recognition of a broad 'functional field'. Such a field is loosely defined by reference to zones of inter-acting policies, processes and clienteles.

Administrative reorganisation is generally undertaken for a mixture of functional and managerial reasons. An example is the creation of new giant departments in Britain, which was begun by the Labour Government in the late 1960s and completed by the Conservatives in 1970. These were Trade and Industry (incorporating the Board of Trade, Technology and Power); Environment (Housing and Local Government, Public Buildings and Works, Transport); and Social Services (Health, Social Security and Children's Services from the Home Office).

The explanations given by the Government were that organisation should serve policy, and that policy issues which are linked should be grouped together within the same organisation. This was described as the 'functional principle'. This description is of course much too simple since a grouping of clients (industries in the case of Trade and Industry and local authorities in the case of Environment), and a grouping of processes (technological resources in one case and constructional resources in the other) could also have been adduced, and were in fact without their difference from the 'functional principle' being noticed. Additionally the Government argued that the new departments would facilitate resource planning, and contribute more effectively to the formulation of overall strategy.[24]

As would be expected in such a situation, the Government stressed the many gains which could flow from the removal of departmental barriers, without considering the advantages of smaller departments. On the managerial side, these advantages include the tailoring of the workload to the capacities of a minister and his chief officials (the Chester-Willson 'principle' mentioned earlier), and the greater strength of personal and informal relations within a small department. On the functional side, they include the political and professional appeal of concentrated attention to some important task; for example a ministry responsible solely for a national health service has clearer duties and goals than a ministry for the social services. A giant department necessarily entails a much more complex structure, at both political and administrative levels, and a range of tasks whose unifying principle may not be very apparent on the ground.

The success of these developments can only reasonably be judged in terms of how the opportunities for internal reorganisation within a large department are in fact utilised. The problems of managerial control inevitably require increased attention from the top career officials. The treatment of policy co-ordination is a more open question. At a minimum, the structure of services may be left much as before, with policy conflicts arbitrated at the top of the department instead of being left to inter-departmental machinery. At a maximum, the existing services may be substantially reorganised so as to correspond to a new policy framework.

These issues of departmental size illustrate the necessity, and the problems, of fusing managerial and functional perspectives. In managerial terms, large departments may be seen as a simple application of span of control theory to conditions of more complex government. The existence of a large number of departments may be managerially satisfactory for each department, but impedes central co-ordination and planning. The creation of a much smaller number of large departments facilitates such planning, through reducing the number of participants, but in turn entails a double-deck system of top management within each large department. This system entails a more hierarchical structure of political management. Such changes are more likely to be acceptable if the political leadership has (or believes that it has) a general policy and resource strategy that needs to be imposed upon the administrative system. This will quite likely be the belief of an incoming government, especially if its leaders are impressed by general theories of managerial efficiency. In political terms, though, the new structure loses much of its appeal if the realisation of this general strategy comes to seem less important, or more difficult, than the realisation of specific functional goals. The structure will then be tested more by the latter yardstick.[26]

Managerial co-ordination requires, ideally, a systematic grouping of functions in roughly equal blocks, while functional considerations are intrinsically resistant to such tidy patterns. A compromise will therefore be struck between functional and managerial considerations. The purposes of the reform can be seen either as facilitating some goal of functional integration (for example environmental planning) at the cost of managerial complexity, *or* as improving the management system at the expense of some functional untidiness or lack of effectiveness. It is interesting that Sir Richard Clarke has given a careful exposition of the problems and the rationale of large departments in managerial terms, without mentioning the problems of functional co-ordination. Ultimately though, the system can only be judged from interacting perspectives, which assess the extent to which managerial change has been for functional profit.[25]

There is a parallel to be drawn between the creation of stronger departments within central government and the creation of stronger systems of local or regional government. A system of enlarged local authorities is an answer to functional pressures for enlarged areas of operation, and also has the managerial advantage of facilitating the general planning of resources through reducing the number of authorities with which central departments must deal. Such developments run contrary to the political or social appeal of 'localism', and also to the case for organisational variety and polycentricity (see Chapter 3).

The mutual adaptation of functions to administrative structure, and of structure to functions, is an ever-changing and complex process. However, we can conveniently summarise some conclusions.

a) Functional organisation is torn between processes of lateral specialisation and reintegration. In technical and professional terms the former process dominates, although with some significant counterpulls.

b) Functional organisation also tends towards a more complex vertical division of functions, and towards increased centralisation of specialised services and supervisory authority.

c) Attempts to develop autonomous functional structures have had some limited success, but founder upon the unifying political and financial elements of the administrative system.

d) Functions have to be slotted into the managerial framework for the control of resources within each multi-purpose organisation and throughout the whole system.

e) The increasing interaction of public policies across loosely defined 'functional fields' creates demands for broader functional groupings.

f) The pressures for functional co-ordination combine to some extent with those for closer managerial integration to favour large departments and strengthened systems of general-purpose government.

   g) The success of such experiments depends largely upon complex issues of internal organisation within departments.

REFERENCES

1 *Report of the Machinery of Government Committee of the Ministry of Reconstruction*, Cmd. 9230 (London, H.M.S.O., 1918). Luther Gulick, 'Notes on the Theory of Organisation', in L. Gulick and L. F. Urwick (eds): *Papers on the Science of Administration* (New York, 1937).

2 Poul Meyer, *Administrative Organisation* (Copenhagen, 1957), pp. 200–3.

3 For the transfer of the Children's Bureau, see Harold Stein, *Public Administration and Policy Development* (New York, 1952), pp. 15–31.

4 Alfred C. Wolf, 'The Blending of Area and Function', *Public Administration Review* (Autumn 1949).

5 Sir Maurice Dean, 'The Ministry of Technology', *Public Administration* (Spring 1966).

6 David T. Stanley, *Changing Administrations* (Washington, Brookings Institution, 1965), Chap. 6.

7 D. N. Chester and F. M. G. Willson, *The Organisation of British Central Government 1914–56* (London, 1957), p. 343.

8 See G. A. Campbell, *The Civil Service in Britain* (London, 1965), p. 246 (table).

9 Chester and Willson, op. cit., p. 82.

10 For problems of aviation policy, see David Corbett, *Politics and the Airlines* (London, 1965).

11 *Report of the Committee on Higher Education*, Cmnd. 2154 (London, H.M.S.O., 1963); and *Report of the Committee of Inquiry into the Organisation of Civil Science*, Cmnd. 2171 (London, H.M.S.O., 1963).

12 Meyer, op. cit., p. 80.

13 P. Self and H. Storing, *The State and the Farmer* (London, 1962), pp. 77–8.

14 H. Simon, D. Smithburg and V. Thompson, *Public Administration* (New York, 1950), pp. 263–6.

15 Chester and Willson, op. cit. This study is supplemented by periodic reviews of developments of the machinery of government in *Public Administration*.

16 Herbert A. Simon, *Administrative Behaviour*, 2nd ed. (New York, 1957), p. 42.

17 Chester Barnard, *The Functions of the Executive* (Cambridge, Mass., 1964), Chap. 10.

18 See J. A. G. Griffith, *Central Departments and Local Authorities* (London, 1966), Chap. 2.

19 For agricultural reorganisation in the U.S.A., see Charles Hardin,

The Politics of Agriculture (Glencoe, Illinois, 1952) and Stanley, op. cit., Chap. 5 For British reorganisation, see Self and Storing, op. cit., Chap. 6.

20 For problems of town planning control, see Evelyn Sharp, *The Ministry of Housing and Local Government* (London, 1969).

21 John D. Millett, *Organisation for the Public Service* (New York, 1966), pp. 77–101.

22 Simon, Smithburg and Thompson, op. cit., Chap. 12.

23 *Report of the Committee on Local Authority and Allied Personal Services*, Cmnd. 3703 (London, H.M.S.O., 1968).

24 *The Reorganisation of Central Government*, Cmnd. 4506 (London, H.M.S.O., 1970).

25 Sir Richard Clarke, *New Trends in Government* (London, 1971), Chap. 1.

26 Between 1971 and 1976 one giant department (Trade and Industry) was redivided into three, and in 1976 Transport was separated from Environment. These retrenchments fully support the analysis in the text, confirming the point that particular goals and problems – for example in transport – will become more important than policy co-ordination once a Government loses its initial impetus and strategy, especially of course if the policy co-ordination proved not very effective.

Chapter 3

ADMINISTRATIVE COMPETITION
AND CO-ORDINATION

THE VALUES OF COMPETITION AND CO-ORDINATION

One of the most interesting of administrative phenomena is competition and conflict between departments or agencies. The two words shade into each other. Competition arises from the demands of agencies for adequate resources and powers to pursue their goals successfully, or to enlarge their zones of jurisdiction. Agencies also compete sometimes for clients and for political sources of support. Even where an agency does not act assertively, it often finds that it cannot achieve its tasks effectively without changing the policies of an agency in some related field.

Administrative competition shades into conflict as these relationships between agencies become more direct and intense. Administrative conflict also arises frequently between agencies who share powers for the performance of some service. In this case, any differences of view-point will lead directly to administrative friction and conflict, whereas competition occurs as a more indirect relationship between agencies who in principle have separate jurisdictions and programmes.

Anthony Downs offers a territorial analogy of conflict between agencies. Each agency is pictured as occupying a policy zone which comprises a heartland, an interior zone, a no-man's land, and a periphery. Agency A's heartland is its exclusive zone of operation, but A's interior zone, though mainly under its control, may be a peripheral zone for other agencies. No-man's land is where agencies compete on roughly equal terms. This model corresponds to the tendency of the political system to allocate goals to agencies which overlap or conflict when they are made operational. However, the model assumes a degree of assertive action by agencies, and an absence or weakness of co-ordinative action, which may be quite untrue. It also offers a simplified version of a phenomenon which is considerably more complex.[1]

The treatment of competition and conflict is related to the character of administrative systems. A pluralistic system is marked by the proliferation of separate agencies, both 'horizontally' at the same level of government, and 'vertically' at regional and local levels. Partly as a consequence, the autonomy of each agency is relatively greater than under a more unitary system. The latter system, on the other hand, limits the multiplication of agencies and polices their powers and mutual relationships. Constitutional factors, such as the separation of powers and the Federal system, and the frequent right of local majorities to create new units of government, have made American administration highly pluralistic. For constitutional and historical reasons, most European systems are relatively unitary, although most systems become more pluralistic as government expands.

These institutional patterns are supported by different cultural values. Indeed, the clash of values on this point is surprisingly strong. Thus in Britain, as in most European countries, administrative competition and conflict are usually regarded with considerable disfavour, and any 'failure of co-ordination' constitutes serious criticism of public administration. These attitudes are rooted (especially for administrators themselves) in historical acceptance of the unity of the Crown and the desirable harmonisation of all public action, supported in modern times by the political capital to be gained through exposure of administrative conflict or waste. In the U.S.A., however, administrative competition and conflict are more readily tolerated as the necessary price of a pluralistic system, or even praised as indications of administrative vitality or as analogues with economic competition between firms.

Organisation theory does not provide much help with the evaluation of administrative conflict. The scientific management school stressed above all the value of a rational allocation and co-ordination of functions, but some modern students of organisation regard this ideal as fatal to administrative innovation. Most thinkers would admit that in some circumstances competition is highly desirable; for example, a business firm needs internal co-ordination primarily in order to compete effectively with other firms, and competition for posts within the firm may contribute to this result so long as it does not destroy the acceptance of a common goal. But the difficulty with public administration is to know what (if any) are the relevant units of competition. Sometimes the whole system must be energised so as to compete effectively with other governments, as in war or through international economic competition, but in most circumstances the function of the system is to serve society. Organisation theory is silent on the question of how much and what kind of competition is desirable between parts of the administrative system, or how this competition should be structured.

A more fruitful approach to the evaluation of administrative competition is through political theories of pluralism and integration. Political pluralism sees society as composed of competing groups and interests, and accepts or recommends that the administrative system should mirror these social demands. Various agencies will be created to respond to the demands of various social groups. A multiplication of agencies, far from being reprehensible, may reflect an increasingly sophisticated response to variegated social requirements. There is an obvious link here with the 'client' principle of work specialisation discussed in the last chapter, only on a pluralist view it is the demands of clients not the opinions of experts which should control specialisation. On a full pluralist approach, one is bound to accept administrative duplication since the needs of clients overlap; and also administrative conflict since this parallels, at least to some extent, the conflicts between social groups.[2]

These views contrast with traditional democratic theory, which holds that it is the task of political parties and leaders to synthesise the demands of social groups, and produce a coherent and consistent programme to be implemented through the administrative system. The policy of each agency may change when political leadership changes, but administrative conflict is a reproach to the unity of the government of the day. British administrators would still subscribe to this ideal of administrative action, although increasing political pluralism in the society is causing rather more tolerance of administrative competition. Conversely, in the U.S.A. the doctrine that administration should reflect pluralist demands competes with the doctrine that agencies should be responsive to the unified programme of the current administration.

The administrative treatment of unorganised or weakly organised groups provides a critical test for these various theories. Such groups have a latent voting power which can be harnessed by political parties and leaders who act (or appear to act) on their behalf. This circumstance is reflected in the structure of American politics; Congress responds mainly to well-organised or localised interests while Presidents are more responsive to the supposed wishes of 'silent' majorities and minorities. However, under any system organised interests are relatively powerful.

A pluralist theory could be criticised for allowing administrative structure to be dominated by the demands of the more powerful groups. The attempted answer to this situation is the creation of additional agencies to meet the specific needs of underprivileged groups, a strategy which was an integral part of President Roosevelt's 'New Deal' and was later followed by President Kennedy. This strategy meets the needs of such groups as small farmers, unemployed, and the inhabitants of city 'ghettos' through the creation of special agencies, instead of through attempting to shift the policies of established agencies. The drawback to this strategy is that it produces continuing conflicts between the rival agencies, with an inevitable tendency for those agencies which are supported by the stronger groups to wax more successful.

Conversely British administration provides a more paternalistic treatment of underprivileged groups, who are supposedly protected by the 'public spirit' of both politicians and administrators, activated on occasion by latent voting power. These notions of administrative equity and fairness are not simply a myth, but they have to be set against the direct influence upon administration of well-organised groups. Equity thus shows itself most clearly in the administrative consideration sometimes shown to small organisations who have a plausible claim to speak for underprivileged groups or on behalf of some weakly articulated 'general interest'. One can only conclude that in democracies there is no sure recipe for making administration responsive to weakly articulated interests.

Related to arguments for variety are those for the maximum possible organisational autonomy. The relevant theory is supplied by the case for polycentricity discussed in the first chapter. This theory stresses the notion of 'goal effectiveness' as defined particularly by those responsible for the provision of some service and by those who are intended to benefit from it. Goal effectiveness will be maximised if the relevant agency is given as broad a mandate as possible to 'get on with the job', and is trammelled as little as possible by requirements for consultation. The pressure of public policies that cannot lightly be ignored easily explains the frustration of officials who find their primary goals blocked by the need to consider what (for them) are secondary or irrelevant goals. Failures of administrative co-ordination can be accepted as the necessary price of strengthening goal effectiveness. Within this context it is easy to understand the frequent demand that some function should be 'cut free of red tape', or taken outside the regular machinery and handed to a special agency devoted exclusively to its performance.

The counter-arguments to polycentric theory turn upon questions of policy control and co-ordination. The effect of increasing agency autonomy will be to weaken general political control in favour either of professional control or sectional influence, or of some mixture of these elements. Policy co-ordination will be weakened by more agency autonomy to the extent that the agency's function is or ought to be linked with some other function. We can summarise these points by saying that the more self-contained is any function, and the clearer is the policy guidance laid down by political leaders, the more practical it is to increase agency autonomy. This conclusion would hold for *any* system, the differences residing in the tolerance of systems towards accepting the risks of greater autonomy.

An example is road construction. A highway agency is much more likely to maximise the output of roads in accordance with the wishes of road users if it has a fair degree of autonomy. However, the co-ordination of roads with town planning, regional development, and the protection of the countryside will get less attention in this situation; indeed that is a necessary consequence of concentrating highway administration upon its primary goal. One consequence is that the enhanced satisfaction of road users will be offset by dissatisfaction among other groups who are affected indirectly by the road programme. By contrast, the operation of nationalised railways has much less indirect effects of this kind, because new railways now are only rarely built. Consequently, functional co-ordination is much less necessary in the case of railways than of roads, which explains why the former function is usually entrusted to a public corporation while efforts to establish a special agency for highways usually fail.*

More organisational autonomy can be claimed to achieve better value for money, through its concentration upon simplified objectives and its possible morale-boosting effects. On the other hand, a multiplication of agencies operating in related fields will often duplicate overhead costs and lose possible economies of scale and specialisation. Additionally, there are indirect costs and benefits imposed by agencies upon each other and upon various sections of the community. These side-effects represent the economic aspect of the case for goal co-ordination, but it is easier to claim their relevance in some specific case than to develop a satisfactory theory of resource co-ordination. While administrative competition cannot be

---

* More often this difference is explained by the fact that railways are directly, but roads only indirectly, supported by their users. However, it would be possible to set up an independent highway authority charged with getting 'value for money' out of some allocated budget or fund, however this was determined. Technical problems of financial control are in fact a less important administrative issue than problems of goal co-ordination.

defended upon the same grounds as business competition, since market tests of efficiency are lacking, administrative integration can find no adequate basis in theories of resource planning. However, administrative pluralism is often vulnerable to demonstrations of specific dis-economies.

Some of these issues are reconsidered at the end of the book. An immediate conclusion is that administrative competition and co-ordination are linked with the pluralist and unitary tendencies of systems, and as such reflect conflicting values about the location of authority and about the relative importance of goal effectiveness versus goal co-ordination. Our next concern is to look more closely at the determinants of the behaviour of agencies, and then at the types of competition and conflict to which such behaviour gives rise. Finally the chapter will cover a few examples of administrative reorganisation which will help to show the conditions that are necessary for measures of administrative integration to succeed.

AGENCY 'PHILOSOPHY' AND INDEPENDENCE

An administrative agency is not simply a compliant instrument for the implementation of political goals. It generates its own interpretation of those goals. Everyone concerned with public administration testifies to the reality of agency or departmental 'philosophy';* but the causes and character of this phenomenon are largely unplumbed. The distinctive attitudes of an agency can be seen as the product of accumulated experience and tradition, created by familiarity with a particular set of tasks and problems, and influenced perhaps by the personalities of leading administrators. A new recruit to the staff is inducted into established methods and attitudes, which unless rebellious he will tend to copy and emulate. Departmental philosophy appears to spread by osmosis among participants and to produce a kind of collective personality. The Treasury, the Foreign Office or the Pentagon project distinctive images upon the public and are expected to behave in certain ways. The very buildings in which they are housed impart a grey quality to their personalities.

These popular images may not be remote from the truth, but they are vague and simplified. Clearly the potency of 'agency philosophy'

* There is a difficulty of terminology here. *Departmental* philosophy is a more natural description to a British audience, but for the purpose of American comparisons is misleading because the subdivisions of departments (bureau) are the main source of distinctive view-points. The general phrase 'agency philosophy' will therefore be used.

will vary considerably both between governmental systems and between particular agencies. Agency viewpoints are much more fully and aggressively articulated in American than in any European type of government. Differences between agencies depend partly no doubt upon antiquity or tradition – Professor Beer, for example, considers antiquity to be a main explanation of the Treasury's character and influence – and partly, too, upon the more random impress of powerful personalities – once again, modern Treasury attitudes would certainly have been different if Sir Warren Fisher had not been its chief official for twenty years.[3] It is impossible to generalise about such influences. However, certain elements in the creation of agency viewpoints can be treated more systematically, and these include the nature of an agency's work methods and clientele, or, in other words, the influence of the process and client factors upon the attitudes of agencies.

In terms of methods of work, a distinction may be drawn between the more bureaucratic and the more technocratic type of agency. The work of the former is governed closely by laws and rules, and is concerned usually with the enforcement of regulations or the provision of services of a fairly standardised nature. Uniformity and impartiality are requirements; discretion is very limited and is guided by detailed rules, not by professional or technical judgement. The work of the latter type of agency is concerned with more flexible services and tasks which require a considerable degree of professional or scientific discretion. This discretion is oversimplified, but corresponding types of agency can be easily recognised. Thus a social security agency or a factory inspectorate fall in the first category; and agencies providing welfare services or conducting scientific research in the second.

The first type of agency will be more disposed towards a generalised and legalistic view of its functions, than will the latter type, which will tend towards more discretionary and particularist interpretations of its goals. The second type of agency is more likely to have a distinctive or assertive view-point, particularly if it is manned by a strong professional group dedicated to a certain view of agency goals. The extent to which professional groups do behave in this way varies widely, and partly depends upon recruitment and training (see Chapter 6).

The more usual distinction between regulatory and service agencies is different from that above. Some newer regulatory agencies exercise considerable discretion, particularly over the control of economic competition, and cannot follow bureaucratic work methods; some service agencies provide standardised benefits.

Many agencies, particularly those charged with the welfare of some industry, have both types of function. In general, however, regulatory agencies incline towards an arbitrative view of their duties, while service agencies are concerned with goal achievement. In the former case, a liberal view of the State sometimes still prevails, and the agency may be disinterested or even hostile to an expansion of its powers, whereas service agencies generally want to maximise their outputs. It is usual for agencies responsible for building roads or providing welfare services to believe that an increase of their activities is highly desirable.

Secondly, agency philosophies are shaped by relationships with clients. The client group may be small and ill-organised, or it may be the opposite. In the former case, the professional staff of the agency will probably regard themselves as protectors and defenders of the client group, and interpreters of its needs. An example is problem families. In the latter case, the clients will articulate their own demands effectively, and the agency will face the problem of squaring these demands with its interpretation of public policy. An example is farmers.

The nature of these agency-client relationships depends very much upon the political system. In a highly pluralistic system such as the U.S.A., agencies and client groups frequently form alliances for the purpose of expanding the provision of some service. The agency is not necessarily subservient to the group's wishes but is quite likely to have promoted or sponsored the group as a way of increasing support for its own policies. Competition occurs between rival coalitions of agencies and groups. In Britain, coalitions of this type are much more limited and less explicit, and the usual relationship between a government department and a large interest group is one of frequent consultation and cautious bargaining within certain policy limits. However hard the department may fight the group on occasion, it will still tend to champion the group's needs as interpreted by itself in inter-departmental controversy.[4]

There is again a difference between service agencies and agencies whose task is to regulate the actions of some group according to some concept of public interest. In the latter case, the 'true' clients of the agency may be conceived as the latent group whom the agency is benefiting. For example, the Monopolies Commission is ultimately serving consumers, and the Board of Trade's control of industrial location is exercised on behalf of the inhabitants of the less prosperous regions. In such cases, the agency is being pushed from behind by political goals, rather than pulled from the front by client needs. However, it still must attend to the requirements of the group being regulated, especially where it needs to utilise persuasion as well as coercion, and it is the regulated group with which it directly deals.

This situation leads to the frequent accusation, particularly in the U.S.A., that an agency has been 'captured' by the interest it is supposed to be regulating. A more frequent situation is to produce great difficulties for the agency over balancing policy goals against the view-points and problems of those being regulated which it comes to understand much better than do ultimate political controllers. Whether the agency then tends towards a cautious interpretation or modification of its original goals, or whether it tries to ram them through, regardless of obstruction, will depend considerably upon the political balance; how much support has the original goal and how strong and persuasive is the regulated group?

It is clearly difficult to distinguish between the internal and environmental factors which shape the attitudes of agencies. An agency's interpretation of its goals is shaped by pressures brought to bear through the political process and its dealings with clients. Its own resources and methods of working also govern its response to these challenges, although vigorous leadership on occasion can expand those resources and change those methods. Thus one can point out some of the factors which shape 'agency philosophy', without being able to provide any adequate taxonomy of its constituent elements.

An agency's view-point will also differ according to whether it discharges heterogeneous or homogeneous functions, and deals with one main client group or with many. Clearly, the larger and more complex the agency the less likely is it to have a distinctive philosophy at all. However, if central management of the agency is a reality, the views adopted over the discharge of its most important tasks will influence its approach to other tasks. The Board of Trade has for long been concerned with the regulation of international trade, and has favoured a policy of liberalisation wherever possible. This concern seems to have shaped its attitude to the problems for those industries for which it is responsible. The Board was certainly more reluctant to concede protection to the cotton industry during the 1950s than were the Departments of Agriculture and Aviation to succour their industries. A further factor was that the Board covered many industries, not just one.[5]

The assumed 'dominant philosophy' of agencies is an important factor over the allocation and regrouping of functions. Much criticism was expressed at the location of the children's service in the Home Office, on the grounds that the arbitrative and sometimes coercive attitudes relevant to the maintenance of law and order (the department's principal concern) are not favourable to a welfare philosophy. The original reason for assigning the care of children to the Home Office was the legal issues which arise over adoption and the prevention of cruelty, as well as the problems of juvenile delinquency. The demand to put the service elsewhere may look like an assertion of the client against the process principle; but it is also close to a clash of process principles (regulative versus welfare techniques) since it is welfare workers who articulate these clients' requirements. Many similar examples could be given of how the 'image' of an agency influences the allocation of functions, both negatively and positively.

The degree of independence which an agency possesses depends upon a mixture of political and managerial factors. Tasks vary considerably in terms of their political and technical elements, and the mixture of these elements much affects the kind of discretion which an agency can possess. Often a function is much more political in its early stages, but then settles down into a managerial or professional routine. Administrative precedents are set and professional discretion is exercised in ways which gradually settle the agency's interpretation of its work. These routines usually possess considerable durability and survival value.

Where a function has a high political content it may seem misleading to talk of agency autonomy at all. The political content is supplied by political leaders, interest groups and other transient or external sources which are not built into the agency's structure in any durable way. Curiously though, functions with considerable political content are not infrequently 'depoliticised' in a formal sense through being handed to a semi-independent agency. It is worth considering what seem to be the three main reasons for this treatment.

First, an *altruistic* reason is acceptance by the Government of the idea that the direct performance of some function is contrary to democratic values. The obvious example is management of mass communications, as represented in Britain by the assignment of broadcasting to an independent corporation. The second reason is *judicial*, but this notion may mean no more than that certain definitely political issues should be tackled through somewhat judicialised procedures. An independent agency is set up to decide individual cases seriatim in an open and public manner, within a framework of broad policy guidance which the agency will attempt to substantiate through the development of rules and precedents. Essentially this is a device for trying to stabilise the treatment of controversial issues of public regulation, through a partial insulation of decisions from shifts of government policy and from the pressures of private interests. The third reason is *persuasive*, which means that the Government wants to make some programme more acceptable to affected interests, through reducing its direct control and appointing executors who are better trusted by potential critics.

Both the second and third of these reasons imply the existence of a delicate and controversial balance between public and private interests. In the second category, public policy is often vague or erratic, while the existence of conflict among private interests supports the case for a partly judicialised body.

In the third category, the problem is effective implementation of a public policy which arouses hostility among affected groups. Thus the 1965–70 Labour Government in Britain sought to implement part of its industrial policy through an Industrial Reorganisation Corporation and its land policy through a Land Commission instead of through ordinary departments. These devices at least reassured critics that the programmes would be guided by reputable business or professional men appointed to the boards of the new agencies.

In a formal sense quasi-judicial agencies have a very high degree of autonomy indeed. However, the agency may possess little real coherence and serve mainly as a forum for fights between contending outside interests or view-points. Independent Regulatory Commissions in the U.S.A. are often divided between consumer advocates and industry advocates, or between supporters of different economic interests.[6] The establishment of an independent agency for persuasive reasons often has the effect of giving a very influential role to the co-opted chairman, particularly over modifications of policies so as to make them more acceptable. Unfortunately, detailed studies of the roles played by such individuals are lacking, although it is known (for example) that the chairman of the Central Land Board in Britain persuaded the Labour minister who appointed him that for *technical* reasons development charge must be levied at 100 per cent. This is a case where a professional view-point did not make the measure more acceptable, and indeed contributed to the demise of the agency.[7]

In contrast with these political situations, agencies or divisions responsible for specialised technical tasks generally have considerable discretion, whatever their formal status. Agencies responsible for scientific research or technical advice suffer mainly from the burden of centralised financial and administrative procedures, not from policy controls, and it is the hope of cutting free from such restrictions that inspires demands for greater formal autonomy. This ambition is usually vain, unless a substantial source of user-supported finance is available to the agency. In Britain, independent boards are usually only created for managerial reasons if this condition is satisfied, as is the case with the nationalised industries. Sometimes, however, a public board is set up for a mixture of managerial and political reasons. Bodies such as the Forestry Commission and the White Fish Authority perform fairly self-contained technical tasks, and also are vehicles for establishing sympathetic relations with a particular industry. In the U.S.A., the proliferation of special agencies is helped along by greater political willingness to concede to them special taxing rights or a protected financial status; for example, local school boards must be allowed their taxation requests.

If one asks what are the special circumstances which maximise the effective independence of an agency, they are probably threefold. First, a real abnegation of governmental policy control, sometimes for reasons of principle and sometimes because there are several governments involved who can agree only upon appointing an independent body; secondly, the existence of a task or tasks which can be treated in relative isolation from the rest of government; and thirdly, the existence of an adequate and independent source of revenue. One should add to this list an absence of any powerful interest group of clients or suppliers who can substitute their control for that of the withdrawing government. Examples of very different agencies which satisfy these conditions fairly well are the British Broadcasting Corporation (Britain) and the Port of New York Authority (U.S.A.).

The use made by an agency of such independence as it gets is of course another matter. A critical question is the old one of how far it is effectively geared to particular goals. Paradoxically, an increase of autonomy may actually reduce goal effectiveness, because policies become the concern of shifting balances among directors and staff – the 'politics of oligarchy' – instead of being settled in more dogmatic political and professional ways. This has been a problem for the B.B.C. since its more dynamic early days. There can also be conflicts between internal and external tests of achievement; to quote the B.B.C. again, concentration upon the popularity ratings of programmes is a way of demonstrating that the Corporation can compete successfully with commercial television and thus deserves higher licence fees, but acceptance of this test also destroys much of the Corporation's cultural tradition and rationale.

In conclusion, it is clear that the behaviour and attitudes of a public agency are the result of complex factors, and that agency discretion has no single or simple meaning. But agency behaviour is guided along fairly predictable lines by (i) the strength and balance of its client groups; (ii) the nature of its staff resources; and (iii) the extent to which its work is bureaucratic or professional. The interplay of these factors explains the different 'images' of agencies, which is an important factor in relation to the allocation of new functions. So far as managerial factors are concerned, an agency's discretion grows with the technical content of its work and with the self-containment of its task, but the gradations are minor, and formal independent status is unlikely unless the service is self-financing or there are political arguments for some degree of detachment. Agencies with high formal independence are some-times simply battlegrounds for contending interests, and a consider-able degree of effective autonomy does not necessarily imply that the agency will have positive goals.

FUNCTIONAL DUPLICATION AND POLICY CONFLICTS

Having dealt with some of the meanings of 'agency philosophy', we can better analyse the causes and results of competition and conflict between agencies. We will do this by considering two types of problem – functional duplication and policy conflict.

Functional Duplication

Since two agencies never perform precisely the same tasks, the extent of functional duplication is a matter of judgement. Duplica-tion can be said to arise when two or more agencies provide very similar services for very similar publics, or pursue activities which have substantial overlap in terms of their technical and professional requirements.

In Britain, considerable care is taken to avoid obvious examples of functional duplication. The Treasury is alert to prevent over-lapping jurisdictions as a likely source of financial waste and administrative confusion, and its position is supported by the political authority of the executive and the values of the administra-tive class. On a broader perspective, duplication does of course occur. For example, in 1969 the Ministry of Technology was striving to modernise certain industries with the aid of recom-mendations from joint working groups, while the Department of Economic Affairs was promoting the efficiency of the same indus-tries through the work of industrial advisers and sponsored economic development councils. Aid and exhortation to industry is less tidily organised than responsibility for public services and statutory regulations. Even for industry, however, the post-war system of sponsoring departments ensures that every section of industry is the particular responsibility of some part of a department.[8]

The American system, by contrast, produces extensive functional duplication. The rivalries of Congress and President prevent effective policing of functional allocations, other than intermittent and very limited efforts by the Bureau of the Budget, and lay the door open for the type of alliance between administrative agency, client group, and Congressional sub-committee which defends the agency's sphere of influence. These 'policy sub-systems' are not of course autonomous – they are variously controlled by superior executive authorities as well as by the complex bargains struck within Congress – but they are particularly effective at resisting efforts at administrative rationalisation and reorganisation. At the same time, the existence of three tiers of government (Federal, State and local) which have substantial functional autonomy and are strongly resistant to structural change, means that national programmes acquire most bite if executed by special local agencies. Vertical is added to horizontal proliferation.

The American administrative system is 'goal-oriented' in the sense that agencies are frequently assigned a broad and challenging objective. Because of strong political opposition to administrative reorganisation, the political urges to innovate can often only be satisfied through the creation of a new agency. The actual effect of the new agency may be mainly to impart a rather different direction or momentum to already well-established programmes. The emphasis on the redefinition of basic goals tends to disguise functional duplication in a way less likely to arise where tasks are more specifically and prosaically allocated.

For example, the Office of Economic Opportunity was created in 1964 for the broad purpose of combating poverty. It was given a number of powers for assisting educational and training schemes, issuing small loans, and operating local community action programmes, the last being its most novel feature. However, much of the work of the O.E.O. had to be carried on through other agencies such as the Small Business Administration. Moreover, its local programmes overlapped considerably with the various measures taken by several other agencies to assist impoverished areas; such as the large area redevelopment programme of the Department of Commerce, the model cities programme of the Department of Housing and Urban Development, the rural assistance measures of the Department of Agriculture, and the work of the Appalachian Regional Commission.[9]

The elaborate pattern of Federal financial grants to State and local agencies demonstrates the extent of administrative duplication. An enquiry found 170 or 240 such programmes, depending upon the method of counting. Some of these grants are very broad in scope, like forms of assistance to problem areas, while others are very narrow and specific. Each sponsoring agency establishes separate procedures and requirements, operational areas, and local supportive organisations. While the goals and 'philosophies' of these agencies ostensibly differ, many are concerned with the same type of end-product, particularly the construction of public works. Thus a local project is often constructed with funds provided from many Federal sources, and it is not exceptional to find five agencies prepared to help build the same sewage treatment plant. According to the Executive Director of the Appalachian Regional Commission: 'each programme has its own criteria, its own priorities. Some are so narrow as to be virtually unusable. Others duplicate each other and compete for clientele as if they were the corner grocer.' One result is considerable ignorance, even among administrators themselves, as to what programmes exist. A computerised list of Federal programmes for community improvement in the State of Maine ran to forty-eight pages.[10]

Administrative competition of this kind need not lead to conflicts which must be resolved by higher authority. (Competition and conflict are not the same though they shade into each other.) There is no necessary limit to the number of grants-in-aid which can be offered on different conditions towards the costs of similar end products.* To take another example, in most rural counties there are field staff from five or more agricultural agencies, and farmers must be found to serve on a variety of elected supporting organisations. These agencies are responsible for various technical and educational services, as well as financial assistance and production control, and there is a good deal of overlapping activity; but allied with different interest groups it is possible for the agencies to sustain this type of competition indefinitely.[11]

Competition must become direct conflict only in those cases where

* Recent forms of aid tend to be broad packages of familiar forms of assistance. For example, the model cities programme is not concerned specifically with physical renewal but with assistance for almost any type of statutory activity which can be argued to be beneficial to the inhabitants of a selected locality. The programme is determined through competitive bidding by cities.

some task is indivisible but two agencies have the powers and the wish to do it. The prime example is the conflicts between the Bureau of Reclamation and the Army Corps of Engineers over the construction of high dams and hydro-electric works. The interest of the two agencies in integrated water resource development started from opposite ends – the Bureau from land reclamation and irrigation, the Corps from navigation and flood control. The Bureau coming down the river met the Corps moving up. In the King's River case, Presidential backing for the 'dominant interest' of the Bureau in the proposed project could not overcome Congressional preference for the Corps or the Corps' own recalcitrance. Similar inter-agency conflicts in the Missouri Valley were temporarily resolved by a sort of negotiated treaty between leading officials known as the Pick-Sloan Plan.[12]

How far does this kind of administrative competition possess its alleged advantages? The analogy with economic competition between firms seems a misleading one. Firms risk their own resources to compete for profit whereas agencies compete for clients and supporters with public money voted by Congress. (It is true that Congress has prohibited direct expenditure on public relations by agencies, but the ban is not very effective.) Again economic competition would probably bring about rationalisation and mergers, whereas political competition prevents this result and allows 'bureaucratic free enterprise'. The argument that competition keeps agencies on their toes also backfires. Possibly the partisan if parochial attitudes of bureau chiefs have value for goal achievement, but they are dedicated to very narrow and rather formalistic interpretations of their goals. They seem also to be easily satisfied with the particular procedures and tests laid down by their own agency, and to have little concern with broader questions of good government.[13]

Administrative sociology certainly supports the political and constitutional causes of administrative fragmentation. The lack of any general class of Federal administrators does much to explain the weakness of inter-agency committees. The specialised skills and narrow governmental experience of many bureau chiefs and their assistants create barriers to mutual understanding and strong attachment to the procedures and 'philosophy' of the bureau. This is patent in such a case as the Army Corps of Engineers, but it is present to some extent in all agencies. The officials in the Bureau of the Budget act as administrative advisers and adjusters rather than co-ordinators. The growth of the President's powers and office, and the multiplication of Federal programmes, have produced increased recognition from officials of the need for co-ordination; but while the principle is accepted, its application is turned in narrow and partisan directions. Indeed the possibility that Federal administration might seem wasteful and cumbrous to an outside observer but rarely occurs to officials themselves or to most Americans.

Policy Conflict

This is different in principle from functional duplication, although the two phenomena overlap. Conflict arises from disagreement between agencies over the desirable action to be taken on some matter of mutual concern. This very general situation has many applications. It is worth asking the naïve question: how and why do such agency conflicts occur?

A basic cause, mentioned earlier, is the frequent inconsistency or vagueness of public policy goals. These difficulties are not necessarily noted during the phase of general policy formation, but may become apparent when policies are translated by agencies into specific programmes. Alternatively, a conflict of aims may be recognised politically but be deliberately remitted to the administrative process for solution.

There are two forms which this deliberate institutionalisation of political conflict can take. One is the creation of a regulative or co-ordinative agency which has the task of adjudicating between competing interests. Secondly, agencies may be deliberately created to pursue conflicting aims and told in effect to fight it out.

Clear examples of this second situation are naturally rare. Political leaders do not readily admit that they are incapable of solving problems, or invite the reproach of creating administrative conflict. The situation primarily arises in relation to staff assistance. Political leaders may wish the benefit of hearing conflicting advice of a detailed kind before reaching decisions, and may hand out assignments or even create special agencies to secure this result (see Chapter 4).

Sometimes, however, the rationale of such 'creative conflict' is obscure. The creation of the Department of Economic Affairs by the Labour Government in 1964 was certainly intended to institutionalise an expansionist approach towards the economy, as opposed to the supposedly restrictive view-point of the Treasury. This might have made sense if the two agencies had fed in their conflicting advice to the Cabinet for decision (a staff agency concept). In fact, however, the D.E.A. attempted to operate as a second co-ordinator of the economy and public planning, and encountered the inevitable result that the agency having the stronger leverage for co-ordination wins the day.

The more normal situation is not engineered policy conflicts, but unintended and unforeseen ones. These do not arise from mere inconsistencies of policy. The critical need for an agency is to establish and achieve a workable programme, and so long as this is possible, the agency need not necessarily worry (or even realise) that its programme is in some broad sense contradictory to that of another agency. The problem arises in an acute form when its programme is blocked by that of another agency, and in a mild form when it would be advantageous to the first agency to persuade the second one to act in a certain way.

We can illustrate these points from physical planning. The fact that some agencies are encouraging employers to quit congested areas (for example through the new towns programme), while others are assisting them to remain (for example through subsidised fares and special housing programmes for workers), may be an example of inconsistent public policies, but does not thereby prevent any agency from executing its part of these programmes. However, a British new town development corporation cannot achieve its prescribed goals unless it can secure a steady build-up of industrial employment. The control of industrial location is handled by another agency, the Board of Trade, whose main goal is to steer industries towards development areas which are defined by liability to unemployment. There has not been enough mobile industry to satisfy all the needs of development areas and new towns, and indeed other 'problem' areas. Formally, the Board's mandate is a general one – to achieve a satisfactory distribution of industry – and was in fact obtained under a Planning Act, but there is no doubt that the Board's interpretation of its goals accords with political support for its powers. When it was demonstrated that the new towns could not succeed without getting more industry, the Board conceded to them a second preference status – a compromise which has not of course avoided many specific disputes but which has enabled most of the new towns to achieve their goals.[14]

This type of conflict can also be pictured as related to the use of resources. Organisational resources represents inputs of money, staff and legal powers. The most obvious type of administrative competition is over budgeting – competition more than conflict since the encounter is many-sided and need not involve obstruction to any agency's goals. However, the supply of regulatory authority is also limited. Such powers cannot be extended beyond their political acceptability or feasibility so that there will be conflict between interested agencies over their use. A similar situation exists wherever government takes powers to allot monopoly franchises. Land use conflicts, for example, are often assumed to derive from the scarcity of land itself but more accurately represent conflicts over the exercise of regulatory powers. When several applicants, public as well as private, want permission to use a piece of land, they cannot all be satisfied. Similar regulatory conflicts arise over transport, radio or television franchises; often conflict occurs between public agencies on behalf of sponsored or favoured clients, rather than for their own requirements.

The mere institutionalisation of functions creates a tendency to conflict on all matters of common concern. The multiplication of governmental powers and (in some countries) the countervailing efforts at planning and co-ordination mean that numerous decisions are of concern to more than one agency. In all such cases an expression of conflicting view-points is to be expected – sometimes indeed an agency may feel itself to be inferior if it has not a specific view-point to offer. These departmental contributions may reflect a deep or shallow interest and knowledge, but to some extent can be deduced simply from institutional position. A department must speak for its clients, even after fighting them; it must defend and preferably expand its own programmes and works; and often it can be expected to react in almost Pavlovian style. A finance ministry is expected to discuss and articulate the needs of economy on every occasion, and an agricultural ministry must be ready with its own version of a farming view-point.

Devices for the reconciliation of agency conflicts are the same in almost all governmental systems. They entail a very full use of inter-departmental committees, supported by the possibility of appeal to ultimate political authority. It is necessary to the conduct of business that the number of issues taken to a Cabinet or a President should be relatively small, so that the main load of business falls upon committees of varying importance and durability. In Britain, the top tier consists of Cabinet committees, below which are numerous committees of officials, some fairly permanent but many formed to tackle some issue and then dissolved. Considerable use is also made of informal consultations.[15]

Despite the stress upon administrative competition in the U.S.A., the committee system there is at least equally elaborate. For example, the Department of Agriculture (a large department with many sub-agencies) is represented on 263 inter-agency committees and chairs 47 of these; it also attends 24 committees concerned specifically with the co-ordination of grants-in-aid.[16] Presidents attempt to resolve disputes according to 'dominant interest' or 'sphere of interest' doctrines. For example, President Johnson signed an Urban Convenor Order in 1966 which empowers the Secretary for Housing and Urban Development or his representatives to convene meetings and task forces for establishing consistent urban policies. A Rural Convenor Order in the same year assigned a parallel role to the Secretary for Agriculture.

Differences occur over the results rather than the methods of administrative co-ordination. In the American case these are far from impressive. It seems to be a major achievement for an inter-departmental committee to standardise the procedures for two closely similar types of grant-in-aid. Any real attack upon the idio-syncrasy and complexity of agency methods for tackling similar problems is beyond the capacity of the machine. Even the President's ruling in cases of sharp conflict is not necessarily accepted in practice. The Presidential device of assigning spheres of influence is simply a device for lending political weight to the efforts of some Secretary to act as a tentative co-ordinator, rather than a real mandate to resolve disputes or reduce duplication. Given the strongly partisan attitudes of agency representatives, and the lack of a strong co-ordinating centre, little other result is to be expected. A broader survey of problems of co-ordination occasionally emerges from a Presidential advisory committee or a reforming Congressional committee such as the Muskie Sub-Committee on Intergovernmental Relations; but it is a long step from exposure to reform.

In the case of Britain, administrative co-ordination is much more thorough. Inter-departmental committees are adept at reconciling, or appearing to reconcile, policy conflicts, while standardisation of procedures is also easier to achieve where clearly desirable. Even so, the machinery does not easily bite deep and the results can perhaps be best described as 'negative co-ordination'. In a sense, this is inevitable. Most decisions are the statutory responsibility of some department which holds the initiative. The department may be persuaded to modify its intentions if injury is demonstrated to the programme of another department, but not easily otherwise. Committees of busy officials are an instrument for papering over cracks and making marginal adjustments, but are ill-placed to examine the basic causes of agency conflict. Such exposures can only be achieved as a rule through the political process or by outside investigation. Administrative co-ordination offers no substitute for integrated policy-making or planning.

THE FORMS OF ADMINISTRATIVE CONFLICT

We can supplement this discussion by a typology of the main forms of administrative conflict, which can be related to the analysis of conflicting values at the beginning of the chapter.

TABLE OF ADMINISTRATIVE CONFLICT

	Rationale of System	Cost of System	Example
A. Competition between separate agencies			
1) Over services:	Multiple needs	Resource wastes	Agricultural Services (U.S.A.)
2) Over policies:	Goal effectiveness	Goal inconsistencies or frustration	New towns and industrial location
B. Conflict between linked agencies			
1) Over services:	Multiple channels for conveying needs	Procedural frustrations	Education (delegation)
2) Over policies:	Representation of conflicting interests	Deadlock	Planning (London)

So far we have dealt with Category A, which mainly relates to parallel agencies operating at the same level of government. Category B deals with agencies who share jurisdictional responsibility for some service or policy, and while this situation sometimes concerns parallel agencies its most obvious application is to joint action by different levels of government. In the case of category A, administrative conflicts often arise indirectly and considerable competition between agencies can occur without administrative action becoming essential. Category B conflicts are direct and visible, although often of a minor nature.

There is a similarity between A1 and B1, and between A2 and B2, in respect of the rationale and costs of administrative arrangements. A duplication of services (A1) can be defended by adducing the needs of overlapping client groups, whereas a division of powers between two levels of local government may be justified by the argument that the same clients gain from different articulations of their needs at county and at local levels. Resource wastes and procedural frustrations are the corresponding types of cost. The notion of allowing agencies maximum freedom to pursue their primary goals (A2) is paralleled by the idea of feeding separate articulations of interests into policy formation (B2). The former situation carries the possible price of indirect policy conflicts, while the latter situation can produce a complete deadlock in relations between the authorities.

We can illustrate further some differences between competition and conflict by reference to the relations between the Greater London Council and the London boroughs. The preparation of a development plan was, until recently, a joint responsibility of both these levels of government. However a borough-level view of desirable patterns of development is in many respects very different from a London-wide view. While it may be desirable that both view-points should be effectively articulated, a procedural deadlock naturally occurred in the absence of any effective method for synthesising the plans (B2). Also, the Greater London Council and the boroughs have parallel powers for providing public housing for similar groups of clients, which is one of the rare examples in Britain of straightforward functional duplication (A1). In this case, there is less scope for procedural frustrations, except in relation to site assembly, but there could be a wasteful diffusion of resources. Since, however, the housing needs of Londoners are so considerable and possible economies of scale seem to be limited, the system is very likely justified by harnessing two sets of political and organisational energies to the pursuit of very similar tasks.[17]

If agencies at two levels of government (say a county and a town) are to share powers for the same kind of service, the following four arrangements are possible:

a) A prescribed division of tasks between the two levels which tries to prevent duplication (divided jurisdiction).

b) The smaller authority acting as agent for the larger one with or without prescribed rights (statutory or voluntary delegation schemes).

c) Either authority (but probably the larger) supplementing the work of the other on either a compulsory or voluntary basis (supplementary or substitute administration).

d) Both bodies entitled to provide all aspects of the service (equal jurisdiction).

If the aim is to avoid a duplication of services, then (a) or (b) or an imposed version of (c) is the appropriate arrangement, but the price is likely to be procedural conflicts between the agencies. The first two arrangements have been extensively tried in Britain, but considerable conflict over the working of delegation schemes, particularly in education, has discredited the second device. However, so long as the guiding ideas remain the same, and some powers need to be conceded to smaller units of government within a framework of higher level planning and control, delegation schemes will continue even if called by another name. The alternative of accepting some wastes of duplication in order to liberate administrative energies does not seem to be acceptable.

By contrast, in the U.S.A. the more usual patterns are (d) or the voluntary aspects of (c). As smaller units of government prove incapable of achieving all their tasks, higher levels of government enter the same field without any formal removal of powers or policing of jurisdictions. This policy of 'substitute administration' is often seen as a way of increasing administrative efficiency without creating institutional antagonisms. This analysis makes it clear that attempts to reduce resource wastes often increase administrative friction and vice versa.

ADMINISTRATIVE REORGANISATION

Issues of administrative reorganisation can be viewed in at least three ways. First they concern existing public agencies. An agency may strive to expand its functions, thus incurring the hostility of any other agency whose functions would be reduced. However aggressively agencies behave – and there are major cultural differences in this respect – it is rare indeed for an agency to acquiesce in its demise. Even hybrid organisations having a weak and uncertain rationale, such as the English divisional executives for education, usually entrench their positions through the formation of a joint association or other devices. The view that reorganisation plans are frequently blocked by the 'vested interests' of existing agencies has considerable, though variable, truth.

Secondly, these issues involve conflicts of group interests and view-points. Three general interests can be distinguished: consumers or clients, producers or professional workers, taxpayers or ratepayers. These groups can be aggregated and subdivided in numerous ways; for example, we can identify all the patients of public health services as one group and those requiring treatment for kidney complaints as another, much smaller one; or we can distinguish welfare workers as a whole and the class of health visitors. Since such analytical distinctions are endless, it is tempting

109

to take account only of groups represented by formal organisations, although the representativeness of the organisation must still somehow be tested. However, the interests of weakly or unorganised groups also make their impact through the interpretations of organised groups, professional experts, politicians and others.

Where particular groups are strongly linked with particular agencies, as in the U.S.A., the power of agencies to influence or prevent reorganisation plans will be correspondingly greater. However, even in the U.S.A. it is usually small or specialised groups which make such identifications, the powerful interests being less aligned. In Britain, the interests of consumers of public services are voiced mainly through political channels and to a small but growing extent through consumer organisations. The interests of professional workers are sometimes linked with particular agencies, but professional bodies, sometimes confined to members of the public service, generally adopt a broader view of organisational questions than that of any particular agency or institution. The most devoted supporters of an existing institution are usually its elected representatives; it is much more councillors than officials who are up in arms whenever the existence of a local authority is threatened.

A third view of administrative reorganisation concentrates upon unifying concepts and goals which can provide a possible basis for reform. As Sir Geoffrey Vickers has shown, administrative change must often be preceded by a shift of 'appreciative judgement' – that is, by a fresh identification of problems and possible methods of solving them.[18] Such persuasive reinterpretations of public tasks will not of themselves reconcile divergent group interests or overcome the resistance of established agencies; but their appeal to persons of intelligence and imagination among the concerned audience may be sufficient to bring about some desirable reform.

Each of these three explanations of administrative change is limited and partial, and none is exclusive of the others. To understand more closely the causes of administrative change, as well as the limits of theorising, we will briefly consider three cases. The first (health service reorganisation) revolves around conflicting interpretations of professional and client interests. The second (defence reorganisation) shows strongly established institutions being slowly overcome in the latent interest of taxpayers and clients. The third (traffic in towns) shows the limitations, though conceivably the eventual triumph, of new policy perspectives and goals when faced by conflicting interests and techniques. In these illustrations it is necessary to stick to relevant points extracted from lengthy histories.

Health Service Reorganisation[19]

The British National Health Service Act of 1946 split functions between three types of authority. Hospitals went to regional hospital boards appointed by the Minister of Health, assisted by a second tier of management committees appointed by the boards; various services of an auxiliary, preventive and after-care type (such as maternity and child welfare) remained with local authorities; and the services of family doctors, dentists and opthalmologists were governed by standard contracts and supervised by local executive councils drawn mainly from local councillors and representative professional bodies.

This system was organised according to one possible definition of the process principle, and reflected traditional distinctions of medical care as interpreted by the attitudes of professional groups. Hospitals were separated from local government partly to obtain large catchment areas and partly because the British Medical Association and the Royal Colleges were and are hostile to local political control. The various practitioner services were given a separate and semi-detached status in line with traditional notions of the independent status of the family doctor and the mistrust by such doctors of State control.

From a consumer's standpoint, there was less rationale to the system. A health service patient needs a mix of preventive, diagnostic, curative and after-care services determined according to his particular condition. So long, however, as the tasks of the three branches remained fairly distinct, and co-ordination of individual cases was reasonably competent, clients had no overwhelming reason for rejecting this particular division of work. It was not the dissatisfaction of clients, but the increasing interdependence of the three branches of the National Health Service and consequent shifts in medical attitudes, which built up the pressure for change. Heavy loads and high costs in the hospital service compelled attention to the need for more effective prevention and after-care, particularly for old and handicapped persons. The isolation of the general practitioner finally broke down, and increasing numbers of family doctors developed group practices either on their own or in health centres provided by the local authority. Local health centres, initially suspected by many independent doctors, began to spread during the 1960s, and traditional medical hostility to 'socialised medicine' gave way to an appreciation of the case for more integrated services.

Thus by 1962 representatives of the medical profession were ready to accept a unified health service operating under area boards

111

(the Porrit Report). In 1968 and 1970 this idea was filled out in a series of proposals published as two 'Green Papers' by the relevant minister. The first document envisaged about forty to fifty area health boards for England and Wales (average population about one million) which would administer all personal health services. Each board would work through 'horizontal' committees for planning and operations, staffing, logistics, finance, and a secretariat, in place of the traditional split between different medical services. Additionally the ministry would gain new powers to provide specialised services, to supervise management training, and to arrange for exchanges of staff, as well as continuing with its existing powers to prescribe standards, control expenditure and approve capital projects. The second Green Paper increased the number of area boards to about ninety so as to make the service more localised, and to match the probable areas of local government reform. The controlling powers of the central department were further increased, and regional councils were also proposed, which would act in a purely advisory capacity to the minister.

The service was reorganised in 1974 with still stronger professional and weaker local control. Throughout there was almost complete agreement about the desirability of an integrated structure, and considerable dispute over forms of control. The medical profession remains strongly opposed to local government control, preferring the model of appointed boards containing professional representatives. Local government, however, has a much strengthened claim to take over the health services for two reasons. One is its substantial reorganisation into enlarged units, the other is the severance of local health and welfare services which would otherwise occur and which would be especially inappropriate in view of the introduction of integrated social service departments by many local authorities. Conversely, local government administration of the health services would pose financial problems, since over ninety per cent of the total cost at present comes from the central Exchequer.

This case presents some nice questions about the identification and balancing of interests. The majority views of the medical profession are expressed by the B.M.A., but the medical officers of health in local government have a different view-point. The consumer interest is harder to identify. Local government may claim to represent the interests of clients, on the grounds first of direct local election and secondly of acting as an effective pressure group for better services. The second of these claims, if true, rests upon the circumstance that local authorities are heavy spenders of national funds – a situation which might have to be amended if they were to control the health service. Finally, the taxpayers' champion is presumably the Treasury, which has obvious reasons for favouring agencies which are as economically-minded as possible.

One point about this case is that the opposition of existing agencies is a minor factor, save in the case of local authorities. The regional hospital boards, still more the local executive councils, are essentially vehicles for professional and other interests, and command little independent loyalty. A second point is that the chosen solution will have to balance claims about control against claims about co-ordination. The key here is the existing local government services, which provide both a main point of potential integration within the health services, and also a link between health and welfare or 'social service'. Co-ordinative needs strongly favour at least some partial integration of the health services within local government, while professional and financial pressures suggest otherwise. The third issue is the form and extent of central control. More central control is wanted by the Treasury on grounds of economy, and is necessary to the extent that the area boards are relatively weak units. However, the ministry has relatively weak professional resources, and no career ladder has been built between medical administration in the field and at headquarters. Professional opinion would therefore prefer the creation of a more autonomous set of national and regional boards in place of traditional forms of ministry supervision, and at the very least a reorganisation of headquarters staff.

Defence Reorganisation[20]

This provides an interesting comparison with the health services because it had to be achieved against the opposition of rival professions organised in strong, traditional institutions. The army, navy and air force possessed considerable organisational autonomy, as well as strong *esprit de corps*, and central co-ordination of their activities was largely confined to strategic reviews and the actual conduct of joint operations. However, the development of processes again outmoded these distinctions. The function of the services became more interdependent, and the mounting cost and sophistication of weapons systems made separate procurement an expensive luxury. However, traditional rivalries were too entrenched and institutionalised to be overcome simply by the logic of technical developments.

It is harder with defence than with health to distinguish between

113

client and taxpayer interests, because the former is a collective good which must be purchased by and for the whole community. The obvious interest of the general community in economy or at least in value-for-money is the political factor which has sustained Ministers for Defence in their contests with the separate Service organisations. In the U.S.A., these contests have been fierce and prolonged. It was the distinctive achievement of Secretary for Defence, Robert MacNamara, that he achieved a considerable integration of the defence budget, particularly through the application of techniques of cost-effectiveness to rival weapon systems. He accepted the aim of maintaining a high level of military power, but insisted that both goals and resources should be stated and compared, and duplications of effort at least reduced.

The similar efforts of Ministers of Defence in Britain have been much less spectacular, but integration necessitated successive demotions of the three Service Ministers and conflicts included the resignation of the Under-Secretary for the Navy (Mr Mayhew).

The chief problem of defence reorganisation, in both Britain and the U.S.A., has been to discover new principles for the allocation of work within a vast integrated system. This is partly a political problem. If the pull of Service loyalties is to be reduced, then it is desirable to introduce alternative methods of task allocation. Thus in Britain the three Service Ministers were first reduced to Ministers of State under the Minister of Defence, and then (following Mayhew's resignation) were further downgraded to Under-Secretaries of State, while two new Ministers of State for Administration and Equipment were introduced over them. This was the signal for a partial switch to an integrated treatment of personnel, equipment, finance and operations for the whole defence forces. The difficulty is that the new 'functional' division of tasks has to live side by side with the old Service division, and neither can be given a clear priority. This made the central co-ordination of activities very difficult and cumbersome, and partly explained the need for a large headquarters staff of 16,000 people so designed as to ensure that every relevant view-point was represented in final decisions. A further point is that the political problem of reorganisation has been solved at the cost of creating a sociological one. The reduction of Service loyalties has left a certain void over organisational attachment, since no fully adequate counter-loyalty seems to be available.

In the case of the U.S. Defence Department, P.P.B. (planning, programming and budgeting) is the method used for identifying tasks, costing alternative methods of achieving them, and fixing

114

consequent programmes and budgets. Nine programmes have been identified which include strategic retaliatory forces (No. 1), continental air and missile defence forces (No. 2), and general purpose forces (No. 3). This approach assists identification of the appropriate role of each armed Service, and entails some subordination of Service organisation to the basic programmes. However, P.P.B. by no means solves organisational problems and conflicts. The logic of the system depends essentially upon the priority given to the maintenance of nuclear strike capacity as a basic objective; by contrast such a broad category as 'general purpose forces' does not settle organisational conflicts between the roles of regional commanders and the Pentagon, or between functional and Service principles of organisation. This analysis does not refute the usefulness of P.P.B. in getting 'value for money' if one can accept the somewhat lunatic logic of a nuclear defence policy; but it does suggest the difficulties of structuring organisations according to rational concepts of task allocation, even when the opposition of vested interests has been broken down.

Traffic in Towns[21]

Sir Geoffrey Vickers cites the Buchanan Report on 'Traffic in Towns' as an excellent example of how a major shift in appreciative judgements has (or should have) altered administrative goals and methods. Prior to this Report, the provision of highways and town planning was administratively quite separate and in some respects conflicting; for example, the Ministry of Transport paid a higher grant for roads carrying traffic through a town centre, whereas it was the aim of planners to avoid such through traffic. The Buchanan Report argued that the construction of urban systems should be viewed as a whole, and claims of accessibility carefully reconciled with those of environmental protection. This could be done, the Report suggested, through the replacement of general-purpose streets by roads of differentiated capacities and functions; limitations on vehicle movement elsewhere; the creation of environmental precincts; and the formulation of standards for the control of noise, fumes, safety hazards, etc.

Many of these ideas were not, of course, new, but they were persuasively brought together in the Buchanan Report. The interesting feature of this Report was its impact upon intelligent opinion, which was increasingly concerned with the nuisance of traffic in towns, and the spate of administrative action which resulted. The Ministries of Transport and of Housing and Local Government set up a joint group for urban planning; local authorities were asked to include full coverage of traffic and transport policies in their development plans; 'Buchanan-type' planning became the theme of departmental circulars, and financial grants were revised to take account of the new philosophy.

However, the most interesting application of Buchanan concepts occurred in the case of the Greater London Council. A major reason for the creation of this great authority was the belief that policies for traffic, transportation and urban planning ought to be determined and integrated for London as a whole, not just for its constituent parts. The leaders of the G.L.C. were dedicated to this approach, and constructed their organisation accordingly. Thus maximum co-ordination was sought between the two departments responsible for planning and for highways and transportation, culminating (1969) in a formal amalgamation of the two departments. Both functions were placed initially under the control of a single committee of the council dealing with planning and communications.

Initial results of this experiment were disappointing. The approach and techniques of the two departments were very different, and an effective fusion of programmes did not result. The first outline of the Greater London development plan, issued by the G.L.C. in 1969, contained far-reaching proposals for urban motorways, including a motorway box circling Inner London; but the proposals for urban planning and environmental protection were very much vaguer. This was not altogether the G.L.C.'s fault. Both planning and highway powers were shared between the G.L.C. and thirty-two London boroughs, and co-operation between the two parties is difficult, particularly in relation to the development plan which had to be jointly determined.

It would also seem that the goal of improved communications is more concrete and realisable than the broader, vaguer goals of urban planning. This is particularly obvious for London as a whole, since environmental protection is in many ways a localised concern, whereas speedier movement needs to be planned for the capital as a whole. The logic of this situation seems to have influenced the G.L.C. in 1969 to secure certain changes in the distribution of powers between itself and the boroughs. Their effect was to allot more discretion to the boroughs over urban planning matters, but to increase the power of the G.L.C. in relation to highways, traffic management and public transport.

One can also view these administrative problems of the G.L.C. in terms of a broader conflict of interests. The interest of the consumers of defence services are homogeneous; the consumers of health services have varying priorities but a common interest in an integrated service. There is no comparable unity of interest between the beneficiaries of better roads and those interested in environmental improvement and protection. It is true that a majority of citizens share both interests to some degree, but their priorities vary considerably and attitudes are often ambivalent, depending upon which issue is being considered. Still more to the point, there is frequent conflict of interest on specific issues. Those whose homes are destroyed or whose local environment is spoilt to make way for a motorway are not easily persuaded that this measure accords with a general interest which they share.

Better financial compensation might reduce their opposition, but would not resolve the conflict of values – particularly if those adversely affected are from the lower income groups and attach more priority to housing than highways. This type of conflict has been sharply exemplified by the strength of local opposition to the London motorway box. Conversely, motorists taking short cuts through residential areas are inflicting much minor nuisance upon others which they might resist in their own localities. The drift of wealthy groups to the remotest suburbs or exurbs and the accompanying conversion of inner areas into 'corridor communities' are consequences of a destructive competition to maximise the joint benefits of environment and mobility.

To reconcile such clashes of interest requires not only a unifying vision or ideal, but the availability of resources and techniques adequate to its realisation. The Buchanan approach ideally requires sufficient funds to produce an adequate and insulated road network; but the cost of such a policy requires a second-best solution that vehicle use should be closely disciplined in the interests of environmental protection.

This solution, while certainly enjoined by 'Traffic in Towns', is politically and technically difficult to introduce. Integrated planning must deal with many variables and uncertainties, including the likely availability of finance and powers of control. It also requires more specific techniques than the Buchanan Report itself offers. A new profession of urban and regional planners becomes necessary, who can integrate effectively, and not just notionally, the contributions of engineers, economists, etc. Thus we can say that the aims of Buchanan-style planning will not become operational until both a better accommodation of interests has been reached in terms of resource allocation and political control, and also 'process' techniques have been developed which integrate the contributions of existing disciplines.

117

What conclusions can be drawn from these three brief studies of administrative reorganisation? The analysis has carried us into a broad discussion of the general determinants of social, political and administrative change. It has revealed, for one thing, that theories which picture administrative change primarily in terms of the competing goals of agencies, as some American writers do, are much too narrowly drawn. Organisational resistance has the capacity to slow up change, as over defence, but not finally so even in this case. Conversely, administrative integration is not sufficient to achieve policy integration where interests conflict and goals are unclear, as is shown by the problems of the Greater London Council.

A second conclusion is to stress the significance of changes in the methods of work – the process principle – for influencing forms of organisation. This influence is not a direct one but works through changing the attitudes of both the producers and the consumers of a service. In the case of health, the changed attitudes of the medical profession towards work organisation was the main stimulus to change; in the case of defence, it required the latent power of consumers to impose more rational work methods upon reluctant organisations.

Additionally, the cases illustrate the earlier analysis of functional specialisation. Thus it would be much too crude to view the health service as switching from a process to a client basis. The earlier organisation reflected the convenience to clients of an *areal* separation of facilities ranging from the less to the more specialised (family doctor, health clinic, hospital), as well as the convenience of work processes. The divisions of the new organisation will tend to correspond partly to vertical groupings of clients, distinguished by the nature of their malady, and partly to an increased range of overhead facilities provided for the service as a whole. In a baroque way, the same analysis could be offered of defence organisation. The previous 'clients' could be categorised as divided up by their location on land, at sea, or in the air. In the new system, enemies will be classified primarily on some geographical basis, while organisation will be largely divided on the basis of inputs of weapons, equipment, transport, etc., into the final product of a fighting force.

A third conclusion is that reorganisation often offers a clean field for applying fresh principles to the allocation of work, and that this approach often seems desirable as a means of overcoming previous sectional divisions and rivalries. This situation occurred with defence reorganisation, and will occur when area health boards

118

are created. However, the creation of a rational new structure is not easy, and the result is often to allocate work according to a mixture of old and new principles, possibly with confused results.

Finally, there is the question of the rationality of administrative change and reorganisation. The need for change may emerge from shifts in the desirable methods of achieving existing public tasks, or it may come from the identification of a new social need or problem. Logically the problem should come first; then the adoption of new goals; and then administrative reconstruction so as to meet these. Rarely of course is public action so orderly or rational. A new goal will be impossible to implement, until it is adequately defined in operational terms and achieves sufficient support among interested groups to overcome organisational resistance. This does not imply a deterministic or purely sectional view of administrative change. The concept of interest is flexible enough to allow for rational suasion or enlightenment, and administrative reform (like any other reform) depends upon the continuous reinterpretation of interests and attitudes so as to meet the challenge of new problems.

REFERENCES

1 Anthony Downs, *Inside Bureaucracy* (Boston, 1967) Chap 17.
2 A classic account of the relations between political and administrative pluralism is David Truman, *The Governmental Process* (New York, 1951).
3 Samuel Beer, *Treasury Control* (Oxford, 1956).
4 Truman, op. cit.; A. Leiserson, *Administrative Regulation* (Chicago, 1942); H. Eckstein, *Pressure Group Politics* (London, 1960).
5 Based upon unpublished research by Harvey Lazar, which is gratefully acknowledged.
6 A good summary of the politics of the regulatory agencies is in Peter Woll, *American Bureaucracy* (New York, 1963) Chaps. 2 and 3. A more sympathetic approach to their work by an ex-Chairman of a regulatory agency is William Carey, *Politics and the Regulatory Agencies* (New York, 1966). The classic defence of the value of these bodies is J. M. Landis, *The Administrative Process* (New Haven, 1938).
7 For history of the Central Land Board, see P. Self, *Cities in Flood*, 2nd ed. (London, 1961) Chap. 7.
8 J. W. Grove, *Government and Industry in Britain* (London, 1962).
9 For U.S. anti-poverty programmes, see James E. Anderson, 'Poverty, Unemployment and Economic Development', *The Journal of Politics*, Vol. 29 (February 1967), No. 1. Also acknowledged is help from papers by Dennis Rondinelli.
10 U.S. Senate, *Creative Federalism*, Hearings before the Sub-Committee on Intergovernmental Relations, 88th Congress, 2nd Session. For

number of programmes, see Part One (pp. 2, 26, and 147–89) and Part Two B (appendix). Quotation is from evidence of Ralph Widner, Part Two B, p. 1023.

11 For agricultural conflicts, see Charles Hardin, *The Politics of Agri-Culture* (Glencoe, Illinois, 1952), and Murray Benedict, *Can We Solve the Farm Problem?* (New York, 1955).

12 Arthur Maass, *Muddy Waters* (Cambridge, Mass., 1951).

13 See 'The Federal System as seen by Federal Aid Officials', reprinted in Alan Altschuler, *The Politics of the Federal Bureaucracy* (Toronto, 1968), pp. 263–81.

14 Self, op. cit., Chap. 7.

15 Hans Daalder, *Cabinet Reform in Britain 1914–63* (Oxford, 1964).

16 U.S. Senate, op. cit., Part One, pp. 421 and 457–62.

17 Gerald Rhodes, *The New Government of London: The First Five Years* (London, 1972).

18 Sir Geoffrey Vickers, *The Art of Judgement* (London, 1965).

19 Based upon Michael Ryan, 'Reform of the Health Service Structure', *Public Administration* (Autumn 1968), pp. 315–31; *The Administrative Structure of the Medical and Related Services in England and Wales* (London, Ministry of Health, 1968); *The Future Structure of the National Health Service* (London, Department of Health and Social Security, 1970). For later developments see R. G. S. Brown, *The Management of Welfare* (London, 1975).

20 Based upon Michael Howard, *The Central Organisation of Defence* (London, Royal United Service Institution, 1970), Chap. 1; and D. Novick, *Programme Budgeting* (Harvard U.P., 1965).

21 Based upon Vickers, op. cit., pp. 50–67; and Peter Self, *Metropolitan Planning* (London, 1971).

Chapter 4

STAFF AND LINE IN GOVERNMENT

THE FUNCTIONS OF THE EXECUTIVE

'Staff-and-line' concepts furnish one of the most confusing branches of management theory. We will not enter in detail into the debate as to how these terms ought to be used, but we will consider some of their applications to administrative organisation. Particularly in the U.S.A. these applications have been very influential, and it is easy to see why this is so. American government is a case of what Meyer terms 'defective hierarchy', which means that the lines of control running from the chief executive downwards are often weak and imperfect.

It seems fairly clear that the American founding fathers believed to some extent in 'defective hierarchy' through fear of too great a concentration of authority; but devising their prescriptions for an age in which legislative power was dominant, they did not of course foresee the issues of control and co-ordination which would arise under conditions of 'big government'. To modern administrative theorists, a defective hierarchy is generally anathema because it offends against the doctrine of unity of command and it blurs the lines of control and responsibility. Staff concepts have provided a rationale for strengthening the instruments of control and co-ordination, and for tightening up the administrative framework.

The significance of staff services emerges from an analysis of the functions of the chief executive. According to Henri Fayol, these functions are to plan, organise, command, co-ordinate and control. Rather more elaborately Luther Gulick uses the ugly phrase P.O.S.D.C.O.R.B. (planning, organising, staffing, directing, co-ordinating, reporting, budgeting) to describe the proper tasks of top management. In either description the various activities shade into each other in a continuous line. A simpler analysis is to break these functions down into the three processes listed by Fayol; those of preparing operations, of seeing that they are carried out, and of watching the results.[1]

When one compares these formulae with the actual behaviour of executives, either in government or business, one is struck with

121

their formality and rationality. The busy executive tends to concentrate heavily upon the middle range of activities (the staffing, directing, co-ordinating aspects), and to neglect the preliminary tasks of setting objectives, examining alternatives, making plans, etc. This occurs because the executive tends to take his objectives for granted, and to consider basic issues only when these are thrown up by external or internal pressures. He proceeds, often reluctantly, from the particular to the general, rather than moving, as Fayol and Gulick prefer, the other way round.

Paradoxically, this weakness seems more prevalent in government than in business, despite the much greater complexity of governmental goals. Under commercial pressures, business management has paid increasing attention to planning its choice of products, methods of operation, etc. By contrast, the governmental executive, whether politician or official, is generally so dominated by immediate pressures that his 'forward looks' are flimsy affairs. When the 'scientific' theorists first wrote, these deficiencies were still greater. Public decisions were on a completely *ad hoc* basis, made without any proper information or analysis.

The theorists' recipe for these problems was to borrow and adapt the military device of a general staff, which had proved an indispensable tool for strategic and operational planning in the First World War. They generally have used this notion of staff in a restricted sense. The staff's function is to assist the chief executive by providing information, formulating possible courses of action, co-ordinating decisions, and reporting on results. Gulick views this task as one of 'knowing, thinking, planning', not of actual execution or 'doing'. E. F. L. Brech, a modern management theorist, defines the task as one of providing 'special advisory, informational and interpretative aids' to an *individual* executive.[2] In order to preserve unity of command, the purely advisory status of staff assistance was stressed. The ruling idea was that actual decision-making is the exclusive responsibility of the chief executive, and of the 'line' operators who work under his control, and that staff assistants exercise no power beyond the influence of their ideas upon the chief himself. In this way the model of a hierarchical pyramid can be faithfully respected.

The slight unreality of these conceptions led to a modification by Urwick. He recognised that staff aides do in fact exercise authority, in the sense that their interpretations of their chief's wishes or intentions are generally accepted as equivalent to commands (this is certainly the military situation). He meets this point by arguing that the staff's authority rests upon function not rank;

that they work, so to speak, as an extension of the chief's *persona*, controlling activities in his name and to the extent that he lets them.[3] By contrast, line officers discharge institutionalised duties and possess a more durable degree of delegated authority.

The only realistic description of personal staff assistance is that given by Urwick. However, if the staff do function as extensions of their chief's *persona*, it is clear that their tasks cannot be precisely specified. They will have to attune themselves to the chief's personal predilections and style of administration, and concern themselves with those matters which he considers most urgent. What the chief will want is more likely to be deft executants of particular chores and assignments rather than systematic policy planners in the Gulick or P.O.S.D.C.O.R.B. sense. Further, the amount of personal assistance which any executive can use is bound to be limited by the capacities of one human brain and body, whatever the extent of his theoretical responsibilities. The executive has to concern himself with many more important persons than his own assistants, whose work he can direct only intermittently and to a limited extent unless they are very few. Very quickly more staff assistance of this kind will yield diminishing returns even if the executive is very capable and hard-working; and the quality of the assistance will count for more than its quantity.

If on the other hand a series of special units are created to perform P.O.S.D.C.O.R.B. functions under the general supervision of a chief executive, their work will become less personalised and more institutionalised. The functions which these units perform will be executed in the chief's name and under his formal authority, but so will the activities of the line agencies or officials for whom he is also responsible. Any controls exercised by such staff units over line officials will rest upon organisational rules and conventions rather than upon the personal wishes or decisions of the chief himself. The chief will necessarily be unaware of many of the problems and tensions which arise between staff and line unless called upon to arbitrate, in which event there is no certainty as to which side he will back. In large organisations, the probable slowness of demanding his arbitration will mean that almost all such issues are settled or compromised at a lower administrative level. The role of the chief himself will be mainly that of conferring his approval upon organisational arrangements which give certain rights to the staff units. Once done, these units will not necessarily have a greater share of his personal interest or support than any other part of the organisation.

Of course, there are many intermediate positions between personalised staff assistance and institutionalised 'staff' units. An executive may be particularly interested, for example, in the work of a planning unit created in his office, while largely ignoring the work of other specialised units for which he is equally responsible in a formal sense. Such variations will depend upon the view-point of the executive himself as well as upon the size, character and structure of his organisation. What can be said is that in any large organisation many of the top-level management functions become specialised and routinised, and cease to work as the personal instruments of the supreme authority.

Thus it is very difficult to link the notion of personal staff assistance favoured by Gulick, Urwick and others with the notion of a systematic treatment of the P.O.S.D.C.O.R.B. functions. These functions can only be made operational if they are institutionalised, which reduces the element of purely personal assistance. Also in governments usually, although less so in Britain, the task of personal assistance is handed to political sympathisers, whereas routinised tasks of planning, reporting, budgeting, etc. are handled by civil servants who work in effect through 'line' controls.

One way around problems of definition is to use a triple classi-fication of line, staff (in the Urwick sense), and auxiliary or 'housekeeping' services. This classification corresponds roughly with the tasks of combat troops, general staff and logistic services in modern armies.

Unfortunately, this distinction between staff and auxiliary is based upon competing and overlapping view-points. Thus to a chief executive, staff services will comprehend all matters of special importance for top-level decision-making. One would expect these to include some aspects of finance and personnel, information services, policy co-ordination, etc. The list is bound to be inexact unless one can accept some clear-cut theory of the key functions of an executive; and even then there will be considerable difficulties in drawing a line between those activities or parts of some service which do or do not need his personal supervision.

The list of auxiliary services, by contrast, will derive from an organisational view-point. The services of finance, personnel and legal advice can be viewed as providing the indispensable inputs of money, staff and legal authorisation, without which no organisa-tion can function. Other auxiliary services, such as research and informational aids, can be viewed as 'optional', in the sense that line activities might get along without them. The same can be said of various kinds of co-ordinating units. The existence of any of these services may be due to a line request, to expert advice or to the

124

personal views or ambitions of some executive – or to a mixture of these factors. A co-ordinating unit may be the inspiration of a chief executive and work to some extent under his personal supervision; or it may emanate entirely from organisational pressures and be placed in the executive's office as a matter of convenience. Whether we describe such a unit as 'staff' or 'auxiliary' will depend not a little upon whether we take a personalised or an organisational view of the reasons for its existence.

A close look also produces grave difficulties in distinguishing adequately between 'line' and 'staff'; once again we are often dealing with differences of perspective, rather than with tasks which can be clearly defined. Definitional problems apart, however, there can be no doubt about the growth of various kinds of controlling, co-ordinating and advisory units in modern governments. Lumped together, these units are sometimes described in the U.S.A. as 'staff agencies' and sometimes as overhead units. The next two sections will explore the significance of these developments under the different conditions of Presidential and Cabinet government.

STAFF AGENCIES IN AMERICAN GOVERNMENT

The administrative theorists started from the simple and acceptable proposition that chief executives need personal assistance in exercising their broad responsibilities. Anyone who dislikes the fissiparous tendencies of American government will favour a tighter skein of co-ordination, running from the top downwards, as an end in itself. This will be especially so if the observer is a champion of the executive branch of government against legislative intrusions. The scientific theorists have had this predilection, which accords with the general tendency of administrative thinkers to value the internal consistency and effectiveness of government more highly than they value its responsiveness to shifting political currents. They like government which steers, not floats.

President Franklin Roosevelt got the support of the eminent experts who comprised his Committee on Administrative Management in building up staff assistance. This assistance was more personalised and less institutionalised than it later became. His press secretary, appointments secretary, special counsel and even his budget director worked under conditions in which the President himself kept the effective controls, while giving his aides considerable discretion to execute special assignments. Roosevelt liked to 'play the field', by welcoming a diversity of conflicting advisers and by allowing the number of overlapping jurisdictions and assignments to multiply. Such a performance was possible only for a master politician, yet it illustrates the truth of Richard Neustadt's remark that 'to a degree the needs of bureaucrats and presidents are incompatible'. Good service to the latter may entail delays and indecisions for the former. These results were rather different from the improved co-ordinative procedures at which the President's Committee had aimed; yet its distinguished chairman, Louis Brownlow, subsequently accepted that the Committee's value lay simply in the strengthening of Presidential will, not in the application of P.O.S.D.C.O.R.B. Strengthening the President is not quite the same as improving administrative efficiency, although the scientific theorists wanted both.[4]

In 1939 the Executive Office of the President came formally into existence, and from that date onwards increasing differentiation occurred between this office and the personal White House staff. The largest element in the Executive Office is the Bureau of the Budget (now Office of Management and Budget) which contains separate sections dealing with budgetary co-ordination, statistical services, administrative organisation and legislative programming. Additional small staffs serve the National Security Council (created 1947) and the Council of Economic Advisers (created 1946) which is headed by a chief economic adviser to the President, and in 1969 there were ten other agencies in the Executive Office. A missing element in the system is personnel management which is vested in a Civil Service Commission that is outside the President's direct control. This arrangement is, however, a historical legacy of the movement to free the civil service from political patronage, and does not correspond at all to modern management theories. A frequent aim of the theorists, and of Presidents themselves, has been to bring the Commission under some degree of Presidential direction. In 1953 and again in 1961, the chairman of the Civil Service Commission was made personnel adviser to the President in order to strengthen links.[5]

A President certainly imposes his style upon the whole Administration. His personal views, for example on legislative or budgetary priorities, will be known in his own office which will do its best to apply them to numerous situations; but the scale of the Executive Office (which had by 1963 about 1,500 employees) is much too considerable for all its decisions to reflect, in any meaningful way, the President's wishes. A President will not necessarily give close personal attention to the work of his staff agencies or favour them over the line agencies in case of dispute. Indeed, some observers have thought that the Bureau of the Budget is handicapped by the

126

low political weight of its director, although the situation will vary with Presidents, and the Bureau is always an indispensable tool for imposing Presidential wishes upon dissident agencies.[6]

Moreover, housekeeping units are manned by specialists who are motivated not only by Presidential directives but by attachment to their own standards and techniques. The familiar tension between the line operator concerned to improve services and the budgetary controller concerned to save money cannot be dissolved by the simple assumption that the chief executive is on the latter's side. Still more obvious is the point that a statistical specialist insisting upon standardised returns is primarily an emissary of administrative 'efficiency'; and whether he is a good one could probably only be decided by another specialist. Of course, the chief executive is interested in efficiency, but it does not follow that he will always get it from a multiplication of controls and standards imposed in his name, and sometimes resisted in his name as well. The various groups of officials play out their contrasting roles, and the health of the whole system requires subtle judgements which must transcend any simple dichotomy between line and staff.[7]

Now that the capacity of any President to use more personal assistance has probably been exceeded, the further creation of staff units becomes a way of limiting the interplay of agency rivalries and Congressional interventions through new forms of expert co-ordination. Sometimes a staff unit is proposed as a weak alternative to the much more difficult task of reorganising the functions of competing agencies. Thus the second Hoover Commission abandoned its predecessor's proposal to merge the competing functions of water resource development, shared between the Bureau of Reclamation and the Army Corps of Engineers, and substituted instead the idea of top-level review of these agencies' proposals by a Water Resources Board responsible to the President. More often, the intention is to lay down central policies and standards with which all operating agencies are supposed to comply. To this end, the first Hoover Commission suggested the creation of separate staff agencies for the co-ordination of Federal grants-in-aid, central-field relationships, methods of overseas administration, and the selection of public work projects.[8]

The development of staff units increases the uniformity and consistency of administration, and helps to spot or avoid overlap and conflict between public services; but there are also drawbacks. Successive tiers of staff control (at both Presidential and departmental levels) increase overhead costs, delay decisions, and tend to frustrate decentralised initiatives. Moreover, the creation of staff agencies stimulates the creation of 'counterpart' units at lower levels, whose purpose is to help the operating agencies to circumvent controls and to bargain effectively with the controllers. Infighting amongst a mounting number of experts results. The internal co-ordination of the system is certainly improved, but at a price.[9]

Thus the structure of American government has grown somewhat more hierarchical, as the scientific theorists wished, but the capacity of Presidents to control the system has not grown in equal measure.

STAFF AGENCIES IN CABINET SYSTEMS

When we turn to the place of staff services in a system of Cabinet government, rather different issues emerge. In the first place, the 'staff v. line' issue is not bound up with the capacity of the executive to assert itself against the legislature. In Britain or France, the executive has already made that assertion.

In the second place, the lines of co-ordination and control are horizontal rather than vertical. Instead of the problems of a superior authority over controlling strong but subordinate agencies, we encounter the problems of imposing collective disciplines upon a group of parallel departments. Traditionally, this control is enforced by a 'senior' department (such as the British Treasury) which possesses a higher status than its fellow departments only as a consequence of its power to control. It is not, as is the Bureau of the Budget, the instrument of a supreme political authority, since the Chancellor of the Exchequer is only one minister among others. Instead Treasury power rests upon the cohesive backing of a highly integrated political and administrative system. Such a situation by no means eliminates controversial issues, but it does reduce their sting when compared with a pattern of 'defective hierarchy'.

These differences explain why staff and line issues have a smaller place in British or French than in American administrative writing. Yet similar issues certainly exist, although sometimes called by other names. Two related issues need attention; first, the place of personal staff assistance in these systems of government, and secondly, the style of administrative control which prevails in a Cabinet as opposed to Presidential system of government.

Personalised assistance has, as is well known, a much stronger place in the French than in the British system of government. There is no true British equivalent to the *cabinets* of French ministers. Above the departmental level, the British Prime Minister and (at various times) senior co-ordinating ministers have been armed with personal staffs, but always on a small scale. By contrast, under the Fifth Republic, both the French President and the Prime Minister have considerable personal staffs at their disposal.

The causes for this difference derive both from administrative structure and political attitudes. The separate practices and traditions of the various divisions which comprise a ministry are more marked in France than in Britain. The task of departmental coordination is therefore greater and it is performed not by a chief official (as in Britain) but by the minister himself and his *cabinet*. Further, in France it is assumed that the will of the controlling minister has to be imposed upon a department whose compliance cannot be taken for granted; and this assumption has survived the conversion of the controlling instrument, the *cabinet*, from a group of political friends and dependants into a group of mainly civil servants. Personalised attachment by *cabinet* members to ministers have also survived this transition.

The French system shows both the strength and limitations of personalised assistance. The minister has the assistance of a group, some of whose reputations and fortunes are quite closely linked to his, and whose services are wholly devoted to getting him all the information he needs, assisting him with decisions, conveying his advice or instructions, and performing diverse chores. This corresponds to genuine staff assistance in the Urwick sense. Equally, however, the very existence of the *cabinet* produces a bigger gap between the minister and the department than exists in Britain. The differences must not be exaggerated because a British minister works largely through a few senior officials and through his personal and parliamentary secretaries; however, these officials are less personally committed to the minister, and the administrative head of the department is a powerful co-ordinator in his own right. Indeed the difference is partly one between political and administrative forms of co-ordination, subject to the paradox that the French minister has sometimes himself been a civil servant (see Chapter 6).

Above the departmental level, different considerations prevail. Much will depend, in the provision and location of staff assistance, upon how genuinely a style of collective decision-making prevails. A Cabinet system of government may be more or less hierarchical. In Britain, ministers vary in weight, according to the importance of their departments and their own political standing, and some departmental ministers are not in the Cabinet. Nonetheless, the system is still genuinely horizontal and collective, in the sense that the main instruments of co-ordination remain Cabinet committees and the administrative committees of civil servants which parallel them. Co-ordinating ministers, when appointed, have not in general proved a success. This is because the capacity of their small staffs is heavily outweighed by departmental resources, so that they can succeed only when pursuing a clear policy which has the backing of Prime Minister and Cabinet. Thus they are only likely to achieve anything when acting on a short-term basis as the executants of special political missions. The co-ordination of defence policy succeeded only when it was followed by full administrative integration so that the Minister of Defence became the head of a strong department with the three Service Ministers as his recognised subordinates. A considerable degree of administrative integration seems to be the indispensable condition for this form of policy coordination.

The Cabinet in general and the Prime Minister specifically have staff assistance from the Cabinet Secretariat. As the work of policy co-ordination has grown, the Secretariat has been strengthened and the arrangement whereby the same official was permanent secretary at the Treasury and secretary to the Cabinet was ended in 1962. Nonetheless, the size of the Cabinet Secretariat, even adding to it the Prime Minister's personal staff, is extremely small when compared to the U.S. President or to the French Prime Minister.

The functions of the Cabinet Secretariat also remain limited. Its main task is the formidable one of servicing the proceedings of the Cabinet itself and of the complex array of Cabinet committees. Poised at the top of the heap, the Cabinet Secretariat has the essential function of smoothing this formidable work of coordination, and of seeing that 'Cabinet' decisions (which include the decisions of all its dependent bodies) are duly understood and noted. However, the Secretariat is not a control or enforcement agency – that duty rests with the departments– nor is it a very active instrument for policy formation. Policies and plans emerge from the departments within the framework of the general strategy laid down by the Cabinet. On the whole, this strategy has a broad, political character and does not usually include detailed analysis by the Secretariat of possible policies and plans. The Secretariat occupies middle ground between the two main sources of policy-making in British government, which are party policy and departmental policy. Thus the Secretariat performs only some of the minimum staff functions distinguished by Gulick. It is, indeed, as much an instrument for 'doing' as for 'thinking'.[10]

In terms of staff-and-line theory, the position of the British Prime Minister has caused frequent confusions. The power of the Prime

Minister rests upon his right to hire and fire other ministers, his personal and political appeal as party leader, and his role as the chief representative of the nation in foreign relations. All these sources of power are subject to strong limitations, familiarly sketched in textbooks on British government. However, the enhanced significance of all three roles in modern times has exploded the constitutional myth that the Prime Minister is just *primus inter pares*, and has led some commentators to talk of the replacement of Cabinet by 'Prime Ministerial' government, and of the effective elevation of the Prime Minister to a position almost comparable with an elective President.[11]

If these theories were correct, then British government would represent a worse case of 'defective hierarchy' than American government, since the Prime Minister lacks any proper staff services for asserting his supreme authority. He has a small personal office which is primarily secretarial. As head of the Government, he is the senior boss of the Cabinet Secretariat, but this office is not his exclusive instrument. Financial and budgetary policy do not come under his direct control, although he naturally plays a leading (and sometimes a special) role in the Cabinet determinations by which the Chancellor of the Exchequer is guided. In his titular capacity as First Lord of the Treasury, the Prime Minister does have the final decision on top civil servant appointments, but he acts within Treasury and departmental conventions which much circumscribe his personal discretion.

In recent years, there have been some attempts to strengthen the resources available to Prime Minister and Cabinet. However, Prime Ministers have usually drawn back, when it came to the point, from creating staff agencies on the American or even the French model. Labour won the 1964 general election on the issue of economic planning, a cause with which the party leader (Mr Wilson) had closely identified himself. However, the new Prime Minister entrusted economic planning to a new department, not – as much staff theory would have suggested, as well as some of Mr Wilson's own utterances – to a new unit in the Prime Minister's office or in the Cabinet Secretariat. Mr Wilson contented himself with the appointment of one personal economic adviser. Even when he later (1967) assumed a shadowy overlordship of the Department of Economic Affairs, this ministry continued to have normal departmental status under the immediate control of another cabinet minister. As suggested earlier, the treatment of the economic planning function was almost certainly a mistake, for the work in question was basically a 'staff function'. Yet Wilson's behaviour showed well the strong British bias in favour of a flat system of parallel departments rather than a pyramid of co-ordinating agencies.

A further development occurred in 1970 when a new Prime Minister, Mr Heath, introduced a central policy review staff (C.P.R.S.) into the Cabinet Office. Here the influence of P.O.S.D.C.O.R.B. theories was very apparent. The basic idea was that Prime Minister and Cabinet needed to utilise more professional techniques of policy analysis in order to set and monitor their objectives, to review departmental policies and to arbitrate disputes. The creation of new giant departments made it particularly important for the Prime Minister and members of the Cabinet to have better tools for policy review. Yet the C.P.R.S. was very small indeed compared with departmental resources, and seemed much more likely to function as a device for briefing ministers periodically on sensitive issues than as a systematic planning agency. The parallel with the results of Roosevelt's Committee on Administrative Management seems likely to be a close one; except that in Britain it is consultants from business rather than administrative reformers who have provided the top dressing of theory for the new system.

The British system, then, is sparing over the amount of staff assistance it offers to political leaders, even the Prime Minister. Partly this is a reflection of the strong position of the regular civil service as ministerial advisers, of the view of ministers as temporary heads of permanent organisations, and of the distrust of political forms of staff assistance (see Chapter 5). But the system also reflects the persistence of the strong tradition of horizontal co-ordination among departments, and the generalised rather than specific tasks of co-ordination assigned to the Prime Minister. If the Prime Minister is to make policy in detail, he must borrow or appropriate departmental resources, as happens sometimes with the Foreign Office but rarely elsewhere. In consequence, the system avoids the dysfunction of loading the Prime Minister with a greater weight of direct 'staff' responsibilities than he could conceivably manage himself.

When one turns from the advisory functions of staff assistance to the routine functions of general management, one encounters a different mixture of professional and political factors. The Treasury, it is often said, is the 'most political' of departments. This is because it combines the political function of allocating available resources of funds among the various departments, with the professional function of seeing that these resources are well used. These two functions are interrelated to some extent. Political judgements about priorities will be influenced by professional judgements about the value and effectiveness of various types of expenditure. Conversely, professional judgements about the desirable size of public expenditure will influence political judgements about priorities for expenditure.

Nonetheless, it is possible to distinguish these two aspects of financial control, and failure to do so causes a confusion of judgement. When anyone talks of the 'effectiveness' of Treasury control, he may allude to the skill with which departmental requirements are co-ordinated by the Treasury according to some broad scale of priorities; or he may refer to the professional effectiveness of the Treasury in cutting out waste and getting value for money. Of course, both commendations may be intended, but this does not necessarily follow. For example, Samuel Beer rates the British Treasury highly as an instrument of co-ordination when compared with the U.S. Bureau of the Budget; but he also notes that the U.S. Bureau has superior professional resources.[12]

Budgeting is an essential part of the internal co-ordination of any organisation; but governmental budgeting does not necessarily make much use of professional judgements. Despite its professional resources, the Bureau of the Budget must still largely 'play by ear' – studying the President's general priorities and questions of political practicality – and must rationalise afterwards. The professional skills of financial control have to be exercised (if at all) within a bargaining framework. This framework settles both the principal budgetary decisions, and also the ways in which more rarified or specialised financial judgements can make a limited impact. The politics of budgeting are closely related to the functioning of the whole governmental system.

Thus the smoothness of Treasury co-ordination, which Beer admires, is a product more than a cause (although it is also a cause) of the strong 'integrative' values of British administration. The Treasury stands sentinel over all public expenditure, controlling every departmental request to Parliament for funds and deciding what new or additional expenditure will be necessary. Treasury control is a continuous process working through well-established conventions. These include the requirement of 'prior approval' for all projects entailing new expenditure when first conceived; annual budgeting, which is a separate control, although naturally influenced and assisted by the operation of prior approval; and the need for all legislative proposals to receive Treasury comments before presentation to the Cabinet. Whereas Congress can and does vary the estimates prepared by the Bureau of the Budget (often with the connivance of a government agency), Parliament now invariably accepts the financial proposals of the Government. Treasury approval is, therefore, the key also to parliamentary approval; and if a departmental annual vote proves inadequate, the Treasury can authorise the expenditure, and Parliament will simply be presented with a retrospective bill ('supplementary estimate'). Probably the chief impact of parliamentary authorisation – other than to set a time-table for annual budgeting – is that unexpended votes must be returned to the Exchequer; which produces some stimulus in the departments to 'last-minute' spending.[13]

The style of Treasury control also reflects the fact of a general administrative class. Communication is naturally facilitated between administrators who share the same traditions, make similar assumptions, follow interchangeable careers, and take the same detached view of specialised knowledge.

The traditional style of Treasury control is sometimes described as control by 'intelligent laymen'. This is the method (as one departmental witness put it) 'of satisfying themselves (the Treasury) that we are properly satisfying ourselves (the department) about the economics and soundness of particular schemes'. It is a method easy to make fun of. Lord Bridges in *The Treasury* gives a list of the kind of questions which the Treasury officials ask, which (as Ely Devons has shown) are hardly very taxing ones. The departmental officials could and should have thought of these questions for themselves, and if they had not would know how to evade them. Further, the wide range of work which a single Treasury official must cover means that his acquaintance with the field of investigation will be extremely limited, the more so as he will normally 'move around' and specialise even in a very broad field for only a few years. When Beer wrote Treasury supply divisions had about fifty officials, but by 1964 the public sector group had one hundred officials; which meant that two principals instead of one could concern themselves with agricultural subsidies under the general guidance of an under-secretary.[14]

It follows that the Treasury system of probe by 'intelligent laymen' has mainly psychological value. It works as well as it does primarily because inquisitor and victim share the same moderate values which stress the unity of the public interest. Thus their disputations, although real enough, take on a mild air. The Treasury inquisition helps to remind departments of the need for economy without necessarily showing them how to practise it. On the other hand, the system of one intelligent layman quizzing another is perhaps unlikely to elicit radical ideas and innovations.

However, to demonstrate that a system works 'smoothly' is not necessarily to praise it. In British government, the budgetary game occupies a narrower field, engages fewer key players, and follows more gentlemanly rules than it does (for example) in American government. The greater ease of fiscal co-ordination does not prove that the actual decisions are any wiser – merely that the temperature of disputes is lowered by procedures which enjoin compromise and which reinforce the over-riding political requirement for the Cabinet to present a united front. The greatest virtue which might be claimed for Treasury control is that its comprehensiveness should facilitate the application of the same yardsticks to all expenditure, and that no unwanted and inconsistent item ought to escape its clutches.

Thus Treasury methods provide the opportunity to apply consistent standards and techniques to the review of expenditure, but paradoxically they may also reduce the incentive to do so. The Treasury has no rival review agencies to stimulate its performance, save for the sporadically effective but belated censures of the two parliamentary select committees. Supported by the well-oiled and secretive machinery of administrative compromise, and buffeted by the interventions of a few political masters, the Treasury may be more liable than similar agencies elsewhere to succumb to the faults of a polished amateurism. Such charges have indeed been made, and supported by evidence of the very small resources of skilled manpower available for the work of financial and managerial control. The smallness of these resources can be treated as a point of pride – a demonstration of what a few talented men can accomplish. However, in recent years the pressure of criticism has led to some strengthening of Treasury manpower, and to greater attention to the use of professional managerial techniques.

CENTRALISATION AND STAFF AGENCIES

The development of institutionalised staff services and agencies, once these exceed the concept of personal assistance to an executive, can be seen as aspects of administrative centralisation. Simon, Smithburg and Thompson's analysis of 'overhead units' (see Chapter 2) is another way of looking at the complex of controlling, co-ordinating and advisory units which get lodged at successively higher points within administrative structure. Overhead units will usually only be needed if ordinary horizontal processes of co-ordination between departments are judged inadequate, which varies greatly between systems. However, the general pressures for administrative centralisation are universal and are of three main types.

1 *Policy co-ordination.* This need arises either because some task requires a partial co-ordination of many departments or because closer integration of a limited group of departments is required. In the former case, the overhead unit will be located at the apex of the system (even if its work is not highly important), in the latter case it will co-ordinate a group of departments or form a basis for their formal integration. In actual fact, the tasks of policy co-ordination are so diverse, both in scope and importance, that this general distinction is not too helpful. It is a question of policy judgement and organisational 'philosophy' as to whether (say) regional development is assigned to a small agency concerned with many departments, or to a co-ordinating minister for a group of departments, or as an integrating bond for a giant department. However, the example does illustrate the growth of pressures for policy co-ordination; once regional development would have been left to the 'normal processes' of inter-departmental co-ordination.

2 *Resources co-ordination.* The causes of increased co-ordination of governmental financial and economic resources are very familiar. They include increasing centralisation of taxation and capital borrowing due to reasons of social equity and fiscal convenience; the need to relate budgeting to the general management of the economy, and the development of tools for economic management; attempts at co-ordinating assistance to the private sector; stress upon equalising resources and service standards between different parts of the country; and closer attention to the costs, benefits and interconnections of all forms of public expenditure. The need for resource plans not only produces additional co-ordinating units (such as the D.E.A. in Britain, the Planning Commission in France) but also an elaborate network of co-ordinating machinery which becomes entwined with patterns of policy co-ordination (see Chapter 2).

3 *Technical co-ordination.* There are a great variety of skills which may be placed in an overhead unit so as to serve a number of departments. These include legal, purchasing, statistical, medical, public relations, operational research, systems analysis, and many

others. However, the 'skill' argument on its own is usually inadequate to justify the creation of a special unit, because of the obvious advantage of harnessing skills more directly to the work of operating units, and because few of these skills are really so rare or precious as to justify concentration. However, the claims of specialised skills do often provide strong reinforcement of policy or economic arguments for an overhead unit. For example, a central statistical unit may be set up, partly to unify and co-ordinate the data collected by various departments, partly to disseminate from one point the use of the most advanced statistical techniques; and public purchases of land or property may be centralised in one agency partly to satisfy requests for uniform treatment and proceedings, but also so as to concentrate legal and conveyancing techniques.

Again, if an economic case can be made for the centralised purchasing of stores, furniture or equipment, the case for concentrating skills (here a very dubious one) can be used to support it. The most irrefutable case for technical centralisation is where the necessary equipment is highly expensive, for example advanced computers.

A further cause of centralisation which should be mentioned are the pervasive pressures for administrative uniformity which appear in many guises. The wishes of public employees for more equality of treatment over pay scales and career opportunities strengthens the centralisation of personnel management; the wishes of businessmen not to be troubled with too many diverse questionnaires leads to attempted centralisation of survey procedures; and the wish or demands of citizens for equal treatment causes much attention to the determination and enforcement of common standards of regulations and services.

It should be noted that these pressures for centralisation run throughout the administrative system. The same policy, economic, and technical arguments which spawn co-ordinating units in central government machinery also lead to the creation of overhead units within large departments, and to the imposition of overhead controls by central departments upon local authorities or public boards. For example, the technical rationale which caused the Treasury to pioneer the development of computers for government departments is paralleled by the work of the Department of Education and Science in pioneering new forms of school construction for the use of local education authorities. The policy and resource co-ordination exercised by the Treasury over the nationalised industries generally is paralleled by the more intensive co-ordination of the fuel and power industries exercised by the (erstwhile) Ministry of Power.

However, the air is considerably more rarified at the top of the mountain. Here one encounters agencies concerned with the general oversight of some spectrum of activities carried on by a great range of public bodies operating in different ways and at different levels. Such an agency will typically be concerned with setting general standards and rules which all relevant agencies are told or urged to observe; with research and advisory functions; and with developing tentative plans for policy and resource co-ordination throughout its allotted sphere of operations. An example would be the central agencies for the planning and conservation of water resources which now exist in many countries. The 'bite' of such an agency will vary a lot according to the sophistication of its planning, and the unitary or pluralistic tendencies of the administrative system. Quite frequently such a body starts in a wholly advisory capacity and gradually develops mandatory powers. Finally it may manage to rationalise and centralise aspects of the administrative machinery through which it must work.

Although a variety of reasons exist for the growth of overhead controls, it seems that their acceptability varies with political culture. In the U.S.A., the advantages of expert knowledge and co-ordination are stressed; in France, the case for policy integration bulks large; in Britain, much weight is given to the case for satisfactory common standards.

Contemplating these centralising forces, one is moved to ask what countervailing pressures exist and why these are not more effective. As Chapter 2 indicated, one counter-trend is the frequent wish of operating agencies or units for maximum self-containment and autonomy. Another offsetting factor is the case for geographic decentralisation, in both traditional and modern forms, which cannot be explored here.

Reverting to the machinery of central government, it is clear that the universal pressures for overhead control and co-ordination must be met according to the structure and tendencies of the particular governmental system. Overhead units, to be effective, must cluster next to the location of ultimate political authority, and their location then becomes also informative about the political structure of the Government. If, however, the system is resistant to overhead units, as is British government, then the same pressures must be met partly at least through other devices.

For example, French government works formally through a Cabinet system and through mutual co-ordination among parallel departments. In practice, though, the structure is considerably more hierarchical than the British one, and accords a strong role of formal co-ordination to both the President and the Prime Minister. Under de Gaulle's régime, both leaders were directly responsible for substantial, and to some extent differentiated zones of policy co-ordination.

The set of agencies attached to the office of the French Prime Minister bear some resemblance to the American situation, although the subjects covered are somewhat different. These agencies deal with defence co-ordination, economic planning, regional development, scientific research, social policy, the civil service, administrative reform, and even tourism; also attached are the public corporations concerned with atomic energy and space exploration.[16] The list reads as an interesting description of those tasks which in France are held to require generalised policy and resource co-ordination 'across the board'; or which necessitate heavy concentration of scientific resources, or which require the highest political backing to be effective, e.g. the overhead unit for civil service management and reform created in the Prime Minister's office in 1945. The range of policy matters being co-ordinated in this way in France is larger than those lodged in the Executive Office of the U.S. President, although the latter has a central task of financial management which in France falls to the Ministry of Finance. Moreover, the list of co-ordinating agencies might be still longer in France if it were not for the resistance of some strong departments. For example, the French Ministry of Finance successfully resisted a proposal to create an overhead unit for European economic integration.

Naturally the French Prime Minister's direct concern with these numerous agencies is very limited indeed. He is supported by a number of co-ordinating Ministers of State who supervise the actual agencies which are mainly headed by civil servants with titles of secretary-general or delegate-general. The various agencies cannot even be described as the Prime Minister's direct concern in the same sense as the U.S. President controls 'his' staff agencies. One is therefore dealing with subtle constitutional factors which affect the authority of particular agencies, and in some cases (as already noted) the real rationale is not an imperative need for high-level co-ordination, but simply a question of where to locate a task which does not fit naturally into the departmental structure.

In Britain, as noted earlier, high-level co-ordination has traditionally worked through the Treasury and the elaborate and elastic, but basically collective, machinery of the Cabinet serviced by its

Secretariat. Experiments with other conventional departments charged with co-ordinating tasks have not been successful. The Ministry of Town and Country Planning (1943–51) had some direct operating responsibilities in relation to local authorities, but was also supposed to co-ordinate the decisions of the many departments (such as Transport, Agriculture and Board of Trade) concerned with questions of land use and development. It never achieved sufficient political status and seniority to be an effective co-ordinator. As already noted, Labour's experiment with a Department of Economic Affairs also failed. (It might have had a better chance if it had concentrated initially on producing plans, instead of intervening on decisions towards which it had initially little to contribute.) The latest parallel co-ordinating department, the Civil Service Department, was set up in 1968 as a direct response to the Fulton Report on civil service reform, and took over the Treasury's responsibilities for civil service management and administrative efficiency. The arrangement that the Prime Minister should become the titular head of the C.S.D. bears a striking resemblance to the French civil service reform of 1945. But it remains to be seen whether the C.S.D. will outlive its initial impetus of implementing Fulton, or be re-absorbed within the Treasury.

Thus the main British device for coping with the pressures towards more centralisation has been giant departments. This achieves broader scope for policy and resource co-ordination, and greater technical specialisation, within a modified version of the conventional departmental framework. It reflects the British preference for maintaining a collective and lateral framework of co-ordination, even though it necessarily requires a new form of political hierarchy within the large department. This development therefore stands in interesting contrast to the accumulation of overhead staff agencies in the U.S.A. and France. But giant departments may bring about, or be associated with, some strengthening of centralised co-ordination as well. The creation of the C.P.R.S. in the Cabinet Office is a small step in this direction, and Sir Richard Clarke has pointed out that while the number of ordinary departments has been cut, the number of 'central' agencies has grown to three (Treasury; C.S.D.; C.P.R.S. and Cabinet Office). This could foreshadow an increased complexity of centralised co-ordination or it might, as Sir Richard himself hopes, provide a case for again pooling control functions in one place – either once again the Treasury or a department dealing with expenditure and staffing but not general economic policies.[16]

This account of administrative trends needs to be correlated with the deductive theories of the role of the executive which were discussed earlier. The error of the P.O.S.D.C.O.R.B. theorists was to posit a degree of personal executive control which is simply impractical in a large organisation, emphatically so in the sphere of government. The P.O.S.D.C.O.R.B. functions have to be institutionalised so that somewhere within the system each function is adequately executed; but the coherence of administrative action hinges a great deal more upon an institutional division of labour and techniques of co-ordination, than it does upon the impress of executive will.

A great weakness of traditional theory is that it tells us more about the duties than the capacities of individual executives. We do not know at all adequately, for example, how the highest governmental executives spend their time. On a formal chart it may seem significant that some agency is under the control of a President or Prime Minister, but in practice this relationship may mean little to either the agency or the chief executive, save in terms of latent political power. Top governmental executives have largely to pursue their aims through their choice of subordinates. They can only rarely attend to much detail or pursue a subject in any depth. Thus their decisions must largely reflect their own assessments of the opinions proffered by senior colleagues, advisers or supporters.

But how is a chief executive to weigh up these opinions? Even a large personal staff will not enable him to examine an issue as fully or adequately as it has already been considered in the originating department or in a reviewing agency if such exists. If the chief executive attempts to consider afresh the matters which reach him, he will duplicate work that has already been done and probably done better. He will run the risk of having too much faith in his own snap judgements and in the extra evidence or opinions collected by his own assistants. To escape these risks, the executive both has to try to limit his policy interventions to those matters which he considers to be of crucial importance, and also to express his interest or view-point before policies have solidified and alternatives have narrowed so that only a final decision is lacking.

These requirements apply as much to the head of a large department or agency as to a head of government. In the latter case especially, however, the burden of decision-making is so considerable that the executive has to take the greatest care in selecting matters for personal intervention and in evolving techniques for keeping down the volume of unavoidable personal arbitration required over other matters.

Vital tasks of the chief executive's personal staff will be to supply him with enough information to make effective and timely interventions, and to shield him as far as possible from requests and appeals which he has not the time to tackle. The staff cannot do the executive's basic work for him. As already noted, their methods are bound to reflect those of the executive himself. If he insists upon being 'accessible to all', or lays stress upon a role of ultimate arbitration rather than one of timely intervention, their techniques must mirror his choice.

However, whatever the executive's personality and however large or skilled his staff, the severe limits upon his possible scope of attention remain. On many matters he must be guided, at any rate in a democracy, by accumulated balances of political or professional support. Where, as often happens, the scales are fairly evenly weighted between alternative courses, the executive can either deliver a last-minute casting vote or he can intervene earlier in such a way as to change the shape or content of the ultimate decision. In the former case, his decision will probably reflect the personal or institutional weight which he gives to advice received; in the latter case it will reflect in greater measure his personal views.

A hierarchical image of government is not very realistic, inasmuch as the exercise of authority becomes necessarily more indeterminate as one moves towards the top of any large organisation. This is because the procedural rules or conventions which legitimise the ultimate exercise of authority are rarely clear enough to settle beyond doubt what is an adequately authorised act; whereas the rules become increasingly precise at lower organisational levels. In the upper reaches of an organisation, the politics of personalities becomes highly significant: where the issues have to be settled among a small number of individuals, it is difficult to have adequate rules of arbitration since the same individuals have to make or interpret the rules.

Despite the existence of laws and constitutions, these considerations are as applicable to government as to business or other organisations – in some ways more so. One might write an interesting treatise upon whether Prime Minister Attlee exceeded his powers in authorising the construction of an atomic bomb without consulting the Cabinet, or how far the constitution of the Fifth Republic warranted the policy interventions of President de Gaulle. It is not too cynical to say that in high positions a mere ability to perform some act often seems to serve as sufficient legitimation, unless or until accumulated discontents simmer over.

Whatever formal theory asserts, there are limits to the concentration of effective authority. Thus the formal distinctions between a Presidential and Cabinet system overlook the point that in both cases power must be shared among a group of colleagues, and that co-ordination will depend upon the arbitrations effected by interlocking groups of leaders.

All the same, the arbitral load falling upon the head of government does vary a good deal under different systems. The existence of overhead units, formally attached to a chief executive's office, means that ultimate disputes between these units and operating agencies will have to be resolved by the executive himself, even though much can be settled through formal or informal meetings of unit and agency heads. The delays and costs of such arbitration represent a high price that has to be paid for the creation of overhead units. This price is often overlooked, particularly by traditional theorists who stress the need for maintaining the 'direct responsibility' of the chief executive for a great number of matters. This encourages the idea that if the right formal channels of responsibility can be laid down, the decisions will be made. That this is far from being true is shown, for example, by the necessity for the French Prime Minister to resort to frequent evasions and postponements of decisions. Of course, all governmental executives face a queue of unresolved issues, but the situation becomes worse where the ultimate co-ordination of a host of agencies is formally vested in one man.

As already noted, the overloading of the British Prime Minister is less because he has not accumulated the same responsibilities for overhead units. Top-level issues of 'staff versus line' can therefore be largely fought out through the normal channels of the Cabinet, where both types of agency are represented. Power, therefore, is more broadly shared among departments and their heads. This arrangement limits the role of the Prime Minister and his need for staff to the general functions of intervention and arbitration discussed earlier, without the need for also having to co-ordinate a formidable group of overhead units. It would seem that even reforming Prime Ministers and eminent civil servants in Britain are relieved that this remains the case.[17]

Believing in hierarchy, the theorists of scientific administration preferred a Presidential to a Cabinet system. Urwick suggested that the British Prime Minister needed the help of two deputies to establish an effective span of control over the work of his ministers[18]

– a proposal which both misunderstood British government and proposed a dubious remedy for improving decision-making. As hierarchical theories have been modified, there has come increased recognition of the virtues of collective forms of leadership in both business and government. The problems of horizontal co-ordination are seen to be no greater than those of vertical control, and it is better appreciated that the tasks of top level decision-making in government are so great that they have to be as widely shared as possible.

Corresponding to this new approach, the chief executive is increasingly seen as a 'chief planner', concerned primarily with the general health and effectiveness of his organisation, and particularly with its adaptation to environmental pressures. The executive must in particular concentrate upon the external relations of his organisation with other bodies or groups with whom co-operation is necessary, and upon long-term planning for adjusting programmes and machinery to foreseeable needs. This leaves the executive much less time for directing, supervising and co-ordinating current activities, which has to be achieved through a co-operative style of administration rather than the scalar process of hierarchical control.[19]

These ideas which are becoming familiar in business management certainly have some applicability to government. It has always been the case that government executives have spent much of their time upon relations with contiguous organisations, for example a departmental minister has to attend to his relations with other departments and a head of State to his relations with other States. Additionally, much time must go upon relations with the political parties or groups whose support is essential – particularly of course where legislature and executive are separated. Unfortunately, the weight of these tasks, and the political urgency of much current business, leaves the government executive with all too little time for his role of long-term planner; nor are political supporters or administrative subordinates usually sympathetic to this use of his time. They need from him decisions or the appearance of decisions. In this respect, business organisations provide actually a better climate for concentration at the top upon long-term planning, because its importance for the survival or growth of the organisation is better grasped, and because the arbitral tasks falling upon a chief executive are less demanding. It may be claimed that political executives have to show an equivalent degree of foresight in their attention to electoral prospects. Unfortunately, it requires a very special democratic ideology to believe that this type of long-term planning is also adequate for the functional needs of government.

The theory that overhead units fulfil a purely advisory function to some chief executive, whose will they express and supplement, doubtless helps to sustain certain myths about the exercise of authority. As Simon, Smithburg and Thompson suggest, this theory sustains the self-respect of the line official by evading the difficulty that he is often controlled by a staff official of inferior status. The same reasoning may please public and legislators, who like to see responsibility 'fixed'. Unfortunately, this conjuring trick over the exercise of authority obscures actual facts, and enables contradictory recommendations to receive simultaneous justification. The two Hoover Commissions in America recommended substantial additions to the number of overhead units but also stressed the primacy of line controls throughout the system. In so far as the effect of both views is to strengthen the control of higher-level over lower-level agencies, the proposals are perhaps consistent; but in so far as the result has been to increase the number and range of specialised staff agencies, the strength of line controls through the operating agencies has necessarily been reduced. One cannot have it both ways; but the myths of authority are strong enough for the attempt often to be made.[20]

It is clear that many of the developments we have discussed derive not from the assertion of executive leadership but from pressures towards administrative centralisation and specialisation. Where the new agencies which these pressures require are located is settled primarily by the logic of the political system. Thus more comprehensive forms of administrative integration can probably only come about in America by attaching new agencies to the President, in France by adding to the Prime Minister's office, in Britain mainly by departmental integrations or extensions. Of course, the optimum location for any supervising or co-ordinating agency is a matter of subtle deliberation, which must take account of the precise gradings of political authority as well as of administrative resources and linkages. However, the creation of such agencies primarily reflects pressures for administrative integration and uniformity which have to be met somehow despite the mounting load of co-ordination to which they give rise. There is no royal recipe for lightening this load, but at least it seems desirable to seek an allocation of functions which will shield the highest executives from an unrealistic weight of co-ordinating duties.

REFERENCES

1   See the papers by Urwick, Fayol and Gulick in L. Gulick and L. F.
    Urwick (eds), *Papers on the Science of Administration* (New York,
    1937).
2   E. F. L. Brech, *Organisation: The Framework of Management*
    (London, 1960), p. 48.
3   L. F. Urwick, 'Organisation as a Technical Problem', in Gulick and
    Urwick, op. cit.
4   Richard E. Neustadt, 'Approaches to Staffing the Presidency: Notes on
    F.D.R. and J.F.K.', *American Political Science Review* (December
    1963). James W. Fesler, 'Administrative Literature and the Second
    Hoover Commission Reports', *A.P.S.R.* (March 1957).
5   The American Assembly (Columbia University), *The Federal Govern-
    ment Service* (New York, 1965), pp. 55–88.
6   Charles Hyneman, *Bureaucracy in a Democracy* (New York, 1950),
    Chap. 17.
7   Fesler, op. cit.; Simon, Smithburg and Thompson, *Public Administra-
    tion* (New York, 1950), p. 274.
8   Fesler, op. cit., Chap. 13.
9   See Chapter 6 for references on French *cabinets* and ministers.
10 For Cabinet machinery, see Hans Daalder, *Cabinet Reform in Britain,
    1914–63* (Oxford, 1964).
11 For this view see R. H. S. Crossman's introduction to Walter Bagehot,
    The English Constitution (London, 1963). See also J. P. Mackintosh,
    The British Cabinet (London, 1962).
12 Samuel Beer, *Treasury Control* (Oxford, 1956), pp. 58–9.
13 For Treasury methods of control and for Treasury reorganisation in
    1962, see Lord Bridges, *The Treasury* (London, 1964). For U.S. com-
    parison, see Aaron Wildavsky, *The Politics of the Budgetary Process*
    (Boston, 1964).
14 Definition of Treasury Control from 6th Report of S.C. on Estimates
    1957–8, c. 1092. Bridges' questions are in Bridges, op. cit., pp. 51–3,
    and Devons' comments are in *The Listener* (21 May 1964). The number
    of officials is in Bridges, op. cit., Appendix 2.
15 F. Ridley and J. Blondel, *Public Administration in France* (London,
    1969), pp. 75–85.
16 Sir Richard Clarke, *New Trends in Government* (London, 1971), Chaps.
    2 to 4.
17 See comments by ministers and officials in *Whitehall and Beyond*
    (British Broadcasting Corporation, 1964).
18 L. T. Urwick, *The Elements of Administration*, 2nd ed. (London,
    1947), p. 57.
19 For new ideas of control in business management, see Rensis Likert,
    New Patterns of Management (1961).
20 H. Simon, D. Smithburg and V. Thompson *Public Administration* (New
    York, 1950), pp. 280–90.

PART TWO:
ADMINISTRATIVE BEHAVIOUR

Chapter 5

POLITICIANS AND ADMINISTRATORS

INTRODUCTION

The conventional view of the relationship between politics and administration is that of one between ends and means. Politics, in its more specific sense, is concerned with the uses of State power; or, if the word 'State' is regarded as monolithic or narrow, we can substitute for it the powers of all duly constituted public authorities, whether international, national or local. Many theories exist as to how political will is or should be derived; but, however these questions be answered, the conventional view of administration is that it is concerned with translating into practice political decisions which are independently derived from other sources.

I have already noted that this distinction provided the starting-point for the attempted construction of a 'science' of administration, concerned solely with the most efficient means for achieving any given set of political objectives. Here it is enough to repeat that, at the higher levels of administration, so simplified a distinction has never at any time or in any society been very realistic. It is again conventional (and many democratic procedures support this) to draw a distinction between 'policy' and 'administration', but the dividing-line is always an artificial one, drawn as a matter of institutional convenience, between the broader or narrower, and the more general or more detailed, aspects of governmental decisions.

Indeed, the ways in which this elusive dividing-line is drawn, or not drawn, tell us a good deal about the character of democratic institutions. In theory, and to some extent in practice, British central and local government knows nothing of the distinction between policy and administration. Locally elected councillors are formally just as much responsible for deciding upon the equipment of a new school gymnasium as they are for deciding (in so far as central government lets them decide) the general lines of educational policy. Not only this, but a frequent reproach levelled at councillors is that they busy themselves with minute questions of detail, and let large decisions of importance go through 'on the nod'.

149

Supposing this state of affairs to be undesirable, as many administrative theorists contend, it will always remain impracticable to put 'questions of policy' and 'questions of detail' into insulated compartments. A matter becomes political essentially by being made so, if not through the interest of politicians themselves then through that of their supporters or opponents. It is a fact that an individual case often stirs up controversy far more sharply than do generalised decisions, through arousing the latent interests or engaging the passions of people who had either taken no previous notice of public policy in this particular field, or had even given it a generalised (but somewhat ignorant) approval. Quite apart from such cases, many of the decisions which elected officials have to make are highly specific, while throughout history generalised rules have often had their source in administrative experience and convenience.

Another way of distinguishing politics from administration is in terms of careers and vocations. On this view, politics is concerned in democracies with the activities of elected representatives or officials, and of those who elect or influence them, and administration with the activities of professional administrators and advisers. The relation between these two groups is the subject of this chapter. However, this distinction obviously does not correspond with that between 'ends' and 'means'. In modern Britain, still more in France, the top professional administrators certainly wield more influence in policy-making than do average Members of Parliament. Nor is this solely a modern phenomenon. In the age of stronger representative assemblies which preceded the First World War, there were officials who operated as extremely effective policy-makers. Indeed, some of their modern successors have reflected ruefully that really powerful and independent-minded civil servants like Sir Robert Morant, or strong town clerks like Joseph Heron of Manchester, have ceased to exist.[1] No doubt such men were always exceptional; and their eclipse (if this has indeed occurred) may be attributed to the replacement of an individual by a group style in the conduct of modern government.

An alternative distinction between politics and administration is in terms of process. We can envisage an arch with the left arc representing the political process and the right arc the administrative process. The junction at the top represents the critical point at which political will flows into and energises the administrative system: and it is also the point at which influences that have been generated *within* the administrative process flow back into the higher levels of the political process. There is thus, at the apex of the arch, a fusion of political and administrative influences which have been generated lower down the two arcs.

The conventional view of this image would show all, or nearly all, the lines of force moving in one direction – from the political to the administrative. They would show political will being generated by the activities of parties, interest groups, public opinion, elected representatives, etc., and then discharged into the administrative system there to be broken down into successively more detailed stages of application. This picture contains a fair degree of truth since it is generally the case that the stronger drives and impulses originate within the political process. But the picture also overlooks the significance of administrative 'feedback'. This 'feedback' can be expressed as the accumulated reactions of modern bureaucracies to the tasks assigned to them, reactions which limit and guide the formulation of political decisions. In addition, public bureaucracies have become increasingly involved in the consultation and co-ordination of specific interests, which often impinge upon public policy mainly through an administrative route.

As one moves away from the apex of the arch, there is naturally much less interaction between the two processes. Voters and politicians seeking election, for example, have their eyes upon the rungs of the political ladder, and are not much concerned with administrative operations. Administrators down the line are primarily concerned with getting policies or rules effectively applied, without bothering overmuch as to how or why they were formulated. It is this genuine distinction of activity and interest which colours the study of the two subjects, and explains why questions about means and processes generally predominate in administrative studies. Political activity is like lightning, in that it may suddenly strike into any corner of the administrative system, but only rarely does so. The great bulk of administrative operations continues in political obscurity, and the main interactions between politics and administration occur at the top levels of government.

To conclude this introduction, how can we redefine politics and administration? Mannheim suggests that social processes include a rationalised sphere of settled procedures (administration) and a non-rational matrix (politics) which flows into this settled sphere. In simpler words, politics is an area of change and indeterminacy, and administration is one of stability and routine. This is a more realistic distinction than that between ends and means, or between higher and lower levels of value judgements. It allows for the fact that any matter, large or small, *can* become political, even though the great mass of detailed decisions do not do so.

Mannheim's distinction is a broad one, and there is a large, grey area between politics and administration as thus defined. Politicians and career officials mingle within this grey area, and cannot be kept to one side of a line. In the zone of 'administrative politics', the political conditions of change and indeterminacy occur within a more planned and routinised framework than usually happens with party or legislative politics. Systems vary in the extent to which an administrative zone of activity is insulated from politics, and also in the extent to which behaviour in the intermediate zone reflects a political or administrative style of action.

A stress upon administrative style normally means that career officials exercise considerable influence, and that the political heads of the executive copy administrative styles and may even be recruited from administrators. Conversely, an emphasis upon political style extends the power of politicians, and influences the selection and the methods of career officials. Yet in the first case it need not be true that substantial power passes to the career officials, since they may be specifically trained to respect political leadership and may not want power for themselves; administrative style does not necessarily imply administrative power. Conversely, a stress on political style is consistent with very limited power for the 'political leaders themselves if they see their role as brokers for other interests.

POLITICAL AND ADMINISTRATIVE ROLES

We have already indicated the difficulties of drawing any simple distinction between the roles of politicians and administrators. R. G. S. Brown suggests that the differentiation might be made in terms of a spectrum of contributions ranging from a specific-technical-factual end to a general-political-value end. Brown points out that specific and technical contributions are often reviewed from successively broader and more politicised view-points, culminating in review by Parliament as the most general organ for the expression of social values and preferences.[2] While there is some truth in this description, it has to be remembered that political view-points are often narrow and specific, and administrative view-points are sometimes broad. Also, the fact that administrators stress technical factors and politicians claim to decide questions of value may partly be due to the interest of both groups in maintaining the conventions or myths of their relationship.

As Richard Rose has demonstrated, the roles of politicians are numerous and diverse and cannot easily be summarised.[3] Another

152

difficulty is that political contributions are divided between those made by members of the legislative and those made by members of the executive. The executive-legislative distinction is often more significant for the analysis of decision-making than is the political-administrative one. The executive politicans work in close co-operation with administrators, so that their respective contributions are often hard to distinguish.

However, in all systems there are certain typical forms of inter-action which result from the distinctive styles and interests of the two groups of participants. Important areas of interaction include policy-making, the arbitration of interests, the treatment of individual and localised claims, and the balance between political accountability and administrative discretion. In the first two cases, politicians possess formal responsibility, but administrators supply the missing elements of political decisions. In the third case, administrators defend their distinctive methods of uniformity and impartiality against politicians' frequent interest in influencing particular decisions. The fourth case represents an inevitable point of conflict between the needs and interests of the two groups.

Climate-Setting and Specific Policies

The most obvious and universal contribution of politicians to policy-making occurs through the formation of general attitudes, opinions and ideologies. 'Climate-setting' influences the way in which particular issues are approached and the kind of measures which are favourably regarded, but is too generalised an activity to produce specific policies.

A general election is the supreme occasion for changing the political climate, and the programmes and political images indicate the direction of intended change. In Britain, Labour is broadly favourable towards public ownership, economic planning, and public housing, and the Conservatives towards private enterprise and a selective treatment of public social services. In the U.S.A., the Republicans emphasise their dedication to law and order, and the Democrats stress the extension of welfare measures. But these images are very general and their relationship to specific issues is most uncertain, while of course even general party goals may not be realised in practice, as witness the frequent failure of right-wing governments to achieve their declared aim of public economy.

There certainly have been periods of effective programmatic politics, a favourite example being the Labour Government's implementation of its programme of nationalisation and social

153

reform between 1945 and 1950. However, this was a special case of powerful accumulated pressures for change, and the capacity of parties to produce and implement detailed programmes seems to be declining. This situation reflects the weakening of the ideological and also possibly the class basis of parties, the increased influence of interest groups, and the difficulties which parties experience over prescribing remedies for increasingly complex problems with the help only of limited expertise and small research staffs.

Many party leaders, such as Harold Macmillan and Harold Wilson in Britain, prefer to contest elections upon their personal appeal and general competence rather than upon a reasoned programme. The record of parties over honouring such specific proposals as they do advance is not impressive, and British parties seem to do no better in this respect than American parties which are intrinsically more pragmatic.[4] The smaller parties of France and other European countries produce much more specific programmes, but have much less chance of achieving them.

Conversely there has been an increase in the importance of policy sub-systems, dealing with such subjects as agriculture, transportation, science, health, education, and so on. Although no clear boundaries can be fixed for sub-systems, each is defined by the existence of a distinctive set of policy issues, which form the specialised concern of a distinctive set of officials, interest groups, experts, advisory committees, commentators and others. For example, the agricultural policy sub-system revolves around issues of subsidies, production controls, marketing, trade surpluses, technical services and so on, which have a long history and somewhat mystify non-specialists, although comprehensible across international borders.

In comparison with the workings of legislators and political parties, policy sub-systems represent a species of administrative politics, and revolve primarily around administrative agencies who possess considerable discretion to initiate and to vary, as well as to apply, public policies. This does not imply that policies are made by administrators themselves, although they may be, but only that administrative style and experience influence the policy process to a much greater extent than if the same issues were settled by a legislature. The actual influences upon policy in any sub-system are numerous and diverse, and include variable contributions from interest groups, advisory committees, special inquiries, and experts inside or outside the agency in question. However, career officials usually play a major part in obtaining and organising these

154

inputs of information and opinion, as well as in adding some contributions of their own.

The influence of members of the legislature upon policy sub-systems varies considerably with the political system. In the U.S.A., members of Congress contribute actively to these sub-systems through their membership of relevant functional committees or appropriations sub-committees. Indeed, because Congress is so loosely co-ordinated, its influence upon specific subjects is more noticeable than its capacity to formulate general policies. In Britain, however, M.P.s lack any real leverage for policy interventions of this type, and only Opposition leaders assigned to 'shadow' roles have a clear incentive to familiarise themselves with a particular policy field. Nor does an M.P. necessarily enhance his political prospects through becoming expert on some subject, since loyalty to leadership, generalised interests and effective speaking are much more useful for promotion. Of course, many M.P.s are well-versed in specialised politics, for constituency or personal reasons or as supporters of some interest; but the number who can effectively contribute to a given sub-system is usually small, and their influence very limited.

An important effect of a change of political leadership is the opportunity thus provided for changing the policies of sub-systems. However, these changes do not necessarily bear much relationship to party philosophies, but under two-party systems follow the logic of the 'ins' and the 'outs'. All sorts of special interests and viewpoints hang on to the tails of a major party in opposition, hoping thereby to achieve a reversal of the current orthodoxy. Career officials, too, who wish for a policy change can often only achieve it as an indirect consequence of a general election.

Brokerage and Planning

All political systems perform functions of interest articulation and aggregation. The latter must include methods of effecting arbitration or compromise between interests where these conflict. These functions may be performed primarily by politicians or at least partially by administrators; and they may be routed through legislative, party or administrative channels. These alternatives have considerable implications for the roles of politicians and administrators.

An uncontrolled or weakly controlled legislature provides the purest example of political brokerage. Votes can be traded for the support of particular interests. A wide variety of coalitions of support, and compromises within and between these coalitions, is practicable. Calculations can be precise in numerical terms, but the net results are shifting and not easily predictable. The pure politician-broker is concerned with maximising the interests he needs or chooses to support, and minimising those he opposes. Of course, a pure bargaining model exists nowhere in practice, because members are also susceptible to party and personal loyalties and to variable notions of public interest.

Parties often act in support of particular interests, but in two-party systems these connections tend to be limited because of their bad effect upon moderate opinion. Instead, parties will attempt to synthesise or aggregate a variety of interests into some version of the general interest. This leads to the kind of vague policy-making already noted, which is compounded by the undesirability of either endorsing or flouting the wishes of a powerful interest group. Professor Samuel Beer points out that in this situation interest groups play the 'disjunctive' role of helping to break down broad party policies into specific programmes; more accurately this disjunctive function is performed by all the elements (officials, advisers, etc., as well as interest groups) concerned with a policy sub-system.[5] Party policies also tend to be more specific in areas where interest groups are relatively weak; for example, Labour and Conservative parties competed with rival social security and pension plans during the 1960s. In subjects such as agriculture, medicine, science and urban planning, party policies are weaker, because of strong interest groups or of high technical content.

An administrative treatment of interest groups, at least when carried out by general administrators, has some resemblance to a judicial approach working within political parameters. The views of relevant groups will be carefully collected and transmitted in moderate terms so as to reduce partisanship. Co-ordination of views will be attempted where practical. However, attention will be mainly given to the views of well-established and accredited bodies, and novel or radical view-points will have difficulty in attracting attention. The administrative style in Britain is also favourable towards comprehensive bodies which can claim to represent the whole of some distinctive interest. This arrangement transfers much of the burden of interest aggregation to the body in question, which has to co-ordinate a variety of sub-interests into a balanced opinion or set of demands. For example, only the National Farmers' Union has been recognised as speaking for farmers for the purposes of the Agriculture and Agriculture Marketing Acts, despite the periodic claims and objections of smaller bodies.[6] The creation of a peak body for British employers, the Confederation of British

Industries, was largely due to the requirements of negotiations with departments.

It is usual for many interest groups to deal directly with both the legislature and relevant administrative agencies. In Britain and France, well-established industrial and professional interests deal primarily with government departments, and usually seek specific legislative support only when administrative channels prove unsatisfactory. Promotional groups of various kinds, and weak or novel interests, press their case upon M.P.s while seeking a foot-hold in Whitehall. In the U.S.A., administrative agencies typically work in alliance with specific clientele groups which they have sometimes themselves promoted. Instead of the broad integrative approach towards interests of British administrators, administrative action frequently parallels or reinforces the division of interests.

The arbitrative or brokerage role of politicians is inevitably in conflict with attempts at comprehensive forms of governmental planning. Planning requires a harmonisation of interests along systematic lines and on a fairly durable basis. Such planning, however, implies foreclosing and reducing the capacity of politicians to effect variable arbitrations and compromises between interests. It reduces specifically political forms of power, or at least channels political arbitration into a systematic framework of policy co-ordination.

French economic planning provides an example of long-term policy co-ordination within a systematic administrative framework. The core of the system is the *Commissariat du Plan* which is staffed by experts. Representatives of private firms, and to a much smaller extent of trade unions, co-operate with governmental officials upon the various modernisation commissions over the formulation of production and investment targets, but politicians play little part in the process. The advisory Economic and Social Council, which represents various regional and other interest groups, has had only a very sporadic and limited influence upon the preparation of the plans, and Parliament's role has been still smaller.[7] The weaker forms of long-term economic and regional planning developed in Britain have also depended upon the creation of special administrative agencies, and have reduced the scope for radical political changes; for example, the Labour Government of 1964 endorsed an existing plan for the South-East region, despite its incompatibility (as later events showed) with Labour's strong political priority for the depressed regions, primarily because this plan already existed and its implementation had started.[8] In the U.S.A., established administrative programmes can often retain their momentum when political leadership changes, but comprehensive forms of planning would be politically unworkable.

Political Discrimination and Administrative Impartiality

There is always some degree of conflict between the politician's interest in helping his supporters and the administrator's concern with impartial rules and procedures. In all modern democracies, the politician's capacity to secure special favours has dwindled as public services have been purged of patronage and nepotism, and as the spheres of administrative uniformity and of professional (as opposed to political) discretion have been steadily expanded. The considerable autonomy of administrative action within its allotted sphere is now well protected by laws and conventions which politicians themselves generally respect.

The history of political patronage and corruption has cast politicians as villains who will disrupt fair rules for the sake of political advantage. There remain, however, many acceptable and useful ways in which politicians act on behalf of supporters and constituents, as well as considerable points of conflict between political interventions and the maintenance of administrative rules.

The crudest forms of political discrimination consist of the procurement of jobs, business concessions, welfare payments, or other special services for supporters in exchange for their votes or for bribes. The classical examples of this type of action were the machine politics of American cities, of which diluted forms still exist. The barrel of available favours for the politicians to dispense has grown smaller, but still provides an important basis of political support. Where such situations occur, politicians act as entrepreneurs who manipulate the legal and fiscal powers of government so as to secure rewards for themselves and their supporters.

There are still sophisticated political scientists who defend this style of politics on the grounds of its indirect advantages. Thus Banfield contends that the machine politics of Chicago is necessary for assembling sufficient political power to achieve some coordination of contending organisations and interests. In other words, the machine enables the mayor to make some decisions in the interest of the city which otherwise could not be made at all. Banfield also contends that the services of machine politicians, although necessarily partial, humanise the impact of administration upon minority groups such as Negroes, who do not understand or share a middle-class ethic of administrative efficiency.[9]

While it could be contended that machine politics is not the only or best way of achieving the results mentioned by Banfield, these examples illustrate the point that politicians sometimes conceive their roles quite differently from the rational model of systematic policy-making. In many ex-colonies also, the British style of impartial but aloof administration is being modified or replaced by more political styles of discrimination and arbitration. However, these examples have not much relevance to the central governments of Western democracies.

An important and accredited role of politicians is to bring individual claims and grievances to the attention of the relevant public agency. In Britain, certain ground-rules govern this activity, which protect both political and administrative ethics. Thus the M.P. will equally assist any constituent and not just his supporters; he does not expect administrative rules to be broken solely for reasons of political pressure or expediency; and he can exercise his own judgement about the strength of a case (which may just be passed on but can be pressed). Conversely, administrators give careful and prompt attention to all cases which M.P.s raise, they may be sympathetic towards demonstrations of personal hardship, but they will not easily waive rules because of political pressure.

However, there are many cases which are less determined by rules than by public policy considerations. Here the M.P. may achieve the reversal of an individual case, if the relevant policy has been questionably applied or is itself under attack. The famous Crichel Down case, when an aggrieved landowner succeeded through parliamentary action in getting back land which had been compulsorily acquired, is usually treated as an example of 'maladministration', and some maladministration did occur in the form of deceitful communications between officials. Additionally, however, this was a case where an established policy of expanding food production through the use, where necessary, of public ownership, was being pushed much further by officials than was acceptable to the political majority in Parliament, once they realised the situation.[10] However, where there is less divergence between politics and administration than in this particular case, a politician's attempt to question or shift the application of policy to an individual case runs up against the strong tendency of ministers to defend their officials, which is grounded in their own need to secure the latter's full co-operation.

All systems concede the right of elected representatives to press the claims of local interests, but the extent to which such pressure is effective varies widely. These political pressures continually conflict with administrative norms of designing and operating programmes in accordance with objective criteria. In Britain, administrative lines are often drawn so as to minimise political influences of this kind, or to channel them within a framework of established rules and conventions. In the U.S.A., on the other hand, members of Congress can adjust both legislation and appropriations so as to favour local interests, subject to the need to reach mutually advantageous bargains; and also can influence administrative agencies, to a lesser extent, for the same ends. In France, elected representatives depend heavily for support upon their capacity to win special favours for their locality, although substantial areas of administration cannot be much influenced by their requests.

If some local interest can establish its claim to unique treatment, for example an important local industry which is severely depressed, the problem may be made the subject of a special programme. Such measures are sometimes introduced in all countries, but their extensive use indicates the susceptibility of government to fragmented political pressures and a low level of coherent administration. The legislative politics of the U.S.A. favour this result.

The distribution of central government grants to local authorities offers an illustration of the conflict between political and administrative methods. In Britain, this distribution is based upon various objective criteria, such as local rateable values (an index of resources), population (a general index of need), number of school children and mileage of roads (indices of special needs). The criteria reflect general public policies which change over time, but these policies are not themselves designed so as to favour particular localities. However, local authorities can often claim that the results are unfair or do not recognise their special problems, and press for adjustments. While local political influence may play some part in these adjustments, the negotiations are channelled through administrative machinery on the basis of the established criteria. Interventions by M.P.s themselves cannot accomplish much. Similarly, the allocation of resources between regional hospital boards is governed by broad tests of regional requirements, although 'marginal politicisation' in the form of pressures from M.P.s and local interests plays some part.[11]

In the U.S.A., the distribution of Federal funds is governed much more strongly by a balance of specifically political pressures. One frequent result is to distort the original objective in order to include local interests whose support is essential. This happened, for example, to the programme of assistance to depressed areas, where the original intention of concentrating assistance upon the really hard hit areas could not be maintained and Federal aid was spread over very broad areas. Another result is to modify objective tests

160

for programme approval by an admixture of political tests; for example, in the selection of cities to be aided under the model cities programme. Political and administrative styles become interfused.

Political Control versus Administrative Delegation

Politicians are the ultimate controllers of administrative systems, and one of their chief problems is to maintain and demonstrate the reality of their control. Control in this sense does not mean simply (or primarily) making sure that policies which have been made are faithfully executed. It has also the converse meaning of so holding the reins of office that the decisions of administrators can always (if necessary) be over-ruled or amended. It means also establishing an atmosphere in which administrators will continually be aware of political guidelines and constraints.

The political concern, or obsession, with issues of control conflicts with the administrator's interest in effective delegation of discretionary authority. Such delegation is wanted to increase the consistency and promptness of decision-making, and also perhaps to widen the administrator's power or the interest of his job. Administrators will frequently confirm or stress that they welcome effective guidance on policy matters; what they dislike (unless indoctrinated to accept the situation as inevitable or even meritorious) are the rigid and cautious procedures which reflect at root the wish of politicians to keep control without knowing how or whether they propose to exercise their power.

This concern with methods of control is shown in very different ways by members of the legislature and by executive leaders. The former face the long-standing seepage of power to the executive branch, and the diminution of their capacity to control policy subsystems. In this situation, legislatures naturally take pains to protect their traditional prerogatives, and their members often appear more concerned with safeguarding their rights to undertake detailed scrutiny of delegated legislation and public expenditure, than with utilising the opportunities thus kept open. Legislatures and executives have long fought a battle over the amount of detail in which appropriations are presented, with the former giving ground slowly and reluctantly. The methods of financial control still favoured by legislatures remain a formidable barrier to more effective delegations of administrative responsibility.

Whilst legislatures naturally stress their formal powers of supervision, the elected political leaders possess direct hierarchical authority over career officials; but the elected leaders have small resources in terms of their numbers, available time, and administrative experience in relation to the vast machine which they formally control. In this situation, they will naturally stress their right to make final decisions. The meaningfulness of these final decisions will naturally be increased to the extent that their options are kept open, and not constricted by administrative methods of policy analysis and presentation.

The discretion of administrative experts over the preparation of plans or programmes can be controlled in several ways. One device is to require the submission of several alternative plans between which politicians can choose; another is to develop a plan tentatively by successive stages with opportunity for political review at several points; and a third device is to test the plan produced by the internal experts against the views of external advisers. In principle, all these methods have the advantage of broadening the range of policy analysis and establishing political guidelines for administrative investigations; but they can also be used for evasions or postponements of political decisions, with the result that administrative efforts are nullified or delayed.

THE STRUCTURE OF TOP MANAGEMENT

The enormous staffs of modern government are very largely engaged upon the direct provision of public services, or the operation of fairly routinised regulations, or the provision of supporting services for the top echelons of administration. Naturally, it is upon the work of these vast numbers, upon their courtesy, promptitude, understanding and flexibility, that the character and efficiency of the whole public service mainly depends. They mainly create the 'image' of the whole service, and each section thereof. Thus sociological studies of the public service have to dig deep into the system to get results. Political studies, however, will be mainly concerned with the relatively tiny top echelons, because it is they who deploy the extensive powers of the modern State, however important be the sense and direction of lower-level officials for their effective use.

It is at these upper levels that there come into play all the multifarious modern facets of the basic powers of the State: the powers to coerce, to tax, to aid, to provide. It is at these levels that individual decisions of great (and sometimes small) importance must be made, legislation prepared, regulations drawn up, officials of independent bodies appointed, interested bodies consulted, administrative appeals handled, and successive stages of administrative co-ordination attempted. Of course, the number of officials who do all these tasks, or advise political chiefs as to how they should be done, has expanded very greatly. But they remain a small, important, and often overburdened headquarters of a vast system.

The 'top management' of the public service comprises a mixture of political and (professional) administrative elements, and it is the nature of this blend – the ingredients which go into it and the ways in which they are mixed together – which does so much to determine the ways in which the executive uses its great accumulation of powers.

The structure of this 'top management' is a very complex matter. In all modern democracies, a line is drawn between the political executives who owe their positions to facts of political power and choice, and 'career' executives who owe theirs to advancement within a bureaucratic structure on some mixed basis of merit and seniority. But there are significant differences in the rigidity with which this dividing line is drawn, and in the sharpness and clarity with which political and administrative roles are differentiated. There are also important differences in the degree of cohesiveness which each group displays, which depends on what ties bind the group together, how it has been recruited, and how far it has imbibed a set of common attitudes and beliefs. These structural patterns have an obvious effect upon the actual relations between political executives and administrators, and upon the ability of the political leadership to get its way.

As is well known, it is in Britain that the political-administrative division is marked most clearly and rigidly, and associated with a definite and well understood differentiation of roles. Moreover, each of the groups principally concerned is highly cohesive. The political leaders share the same loyalties, have worked together in their party and in Parliament, and have been attuned to a high degree of party discipline. Whatever their disagreements on policy, they have every incentive to work together and ministerial resignations (as opposed to ministerial 'sackings') are rare.

In a wholly different way, the general administrators, who form the élite corps of the British civil service, have imbibed a potent tradition of common belief, attitudes and ethics. Partly this depends upon methods of recruitment, but mainly it comes about through the character of an administrative career. The British general administrator does not regard himself as a specialist in anything save his understanding of the machinery of government and his 'awareness of ministerial responsibility'. Belonging to a general and not a departmental class, he is inducted from the start into a general view of the functioning of government as a whole and an

163

appreciation of the subtle relations between politicians and administrators, as these exist in Britain.

The working of this system turns upon an understanding that neither group will venture on each other's territory. Administrators are appointed on the basis of qualifications and tests operated by the Civil Service Commission, and there is no political influence upon their appointment. It is possible for an incoming government to introduce a few specialised advisers, usually economists, into the system, but despite the attention paid to these 'irregulars' during the 1960s, their numbers never exceeded a score upon any reckoning, and they do not affect the status or promotion prospects of administrators. So far, every new government has accepted the need to apply its policies almost entirely through the established civil service.

The general administrators, for their part, are both protected and restricted by a rigid code of conventions. All acts of a department, however minor, are done in the name of its minister, who takes 'full responsibility' before Parliament and public for everything that is done or not done. The only exceptions are very rare occasions when an official has been personally disobedient or plainly negligent. Administrators do not appear before Parliament to answer questions or accusations, but 'brief' their minister as to how he should answer. (This work of briefing is given the highest priority and takes an appreciable portion of the top officials' time.) They do appear, before the Parliamentary Select Committees, but the scope of these Committees' inquiries is somewhat restricted and their proceedings do not attract much political attention. Particularly in recent years, some administrators have left government for business, but it is rare indeed for one to turn politician. If he should do so, he must completely sever his civil service links and embark on a new career.

Thus the British governmental system turns upon a curious kind of symbiotic partnership between two disparate groups. The partnership is naturally closest between the minister himself and the 'permanent secretary' of his department who is his senior official. At this level, it takes on a close, highly personal quality, since these two individuals spend much of their time either together or complementing each other's movements. The character of this relationship has now been frequently portrayed by participants themselves. They all agree on what are or should be its essential features, and are virtually unanimous in their view that the system works well and is a good one.[12]

All participants agree that the good general administrator must show a peculiar mixture of independence and compliance. It is his duty 'to speak out and then shut up'. Under government rules he occupies the post of confidential policy adviser to his minister, and he should discharge this duty with outspokenness and integrity. One sees here an echo of the qualities of an independent conscience which Burke prescribed for elected representatives, and which still sometimes in Britain involve the Member of Parliament in a conflict with the dictates of party discipline. However, as with the M.P., this independence of mind must not go too far. The senior official has to give not only a personal view (where appropriate), but an accumulated departmental one. Further, his views must be completely innocent of personal alignment with any political party. His task here is not so much to be a political eunuch as a political chameleon. He has to enter sympathetically into the political aims of whatever government is in power, as a duty pointing out 'all the difficulties' in the way of their realisation, but resolutely prepared to try and circumvent them if he is so required.

'The heart of his job' (claims Lord Redcliffe-Maud, a distinguished ex-official), is 'to have a common mind with his minister'. This requires long hours of conversation between the two, in which no subject can be excluded however politically controversial. 'To help your minister make up his mind you cannot confine yourself to the so-called technical or administrative questions; you have to enter as fully as possible into the minister's political thinking, including his relations to the Prime Minister and his other colleagues in the Government.'[13] Some administrators would not accept the rightness of so high a degree of personal involvement and alignment. If the official is so absolute a political chameleon as Lord Redcliffe-Maud suggests, he will need an exceptional degree of mental and emotional versatility to serve the next minister with equal verve. (It is this kind of relationship which American observers find difficult to conceive, and castigate as inhuman or bloodless.) A more conventional view of the relationship sees the official as basing his advice upon his administrative experience, and accepting but not contributing to political direction. In this way the two roles are more clearly demarcated, and the official's intellectual integrity gets better protection. In any event it is agreed that there needs to be the closest intellectual *rapprochement* between minister and administrator; some participants stressing not so much the need for a 'common mind' between the two as the important and difficult task which the latter faces in conveying ministerial thinking to junior officials.[14]

There is no reason to doubt the honesty of these descriptions of political-administrative relationships in Britain, although they are perhaps coloured by the personal satisfactions of ex-ministers and successful civil servants. At the same time these statements are as much prescriptive as descriptive. They make great play with the complex balance of attitudes and habits which officials and ministers need to display if their partnership is to be fruitful. But we cannot be sure that these difficult and somewhat contradictory requirements are always met. The exhilaration of an almost mystical sense of harmonious collaboration, portrayed in retrospect, has a strongly personal quality.

The smooth nature of this British partnership is certainly due in part to the very unspecialised backgrounds of both ministers and administrators. Ministers do not as a rule (although there are exceptions) specialise for long periods in particular policy fields, and they move freely between departments according to their standing in the party and other specifically political considerations. Administrators have no common intellectual background and only a very limited post-entry training, and the senior ones are fairly mobile between departments, and are becoming more so. A study of British permanent secretaries over the years 1900–63 showed that in the post-1945 period 18·2 per cent of these officials had served in four or more departments, while at the other extreme one-third had experience of only one department. Average service as permanent secretary of a department was 7 years, average previous service in the department 13·9 years (these averages, especially the latter, were substantially longer in previous periods). Thus, though not nearly as mobile as his minister, the average chief administrator has spent a large part of his career in other departments.[15]

Thus the style of the ministerial-administrator partnership is pragmatic and flexible, stressing responsiveness to collective leadership and to general political ideas or fashions, while giving much less weight to specialised knowledge or experience. If it be true that this arrangement is a coalition of amateurs, they are powerful and mutually supporting.

The French system of top governmental management is marked by a more assertive and self-confident career bureaucracy. Here the political-administrative dividing line has been pushed upwards in favour of the career bureaucracy. This process started well before the Fifth Republic. Under earlier forms of parliamentary government in France, the absence of majority parties and the necessity for political coalitions meant that French ministers formed a much less stable and cohesive group than their British counterparts, although the individual minister often continued when the coalition changed. During the not infrequent periods of political crisis and stalemate, the French bureaucracy resumed its traditional role as the custodian of the enduring interests of the French nation, and governed by default.

In addition, political posts themselves have been progressively bureaucratised. A French minister governs his departments with the aid of a *cabinet*, which traditionally contained his political friends and supporters. This provided in theory an instrument of political control and supervision which has never existed in Britain, and was more akin to the American system. However, most of the posts in these ministerial *cabinets* had been effectively bureaucratised, and filled with career officials, before the advent of the Fifth Republic.[16]

The bureaucratisation of once political posts has not basically changed the character of ministerial *cabinets*. Although generally career officials, the members of a *cabinet* need political qualities of suppleness and versatility which are less necessary within the divisions or bureaux of a ministry. A *cabinet* often has 'political' and 'technical' wings, concerned respectively with external business and internal co-ordination, the actual structure depending a good deal upon the character of both department and minister. In any event, its organisation must be flexible, relations among its members and with the members of other *cabinets* being governed by political and personal considerations, rather than by the hierarchical rules which apply to most of the bureaucracy. The point is that in France some career officials have the opportunity to fill posts which are distinctly political in character.[17]

Since the appointment of M. Monnet as Commissioner General for the Plan in 1946, the practice has grown of entrusting important tasks not to politicians but to distinguished experts or civil servants. In the early days of the Fifth Republic, the bureaucratisation of top appointments was carried much further. Ministers were obliged to resign from Parliament although they managed to keep their seats in cold storage. The first two Prime Ministers of the Fifth Republic had been members of the Council of State, the third one had been an inspector of finance; there were at various times an ambassador at the Foreign Office, an inspector of finance as Minister of Finance, and an administrator holding the portfolio for administrative reform. Also previously junior ministerial posts such as Secretaries of State were converted into civil service positions.[18] However, under the Pompidou régime there has been a definite reversal to the appointment of politicians as ministers.

167

In many respects, French administrators form a more cohesive and prestigious group than do British ones. Whilst the latter have no common education or training prior to entering the service, the former experience the moulding influences of a long period of shared educational experience. Since 1945, all general administrators in France have gone through the twenty-eight-month course organised by *L'École Nationale d'Administration*, which mixes intellectual study with periods of attachments to prefectures and to nationalised industries or financial institutions. But even prior to this experience, all those entering the general administrative service as graduates had taken the same type of degree, the great majority (87 per cent in 1959) actually coming from the same institution: the Paris *Institut d'Études Politiques*. When one adds the points that internal promotion from lower grades is harder and rarer than in Britain (and also for the administrative corps involves attendance at *L'École Nationale*), that a still higher proportion of administrators than in Britain come from the upper middle class, and that a majority are born as well as educated in the Paris region, one can understand that the social, and, still more, the intellectual background of French administrators is highly homogeneous, and of a kind to inspire feelings of competence and superiority – feelings that are less apparent in the British case.

However, once within the service, there is much less sharing of a common status and loyalties than with British administrators. The 1946 civil service reform established a common pattern of entry and training for French administrators, and set up a new general class of civil administration; but this new class has functioned as an addition to the traditional *grands corps*, such as the court of accounts, the finance inspectorate, and the corps of the Council of State, which have kept their separate identities. These corps attract the most successful recruits, monopolise many of the highest posts, and each has its own considerable prestige and loyalties. The 1946 reforms were extended in 1964, but the *grands corps* have not been assimilated. Additionally, the system of administrative training has produced new tensions between the E.N.A. sophisticates and the self-made administrators who still predominate within the prefectoral corps.

Thus France has a much more splintered top bureaucracy than does Britain, but one with a greater belief in its aptitudes and possibly more inclination to indulge directly in the tasks of policy making. These qualities are reflected in the skilful and sophisticated views on public policy given in the occasional writings of civil servants, which are restricted only by the doctrine of *réservé*: that they should contain no direct attack upon superiors or State authority. The prestige and abilities of this bureaucracy enable it to assume some tasks which in Britain or America would rank as being definitely political.

However, in France political and administrative roles are more mixed and blurred than in Britain. 'Marginal politicisation', for example the ability of politicians to extract specific favours and concessions from the administration, is definitely more marked. Moreover, officials themselves often play political roles. French civil servants are entitled to stand for Parliament, and if elected they keep their civil service rights in storage. Many public servants take advantage of this opportunity, and many high officials have a secondary role as mayors or councillors of *communes*. The political activity of officials, which declined in the de Gaulle period, was sharply on the increase in 1970.

The consequence of this situation is a somewhat ambivalent attitude by officials towards politics. Gournay contends that 'the state of the top officials . . . is a state free of all political ferment', and this may correspond to certain bureaucratic notions of efficiency in France. But an official can also view political activity as a way of increasing his accountability to the public, as well as of achieving some advantages for himself. An official may help to secure favours for the locality with which he is connected, and in return can gain political support which may help his own career. Such acts do not necessarily destroy administrative notions of justice and efficiency, but perhaps express cultural values about the necessity and limitations of political activity.*

In the U.S. Federal Government, as is well known, the only elected officials are the President and Vice-President. The U.S.A. is quite different from any European democracy in having a class of 'political executives' who are personally selected by the President and his advisers, subject to the requirement of Senatorial confirmation for most senior positions. However, the days of wholesale political patronage are now completely passed in America, not only as regards the Federal service as a whole but also for these senior posts. With some significant exceptions, these political executives are members of the same party as the President, but not necessarily particularly active ones. A study of 108 senior executives appointed under Truman, Eisenhower and Kennedy

---

* B. Gournay, *Introduction à la Science Administrative* (Paris, 1966), p. 282. For the local activities of officials see Jack Hayward and Vincent Wright, 'The French Local Elections of March 1971', *Parliamentary Affairs* (Winter 1971).

showed that only 34 had been active politically in party organisations or as supporters of the Presidential campaign.[19]

It is quite normal for the Presidential staff to clear these appointments with the national committee of the victorious party, and through it with the more important State party committees (President Eisenhower issued a directive to this effect). It is also normal to 'sound out' influential senators prior to the official hearings on confirmation. These consultations sometimes result in the elimination of a candidate who is unacceptable to influential politicians, but only rarely do they allow names to be successfully pressed simply upon grounds of party service or loyalty. Indeed, there may be objections from other executives to an appointment which might look like patronage.

The qualities sought in political executives are a mixture of administrative ability and support for the general aims of the new administration. These qualities are found by looking for suitable businessmen, financiers, lawyers and persons already working in some branch of the public services. Inevitably, personal factors enter appreciably into this selection process. The predilections and 'style' of the President himself colour his whole Administration. Presidents who rose through party politics themselves (like Roosevelt or Truman) naturally attached more weight to the value of such political qualities as a probable ability to get on with Congress. President Eisenhower's greater fondness for a 'business' government was well known. President Kennedy introduced relatively more, although not many, academics and intellectuals into top government.

Once a President has appointed his principal Secretaries of State and a few other high officials, their preferences naturally enter into the selection of the next tier of executives who will assist them to make and apply policies. Personal loyalties also play a considerable part in persuading individuals to leave what is usually a much more profitable job for a post in Washington. Nothing is more likely to bring some high-powered industrialist or banker to the capital than a personal appeal from the President himself.

To the outside observer the puzzle about this system is that it works as well as it does. Despite the anti-governmental traditions of America, some fascination and glamour is now attached to high public service, and there are also the dictates of duty and of political or personal loyalty to summon eminent private citizens to the service of the President. Nonetheless, now that simple patronage has been heavily discredited, there is difficulty in finding enough citizens of really high calibre to fill all the requisite posts, at fairly short notice and on a basis that often involves personal sacrifice. Most political executives return sooner or later to the private occupations from which they are drawn. Men who are already at the head of enterprises, and often relatively old, may not find a period of government service too awkward or disadvantageous: but those who are in line in their businesses for top posts may have to risk their career prospects in order to answer the call: and if they do not object to a setback of prospects, their wives may.

Added to this difficulty are the drawbacks of a rapid and rather ramshackle method of recruiting executives when a new President takes office. Most authoritative examinations of the problem have stressed the desirability of more systematic procedures for vetting and selecting possible candidates for office.[20] But while improvements might be made, no selection methods can circumvent the fact that the whole system turns upon the capacity of a single elected official to secure the temporary services of able sympathisers. This fact means that the pattern is bound to be a flexible one too, and places limits upon the efficacy of procedural devices.

The main alternative approach, naturally enough, is to make fuller use of career officials. The history of the American Federal service can be and often is viewed as a steady movement away from patronage and towards the merit system. The Civil Service Commission was created to police the merit system, and the proportion of civilian employees occupying classified posts which come under its control rose from 10·5 per cent in 1884 to 41·5 per cent in 1901, 79·6 per cent in 1931, and 86·1 per cent in 1961,[21] while further posts are excluded from the merit system only for reasons of technical convenience. However these global figures are not informative about the structure of 'top management', where the numbers involved are relatively very small.

There are in all about 1,200 political appointments at the top of the American Federal service, or in regulatory agencies and other public bodies, which are excluded from the normal routines of civil service promotions. These posts are at the President's disposal, but some of them (in regulatory agencies, for example) do not fall due for immediate replacement when a President takes office, and many others continue as a matter of choice or convenience to be filled by the existing occupants. There are about 500 top posts where an immediate change of personnel is normal, and several hundred other less important posts where consequent changes can be expected.*

These figures can be compared with the total of 8,600 key posts

* This estimate of 1,200 political appointments includes 500 posts which form part of the classified civil service. See below, p. 184.

in Federal government distinguished by the Committee for Economic Development. However, this list of key posts includes foreign service officers and military flag officers, and it also includes considerable numbers of staff specialists and professional experts who (significant as their contributions are) do not have executive responsibilities. If one focuses upon the higher executive positions exclusively, it can be argued that the top 'political' executives out-number the top 'career' executives by two to one.[22]

These figures bring out the continuing great importance of the political executive in American government, but they also under-state the modern importance of the career executive and exaggerate the distinctions between the two types of top personnel. Both the structure of Federal government, and the fact of frequent turnovers of top personnel, lead to a considerable concentration of power at the middle levels of the system, particularly in the 100 or so bureaux which still represent in many ways (despite intensified efforts at co-ordination) the key operating units of American government. As a result of the upward thrust of the merit system, most of the posts of bureau chief have now been included in the classified civil service. Many posts which were theoretically 'political' came to be occupied by civil servants who acquired too much experience and skill to be lightly removed, or by political executives who stayed so long as virtually to become professional bureaucrats.

The latter development was particularly fostered by the long years of Democratic administrations from 1932 to 1952, but both developments reflect adjustments to more enduring problems of American government. Unlike the British system, there is no possi-bility of a separate learning of the political and administrative components of executive government. The skills have to be jointly learned and practised in the day-to-day work of government. Thus the career bureau chief has to display as much skill in his dealings with Congress, as much sensitivity to public relations, as much belligerency on behalf of his own agency, as does the Presidential nominee occupying a similar post. In fact, some career executives are definitely more adept at the political aspects of their jobs than are many political executives who may be amazed, on arrival in Washington, to find what their work actually entails. As one of the latter remarked, putting the point a little extremely, the sheltered life of a family textile business is not good training for an alley fight.

Thus American government puts a premium upon the acquisition of certain skills which require rather rare gifts of character and also (preferably) substantial experience of the working of the system. Political executives arriving in Washington without previous governmental experience start at an obvious disadvantage. It may be some time before they can be really effective, and to become so will involve them in adopting different methods from those which succeeded in their business or professional careers. Many political executives find this transition too difficult or uncomfortable, and withdraw with relief after a short period of service. Business executives, for example, often feel frustrated on two different counts: by the rigidity of civil service procedures and promotions which give them less control over their own staff and its operations than they expect to have: and by the continual necessity to adjust their decisions to the views of other government agencies, of Congress, of outside interests, of national and even world opinion – by the whole political process in fact. On the other hand, some newcomers to Washington adjust very well to these requirements, and turn into highly effective Federal executives.

Whilst there is no golden rule for spotting who has, or has not, the qualities that make for success in Washington, the importance of flexibility of attitudes and catholicity of experience are fairly clear. Of the 108 political executives examined in the study already quoted, 24 listed public service as their previous main occupation and a further 43 already possessed (at the time of their appointment to a senior position) appreciable experience of Federal government. Top political executives only occupy their posts for a short average period, but the more effective ones will frequently have had previous relevant experience – either as more junior political executives or else as civil servants who have moved up on to the political rungs of the ladder.

Thus American government produces neither a clear differentiation of politics and administration, nor a cohesive pair of political and administrative élites. The political executives represent a hastily improvised array of disparate individuals, many of whom lack political experience, and do not form a very cohesive group. In fact, their degree of cohesion varies considerably, being strongest when a powerful new President has arrived on the scene with a distinctive style and programme which have widespread appeal. The political appointees lose their capacity to act effectively together when a President's term is starting to run out (especially if there is little hope of his re-election) and the Administration is wearing a 'tired' look. At such times, it becomes difficult to fill top positions with able men, unless they are career executives.

Similarly, the professional bureaucracy lacks the cohesive force

173

which the British or French system produces. Government officials are recruited upon the basis of more or less specialised qualifications, and mostly spend their careers in the same bureau or agency. The system produces a mixture of expert knowledge, parochial attitudes and partisan activity which has no real parallel among European governments. Many proposals have been made for the creation of a mobile cadre of general administrators, who would be neutral on policy issues but skilled in working the governmental machine, such as is presumed to exist in Britain. So far they have always foundered upon American dislike for such a 'bloodless' form of administration, as well as upon more specific opposition from existing interests.

However, it should be added that a type of general administrator is becoming more prevalent in American government, in the form of the 'staff experts' at work in the Presidential office and in the offices of the departmental secretaries. This type of administrative control and co-ordination has much modified the traditional style of American government, and it may be producing a more cohesive form of bureaucratic action. These questions will be considered again in another context. The main conclusion at this point is that the unifying force in American government (in so far as one exists) develops out of the common exigencies which confront executives of all types.

THE INTEGRATIVE ROLE OF GENERAL ADMINISTRATORS

What are the effects upon administrative behaviour of the existence of a class of general administrators? The question is difficult because, although the role of general administrators is often discussed, it is rarely very satisfactorily explained.

Sir William Armstrong has described how the work of the administrative and executive classes in Britain was shaped by the requirements of political and financial accountability to Parliament. While in private business financial and personnel management became separate specialisms, in government these tasks become extensions of the general administrator's responsibility for protecting the legitimacy of all governmental action. He concludes that the best description of administrators is as specialists in ministerial and parliamentary business.[23]

However, Sir William's valid description of the origins of the administrator's role is no answer to the question posed at the beginning of this section. First, while parliamentary accountability certainly remains important, much of the administrator's energies is given to newer consultative and executive tasks. Secondly, it would be as valid to describe a bureau chief in the U.S.A. as a 'specialist in Congressional and Presidential business', and to note that senior career officials in that country are even more preoccupied with administrative and financial legitimation. Therefore, the general need for political accountability does not adequately define the general administrator's role, unless the concept is modified to mean the requirements of a particular political and social system. In that event, the question becomes one of what those particular systematic requirements are, and whether they have changed.

The general administrator is a special kind of co-ordinator and arbitrator. He assists political decision-making through assembling and processing a diversity of claims, opinions and view-points. While co-ordination of views is a major task of officials under any system of government, this task is much more systematically performed and strongly stressed when a general administrative class exists. Co-ordination is the administrator's *forte*, and the attention paid to it is naturally greater where (as in Britain) the policies of government are expected to be formally consistent. The consistency actually achieved may be only skin-deep, but the administrator has a real interest and pride in maintaining at least the appearance of harmonious and smoothly integrated government action.

Linked with co-ordination is arbitration. In Britain, the administrator has some discretion over which bodies and persons shall be consulted, and he decides how to present or synthesise opinions for ministerial attention. Administrators have considerable discretion over the detailed application of public policies; for example, the determination of town planning appeals, the issue of industrial development certificates, and investment priorities between the new schools proposed by local education authorities.

In all these cases, the administrator walks delicately within political guidelines and constraints. He tries to adapt individual decisions to such knowledge as he has of ministerial wishes; for example, when a new minister arrives, administrators will seek his personal arbitration upon a sample of town planning cases so as to assist the thousands of decisions which they must in effect judge for themselves. He is also sensitive to professional or expert opinion; in the above example, administrators would be cautious about over-ruling any firm opinions offered by town planning inspectors or the ministry's own technical planning staff save for known political reasons. A failure to consult some interest group, or a discretionary decision which affronts an industrial firm or a local authority, may result in political annoyance or embarrassment to the minister even if, as will usually be the case, the minister upholds his official.

To some extent these descriptions would apply to any official working within political guidelines. A French minister, M. Robert Buron, has described how one of his directors urgently asked him to approve a series of decisions which on inspection the minister found to be inconsistent. If they had all been signed, the official would have known he had discretionary freedom, otherwise the right bias for his decisions would be indicated.[24] The feature of general administrators is that they are especially selected to exercise discretionary authority in a systematic and non-partisan way.

Administrative discretion utilises precedent where convenient, but is also sensitive to changes of political climate, and fills in the limitations of established rules and policies with pragmatic ideas of fair treatment and common sense. Still, there are occasions when senior administrators at least make stronger policy contributions. These are most likely to occur where party policies are vague, and specialised opinion is inadequate or evenly divided. Administrators are residuary legatees of decisions which nobody else is able to make, although prone to take a cautious view of policy innovations.

French administrators are often said not to be generalists in the British sense. C. H. Sisson considers the legalistic style of French administrators to be wholly at variance with British traditions, and wholly undesirable to emulate.[25] Still, this difference can be exaggerated. French administrators work within a precise and formal legal code, whereas British administrators are more pragmatic and more guided by convention; but both groups are much concerned with equitable treatment of individual cases and with a fair balance between contending interests. As already noted, much of the British administrator's discretion has an arbitral quality and is probably acceptable to the public for that very reason.

In both Britain and France, general administrators are strongly concerned with general forms of control and co-ordination, but achieve their results in very different ways. In Britain, administrative style is pragmatic, flexible and shallow, which follows from the deliberately unspecialised character of administrative recruitment and postings and from the occupation of top posts in all departments by members of the same administrative class. The senior administrator plays something of a chameleon role, not only in relation to successive political loyalties, but also in relation to successive departmental ones. Indubitably, he puts his full energies into pleading his department's case at joint meetings, but he is also trained to recognise the diversity of factors which constitute the 'public interest', the need for frequent compromises, and the merits of smooth co-ordination.

There is a certain barristerial quality in an advocacy which is not strongly rooted in departmental loyalty or professional opinions. In the same way, the financial controller in each department mixes a primary loyalty to the department with recognition of Treasury requirements. This administrative style enables financial control to be exercised more smoothly if possibly less thoroughly than in France, where the Ministry of Finance appoints its own controllers in the various departments.

In the French system, the specialisations of the various *grands corps* do not prevent administrators from interpreting their tasks in a broad and judicious manner. For example, the *Inspecteurs des Finances* view financial inspection less as a technical task than as a form of training in the exercise of economic judgements. However, the specialisation of the *grands corps* does mean a separate articulation of control tasks which in Britain are undifferentiated. Also, the *grands corps* concentrate much more specifically upon functions of arbitration and harmonisation, whereas *polytechniciens* dominate many technical divisions of ministries. The *grands corps* view their duties as the protection of general against special interests, economy against extravagance, unity against fragmentation.[26] The similar attitudes also to be found among British administrators are much moderated by the catholicity of their tasks.

If one seeks justification for the existence of general administrators as such, irrespective of their considerable national differences, this is usually offered in terms of their service to some concept of public interest. Put arrogantly, administrators are custodians of the 'permanent interests of the nation', a claim often made in France but only rarely heard in Britain. Put modestly, their value consists simply in a non-partisan and equitable approach to supporting tasks carried out on behalf of political leaders. Quite clearly, there are considerable differences between France and Britain in the extent to which administrators are trained to depend upon political initiatives or to substitute their own. But in either case, the question still arises as to how far any distinctive administrative philosophy exists for the interpretation of discretionary tasks.

One common and familiar feature is the defensive posture of administrators against special interests and claims of all kinds, whether emanating from pressure groups or from partisan technicians or experts. A central aspect of this protective role, and one which also buttresses the administrator's own special status and

177

authority, is concern with or dedication to public economy. As economy has become a less fashionable political goal, the administrator has switched his image of 'taxpayer's guardian' to that of a prudent and rational allocator of scarce resources. Resource control remains central to the administrator's function, treated not as a technical exercise but as detailed policy judgements made within a framework of broad political priorities. Thus in the British civil service finance is always coupled with policy as the appropriate sphere of the generalist, and the Fulton Committee's suggestion that economic and social administration should become separate specialisms failed (among other reasons) because so many administrators stressed their strong concern with financial control. In France, financial control is the special task of two of the most prestigious *grands corps*. The Treasury and the French Ministry of Finance are the natural homes and centres of the generalist tradition.

However, the absence of an administrative class does not mean that goals such as public economy are neglected. Instead there will be more directly partisan conflict between spending agencies and budgetary authorities, and between agencies concerned with contending interests, such as those of producers and consumers. The idea that some administrators have unique insight into the nature of public interest is a legacy of the *étatist* traditions of centralising European monarchs, which retain little appeal in a pluralist society. Rather do the general administrator's values contribute to the reduction of conflicts and the integration of decisions, but it does not immutably follow that the results are preferable to a more fragmented and competitive style of administration. In France conflict between administrative groups remains strong and the controlling power of the *grands corps* can be defended either by saying that all governments need strong defences against special interests, or else that these groups achieve an ultimate harmonisation of decisions which would otherwise be lacking.

The arbitrative authority wielded by general administrators perhaps reflects social norms which seek to put limits to the exercise of both political and professional authority, as one element within the complex legitimation of the governmental process. How else can we explain the right of administrators to make adjustments to quite minor decisions reached by local authorities,[27] which can be validated both by the political right of democratic election and (in Britain at any rate) by the effective authority conceded to local professional staff of good calibre? A conventional explanation might be that the administrator's act is acceptable because of the high political legitimacy vested in the minister for whom he acts, but it is widely known that ministers do not themselves make most such decisions, and it is uncertain that such acts would be more acceptable if they were directly political.

The acceptability of administrative arbitration of this type varies greatly between societies and depends upon qualities in the administrator himself which are difficult to fix. In France, the discipline for such arbitration is provided by the code of administrative law, though there is plentiful scope for discretion within that code. In Britain, a more pragmatic balance must be struck between considerations of policy and of equity, and the tendency is less towards formalisation of rules than specialisation by policy areas, as is evidenced for example by the increasing authority given to town planning inspectors. These share some of the traditional values of general administrators, from which in some cases they have been drawn, combined of course with a more specialised knowledge of town planning. This provides another illustration of the pressures upon administrators to become more specialised, yet the acceptability of administrative arbitration still depends upon qualities of objectivity and fairness which have been cultivated primarily through the generalist tradition.

The other face of administrative ethics is the capacity to resist illegitimate political demands or pressures, but any code on this matter is weakly and uncertainly drawn. Thus it is very much in the administrator's own interest to resist political encroachments upon the internal self-regulation of the bureaucracy, and generally such resistance is successful on the limited occasions when it is necessary. On such matters as financial accounting and the award of contracts, the administrator has direct parliamentary obligations which can compel him on rare occasions to resist a ministerial command. There is, however, a border-line area where the flexibility of ministerial prerogatives can be used to sanction acts which offend general tests of administrative propriety. An example would be the wish of a minister to fill some appointment on the basis simply of personal friendship, or to spend money in ways that the administrator considers to be undeniably wasteful. It is over such cases that the notion of administration as an independent ethic which should be explicitly upheld comes into its own. Such issues are too little known and (in Britain) probably too rare for generalisations to be possible, but it is probable that the concept of differentiated political and administrative responsibilities has given ground before the concept of a more politically pliant partnership.

Lord Bridges has claimed that the British administrator has some

179

resemblance to both an artist and a don, and Robert Catherine has compared the French administrator to a dedicated monk.[28] These descriptions stress the anonymous and cloistered role of the high official, which derives from an environment that is deliberately protected from personal political involvement, as well as being somewhat removed from direct operational tasks. The Treasury official, for example, controls other departments which themselves frequently exercise only an indirect control over decisions made by private firms or public agencies. The artistic comparison derives from the administrator's skill in reconciling diverse elements into a harmonious composition, usually by means of a carefully written brief. The administrator's quality of ironic and aloof detachment, and his sense of a special duty or mission, are implicit in these descriptions.

The relation between the political and managerial tasks of general administrators is the source of much controversy. In Britain, the Fulton Report stated that administrators 'tend to think of themselves as advisers on policy to people above them, rather than as managers of the administrative machine below them'; and again 'few members of the (administrative) class actually see themselves as managers, i.e. as responsible for organisation, directing staff, planning the progress of work, setting standards of attainment and measuring results, reviewing procedures and quantifying different courses of action'.[29] The Fulton Committee did not of course deny that policy advice and co-ordination were important and officially prescribed aspects of the administrator's duties. Their argument was that this part of the work received excessive emphasis and attention, while administrators were inadequately trained and equipped to do managerial work which could be separately distinguished.

However, it is not obvious that British administrators are especially burdened with their political environment. They must be meticulous over meeting ministerial requests but they are relatively insulated from legislative pressures. It is also most doubtful as to how far managerial efficiency in government can be assessed without reference to the policy process. Effective management is not so much a matter of familiarity with techniques, as an ability to achieve goals within a specific political context.

In systems without general administrators, politics and management interact directly and produce a style which may be labelled 'political management'. The effect of an administrative class is to produce an intervening layer of politically neutral co-ordinators and adjusters. This group will certainly participate in policy conflicts, but to the outside world they will minimise the existence of such conflicts. Overt conflict is a matter for politicians, while the general administrator's task is to maintain the continuity, consistency and impartiality of public action. This work may be seen as a supportive task done on behalf of a collective political leadership (the British model) or as work with a higher degree of autonomous direction (France).

If administrators are trained to respond flexibly to political leadership, which is the British case, they will become somewhat directionless or ritualistic if the leadership is inadequate. This is the truth behind the oft-expressed views of British administrators that they prefer ministers to have definite policies. (In fact, though, if a definite policy already exists from a previous government, the administrator may well prefer to retain it; it is a policy vacuum which the administrator cannot fill.) The tendency of British administrators to look upwards rather than downwards that Fulton criticised, in so far as this is not a feature of *any* hierarchical organisation, is a natural result of the directionless character of administration itself.

French administrators are less dependent upon political direction, and adaptation to change is internalised to some extent within the administrative system through the conflict of viewpoints between administrative groups. Still, as the Presidency of de Gaulle demonstrated, administrative initiative tends to be stronger within the protective umbrella of a strong political leader.

As a rule, political and managerial skills are joined within a particular context. The American bureau chief can combine expert political and managerial knowledge because of his close concentration upon a limited sphere of government operations. In France, the officials in the ministerial *cabinets* concentrate upon policy advice and personal assistance, the *grands corps* upon general arbitration and control, and the *polytechniciens* upon executive management; while the *grands corps* are themselves differentiated according to broadly defined processes. The fact that American officials specialise according to policy sub-systems, and French officials according to broad processes, reflects the political values of these two governmental systems.

Similarly, the deliberately unspecialised character of British administrators reflects such political values as a strongly collective style of government, prompt adaptability to new leadership, and a shared interest in economy, moderation, and flexible co-ordination. While specialisation can to some extent be pressed for purely managerial reasons, such as the improvement of staff records and relationships, specialisation would necessarily change political values. Thus if administrators specialised according to functional fields, general co-ordination would be weakened but greater vigour and experience would be infused into the goals of policy sub-systems. If administrators specialised according to processes, technical skills would be enhanced but the general-purpose adviser of the present system would become less in evidence.

Not surprisingly, British administrators themselves have tended to resist any development of specialisation, save in limited and pragmatic ways which can be combined with the maintenance of their generalised career opportunities. Technical forms of specialisation are liable to be self-defeating to the administrator through blocking him off from the broader career opportunities which are his main prize. Even specialisation in finance and budgeting would undermine the strength of the administrator's position unless it was treated in the very broad French style. Specialisation according to broad policy areas would be contrary to the generalist tradition, if it required concentration upon particular sets of goals and problems, rather than upon working the machinery of government as a whole.

The function of an administrative class, such as exists in Britain, could of course be dissolved into its component parts. Advice to ministers could be handed to a personal staff recruited either politically or bureaucratically. The arbitrative work of administrators could be handled partly by politicians, and partly by expert adjudicators who combined specialised knowledge with some degree of legal training. The control of departmental operations could be handed to managers skilled in particular fields of operations (the bureau chief model). Alternatively, instead of being unhorsed, British administrators could be converted into a more functionally-based class of departmental managers or into a more highly-trained corps of high-level controllers and adjudicators. These developments would point in opposite directions, borrowing respectively from the American and French systems, and would require the very kinds of specialisation which have so far been resisted. If, however, administrators retain a large part of their present qualities and their present influence, the explanation will be their continued usefulness to the political system. Basically the general administrator is a political phenomenon.

POLITICAL CONTROL AND ADMINISTRATIVE INFLUENCE

The capacity of political leaders to impose their will upon career officials is the subject of much inconclusive debate. In this section, we shall look at two aspects of this question; the numerical relationship between the two groups under discussion and their attitudes towards policy-making. Finally, we will consider the factors which produce a convergence of political and administrative styles within the executive branch of government.

It is plain that in terms of *numbers*, political leaders have shrunk in importance when compared with the higher ranks of the public service. However, it is impossible to quantify this relationship accurately because no satisfactory definition can be provided of the higher civil service for this purpose. The number of influential officials is a product not simply of grades and ranks, but of access to decision-making; and this access is itself partly a product of the political system which restricts the number of people (whatever their rank) who can effectively participate in governmental decisions. However, some indications are possible of the direction of change.

In Britain, the total number of political offices which comprise the Government has grown to over 100, and this development has caused frequent criticism or disquiet about the consequent ability of a Prime Minister to control his parliamentary supporters through appointment to office. However, a large proportion of these office-holders are parliamentary secretaries to ministers who by convention and in practice have very small powers of decision. The size of the Cabinet itself has remained very stable in peacetime, at between 17 and 23, and the number of principal ministers has recently tended to decrease with the creation of 'giant' departments. The chief political innovation for coping with the increased scope of government has been a substantial growth in the number of second-ranking ministers who handle some aspect of a department's work under the minister's general control. There were 16 ministers of this type in the Wilson government of 1964, and the Heath government of 1970 contained at least as many. One effect is to reduce parliamentary secretaries to the third tier of the ministerial hierarchy. The extent of power wielded by these second-order ministers is uncertain, and varies a great deal with the behaviour of the principal minister himself.

Writing in 1939, H. E. Dale stressed the small size of the administrative élite which participated in policy formation. His description of this élite (which excluded the foreign service) numbered 550, and comprised all general administrators with the rank of assistant secretary and higher, private secretaries to ministers, and a sprinkling of legal advisers (25) and other specialists (25). Any similar description of an élite of present-day officials would need to include substantially more specialists, although administrators counted for 400 of the 657 members of the new senior policy and management group, created in 1970 following the Fulton reforms. This class started at a higher hierarchical level (under-secretary or equivalent) than that chosen by Dale and an élite specified on a similar basis of rank would now be perhaps three times the size of Dale's group.[30]

In France, the members of the various *grands corps* amount to almost 2,500; but many of these are relatively junior. The size of the political offices which constitute the ministry is smaller than in Britain, and (as noted earlier) some ministerial posts are often occupied by civil servants themselves.

In the U.S.A., on the other hand, President Eisenhower made a determined attempt to enlarge the scope of political leadership through the creation of a new category of 'Schedule C' posts within the classified civil service. These posts, defined as having a policy-making character, were denied the protection of civil service procedures and could be offered to Presidential nominees. They accounted for 20 per cent of the 'supergrade' posts in the civil service, and theoretically raised the total of political executives to 1,200, as compared with 2,000 career civil servants continuing at 'supergrade' level.

While bureau chief and similar posts have increasingly been filled by career officials, political appointments within American government have been organised into a more systematic concept of a controlling hierarchy. This has been done through the creation of more political offices as deputies or assistants to secretaries of departments, with the aims both of strengthening political leadership and of reducing bureau autonomy. On the other hand, Secretaries of State as well as the President have become increasingly dependent upon professional civil servants skilled in such matters as budget analysis, legislative programming and administrative co-ordination. In general, though, it is not inadequate numbers that restrict the exercise of political authority in the Federal government, but the difficulties of recruiting enough able political executives, and their intrinsic lack of cohesion.

The traditional strength of political leadership, as compared with bureaucracy, is its commitment to some ideology or set of policies which provides a spur for common action along agreed lines. By contrast it may be said, as T. B. Bottomore claims,[31] that career officials do not as a rule share any common ideology or political doctrine, at any rate of a positive kind, and may often indeed have been deliberately selected on this basis. Thus they lack the will to make policies, even though they may command the means. By contrast, policy commitments of the politicians help them to overcome what would otherwise prove to be very serious limitations of numbers, knowledge and experience.

This persuasive comparison of attitudes is a great deal too simple. In Western democratic societies, party ideologies are often weak and offer limited guidance for specific policy-making. The programmatic style of politics which is often found in such societies depends more upon the successful synthesis or aggregation of interests than upon ideology or doctrine, and career officials also play a part in this process of aggregation. Conversely, no formal doctrine may be necessary for administrators to share a pragmatic commitment to certain goals. Indeed, a pragmatic approach – whether for politicians or administrators – avoids ideological rigidities and disappointments, and substitutes a flexible intellectual basis for the exercise of power.

How far groups of officials do share strong commitments to policy goals is another matter. Such attitudes are most probable among specially trained cadres of experts (see Chapter 6), but the often considerable policy influence of such groups is confined to particular and limited spheres of government. More broadly-based administrative groups, such as the administrative class in Britain, usually lack any coherent policy objectives, even though their general attitudes certainly influence the process of policy formation. Moreover, the division of the bureaucracy into separate classes, and the strength of departmental attachments, means that career officials as a class are most unlikely to share the same policy goals or viewpoints.

French administrators are sometimes quoted as a contrary example, and are said to share a common social philosophy or ideology. According to F. F. Ridley, this philosophy consists in a strong commitment to economic growth; priorities for publicly supported welfare schemes and cultural activities at the expense of private consumption; an almost Puritan resistance to economic individualism and materialism; and pride in the collective achievements of the State.[32] This philosophy largely amounts to a belief in the importance of the State, meaning the executive branch of central government, for the economic and social development of the French nation, and represents an extension of the professional pride of the senior civil servant in a society which tolerates a considerable degree of public planning and intervention. These generalised attitudes do not prevent considerable disagreement between departments. For example, it is doubtful whether the French

185

Ministry of Finance is any more committed to economic growth than is the British Treasury.

It is conventional to assume (as this discussion has done) that politicians wrestle with a continuous problem of 'controlling' bureaucrats adequately, and that the attitudes and aims of the two groups are likely to diverge considerably at some points. Certainly, there is some truth in this assumption, but the actual position is more complex.

The requirements of these two types of career, where they are clearly separated, appear without doubt to be very different. Politics in its purer forms is a speculative activity; it carries no certainty of reward even for prolonged efforts, and even the successful politician is likely to move upwards and downwards in erratic jumps. Politics calls for gifts of persuasion and manipulation, and for the projection either by eloquence or other means of successful public 'image'. By contrast, professional administration offers the prospects of a stable and evenly graduated career, moving towards positions that can be clearly envisaged. Traditionally such careers have attracted individuals with a preference for security, regularity and anonymity – the very opposite of the qualities which a politician needs.

Nonetheless, at the highest levels, the factors which make for a convergence of capabilities and attitudes are also considerable. It was Henri Fayol who pointed out that the first requisite for both a minister and his chief official was that each should be a 'good administrator'.[33] Whatever range of definition we give to this concept, it will include competence in the assessment of evidence, in the integration of diverse considerations, in expediting action, and so on.

A second quality which both politicians and administrators need is an ability to measure correctly the limits of the possible. This is one respect where they may be claimed to complement each other by undertaking measurements in different spheres. The politician is an expert on political acceptability, being attuned to the party and other pressures generated within the political process. The administrator measures the capacity of his machine to undertake new tasks, and assesses evidence about the probable reactions of departmental clients or other groups. Each party needs to have that delicate sense of feasibility which eschews both an unworkable idealism and a cloying pragmatism.

Turning to the occupational diseases of the two roles, the politician's temptation is to be content with the shadow rather than the substance of political responsibility; that of the administrator is to adopt the same attitude towards public service. These temptations arise from the nature of their respective rewards. To win elections, a politician must *appear* to be applying successful and dynamic policies, and he will tend to claim credit for many developments to which he contributed little or nothing. Politics is always liable, under modern conditions of strong executive government, to become a shadow play in which minute differences of political causation are exaggerated into major effects, to be praised or condemned. One consequence is to exaggerate the real power wielded by political leaders, and to under-rate the strictly bureaucratic contributions: the conventions of identifying political position with effective power, and the interest of politicians in sustaining these conventions, ensure this result. Another consequence is that, in terms of political success, it may do almost as well to appear to be powerful as actually to be so. For the administrator, the problem is that no system of bureaucratic promotion can offer adequate rewards for acting energetically or taking risks. (This familiar point is returned to in a later chapter.) To avoid their occupational temptations, both politicians and administrators require a strong ethic of public service.

Finally among cohesive forces may be counted the experience of working closely together in the service of government. This gives to politician and administrator a shared interest in mastering common problems and achieving effective action, which can make them draw closer in their views and prejudices: just as a minister can feel himself dissociated from his party supporters by their ignorance of the 'realities' of government, while they may be displeased by his aloofness and unreceptivity.

This binding force within executive government is particularly strong when its work is expanding rapidly and there are many positive tasks to be done. It is often said that the American Federal government lacks any cohesive force or binding ethic. This is possibly true, but there is no doubt that these qualities are more evident in Washington than they used to be. The challenges of achieving adequate executive action in the face of legislative and other divisive forces have at least served as a spur towards greater unity. Thus, despite the very different patterns of recruitment, political leaders and their chief officials need to possess many qualities in common, and tend to share some of the same attitudes and prejudices.

This convergence of styles over the conduct of executive government is in its turn moulded by the respective influence of the two principal groups, as well as by the national political system. As already noted, a style of government is more bureaucratic if it pays more attention to systematic methods of decision-making, entailing a fairly high degree of consistency, continuity and formal impartiality. The style is more political, if it is responsive to diverse claims and pressures, which must be continually recalculated within changing levels of support and opposition for particular goals. The bureaucratic style absorbs and modifies the 'non-rational matrix' of politics within a cocoon of routinisation and precedent, while the political style faces the flux of politics head-on. It follows that the former style is much more favourable towards systematic governmental planning, at least in principle, than is the latter style.

In some respects but not in others, the French style of government is more bureaucratic than the British, which is more bureaucratic than the American. These differences owe a great deal to the varying powers of executives in relation to legislatures. Broadly speaking, career officials exercise more influence upon both the style and the policy content of government where legislatures are weak, but this generalisation needs qualification.

The French Fifth Republic was widely represented by its supporters as an assertion of political leadership over the bureaucracy. The powers vested in the President of the Republic did produce more durable and decisive political leadership on some matters than unstable parliamentary coalitions of ministers could achieve. In fact, though, what President de Gaulle did was to reduce the boundaries of political uncertainty within which administrators operated, and thus to concede them more confidence and more autonomy within a broadly defined sphere of operations.[34] President de Gaulle also attempted to strengthen the administrative authority of the prefects, but the reciprocal relations between prefects and local politicians were quickly re-established. Any description of French government as bureaucratic in style must be heavily qualified by the large volume of 'marginal politicisation', and by the political activities of the officials themselves.

Although the behaviour of both groups is shaped by the requirements of the political system, the interests of political and career executives (in the U.S.A.) diverge in several ways. The former group is normally keen to make policy changes – that is why it is in Washington – and is often impatient about Congressional and other constraints upon innovation. But the career executives have to live with Congressional committees and interest groups all their lives, they have a stake in stability and continuity, and they can have only limited loyalties towards political appointees who may relatively soon be replaced.

Thus, the familiar tension between political and bureaucratic styles of government does occur in America in a rather special way. Gawthrop contends that the result is defensive and conservative behaviour within the executive branch, and the discouragement of innovation. Certainly, there are good reasons for concluding that the U.S. career bureaucracy is more conservative as well as more parochial on policy issues than is (for example) the French higher bureaucracy. The question is how far their bureaucratic narrowness is in practice overcome by the stronger doses of political influence injected into American government, even allowing for the weakness of mutual loyalties within the executive branch? While the systems are too different to risk a definite answer, it may at least be concluded that the U.S.A. pays a higher price for its political values in terms of the attitudes of its senior career bureaucracy.[35]

Finally then, the respective contributions and influence of politicians and administrators cannot be assessed within the circuit of high-level executive government, but must be related to the whole political system. It is quite possible for the policy inputs of *both* the political leadership and senior administrators to be declining. In Britain, for example, the capacity of political parties to state and achieve specific programmes may be declining, but it would be wrong to suppose that administrators have usurped the policy-making rights of the parties. Administrators have policy influence as individuals, but appear to be directionless over policy issues as a group. Richard Rose's analysis concludes in effect that Britain possesses neither party government nor administrative government.[36]

Western democracies are becoming more pluralistic in the sense that policy-making is diffused among a greater number and variety of participants. In the U.S.A., power is distributed horizontally between agencies and interests, rather than vertically between politicians and administrators. In Britain, much power has seeped away from party leaders and general administrators to specialised experts, advisory organs, interest groups and other elements within the policy sub-systems. The activities of both political leaders and general administrators extend over a more elevated plateau of governmental action, and they can concern themselves less thoroughly with the lower slopes.

However, the political-administrative relationship remains intrinsically important as well as fascinating. There is not only the question of the balance of capacities and influence between the two groups, but also of the nature of their influence upon each

189

other. In Britain, for example, politicians and general administrators match each other neatly in respect of style and capacities, and have shown little inclination to trespass upon each other's traditional spheres; and yet the very smoothness of this partnership may have bred reliance upon both political and administrative methods of recruiting executives which are too unspecialised for modern needs. In the U.S.A., the system of political executives reduces the capacity of the civil service to attract career officials of high quality, yet is itself obviously incapable of providing sufficient continuity and coherence of government operations. In France, the apparent effectiveness of administrators under the Fifth Republic confirms the inadequacy of the traditional parliamentary methods for recruiting political leaders.

If, then, there is to be a satisfactory balance in democracies between politicians and administrators, continuous attention must be paid to the recruitment of both groups, and any proposed alteration of the qualifications and duties of administrators has to be inspected for its effects upon this partnership.

REFERENCES

1 See quotation from Mannheim in A. Lepawsky, *Administration* (New York, 1949), pp. 71–3.
2 R. G. S. Brown, *The Administrative Process in Britain* (London, 1970), pp. 159–60.
3 Richard Rose, *Policy-Making in Britain* (London, 1969), and *People in Politics* (London, 1970).
4 Richard Rose, 'The Variability of Party Government', *Political Studies* Vol. 17, (December 1969) No. 4, pp. 413–45.
5 Samuel H. Beer, *Modern British Politics* (London, 1965), Chap. 12.
6 P. Self and H. Storing, *The State and the Farmer* (London, 1962), Chaps. 2, 3 and 4.
7 J. E. S. Hayward, *Private Interests and Public Policy* (London, 1966).
8 P. Self, *Metropolitan Planning* (London School of Economics, 1971), Chap. 5.
9 Edward Banfield, *Political Influence* (New York, 1961).
10 Self and Storing, op. cit., pp. 118–19.
11 Harry Eckstein, *The English Health Service* (Oxford, 1959), Chap. 9.
12 For example: Lord Morrison, *Government and Parliament* (Oxford, 1963); Sir Edward Boyle, *et. al.*, 'Who are the Policy-Makers?', *Public Administration*, Vol. 43 (Autumn 1965), pp. 251–87; Lord Bridges, *Portrait of a Profession* (Cambridge, 1950); Sir John Maud, 'Government in Theory and Practice', *Political Studies*, Vol. 13 (February 1965), pp. 15–21; Sir Charles Cunningham, 'Policy and Practice', *Public Administration* (Autumn 1963) and *Whitehall and Beyond* (British Broadcasting Corporation, 1964).

13 Maud, op. cit., pp. 19–20.
14 Cunningham, op. cit.
15 John S. Harris and Thomas V. Garcia, 'The Permanent Secretaries', *Public Administration Review* (March 1966).
16 F. Ridley and J. Blondel, *Public Administration in France* (London, 1969), p. 66.
17 Bernard Gournay, *Introduction à la Science Administrative* (Paris, 1966), Part 5, Chap. 3.
18 Ridley and Blondel, op. cit., p. 51. For details about French ministers, see Malcolm Anderson, *Government in France* (Oxford, 1970), pp. 100 and 120.
19 Dean E. Mann, *The Assistant Secretaries* (Washington, Brookings Institution, 1965), Appendix A. On political executives, see also Marver H. Bernstein, *The Job of the Federal Executive* (Washington, Brookings Institution, 1958).
20 See the conclusions in Bernstein, op. cit., and of a report of the Committee for Economic Development, *Improving Executive Management in the Federal Government* (1964).
21 The American Assembly (Columbia University), *The Federal Government Service* (New York, 1965), pp. 41–3.
22 For these figures see Bernstein, op. cit., pp. 10–11 and 38–9; and Committee for Economic Development, op. cit.
23 Sir William Armstrong, *Professionals and Professionalism in the Civil Service* (London School of Economics, 1970), p. 9. For another view of the British general administrator, see R. G. S. Brown, op. cit., pp. 261–5.
24 Quoted in Anderson, op. cit., p. 116.
25 C. H. Sisson, *The Spirit of British Administration* (London, 1959).
26 Gournay, op. cit., Part 5, Chap. 6.
27 See the description of administrative control in J. A. G. Griffith, *Central Departments and Local Authorities* (London, 1966), Chaps. 2 and 5.
28 Sir Edward Bridges in A. Dunsire (ed.), *The Making of an Administrator* (Manchester University Press, 1956); Robert Catherine, *Le Fonctionnaire Français* (Paris, 1961).
29 *The Civil Service*, Vol. 1, para. 18, Cmnd. 3638 (London, H.M.S.O., 1968).
30 H. E. Dale, *The Higher Civil Service* (Oxford, 1941), pp. 11–16. For the present size of the senior civil service, see Sir Richard Clarke, *New Trends in Government* (London, 1971), Chap. 4.
31 T. B. Bottomore, *Élites and Society* (London, 1964), pp. 81–4.
32 F. F. Ridley, 'French Technocracy and Comparative Government', *Political Studies* (February 1966), pp. 44–5.
33 Henri Fayol, *The Administrative Theory in the State* (1923).
34 See, for example, the analysis in Anderson, op. cit., Chap. 7.
35 Louis C. Gawthrop, *Bureaucratic Behaviour in the Executive Branch* (New York, 1969).
36 Richard Rose, 'The Variability of Party Government', op. cit.

Chapter 6

ADMINISTRATIVE ADVICE AND APPRAISAL

INTRODUCTION

Modern administration requires complex team-work, and the synthesis of diverse contributions and view-points. This synthesis has two main dimensions: the institutional and the intellectual. The organisation of government determines how far particular agencies can act autonomously, and how far they are controlled by other agencies or guided by joint systems of decision-making. In this chapter, we are primarily concerned with the intellectual dimensions of co-ordination; that is, with the integration of different kinds of knowledge and experience in the making of administrative decisions. It has to be recognized, however, that the two processes are intertwined. In many ways, the institutional structure of government influences the kinds of intellectual contributions which are sought and are available; while conversely patterns of administrative recruitment and training have a 'feedback' effect upon the relationships between agencies.

Logically one can separate the taking of a decision from the means for its implementation, even though the same person may be responsible for both activities. Administrative appraisal requires the review of all factors judged relevant to some decision. This can involve a very elaborate marshalling of evidence, both of a factual or scientific kind, and also in terms of the demands and pressures which require consideration. Once the decision has been made, its execution is intellectually a simpler matter, requiring qualities of energy, competence and honesty. Administrative appraisal requires the resources of the system to be fed upwards to the point where the decision can be reached; while administrative execution turns upon a downward flow of orders to the points where action occurs. Appraisal is a more complex and elusive process than execution, and proceeds less easily and satisfactorily through hierarchical channels. Administrative charts are usually better at explaining the steps by which decisions are executed than reached. This is inevitable: where multiple factors must be sieved

192

and weighted through successive stages of consultation and review, the rule book cannot easily state which factor, or which person's advice, will prove most influential. The downward swoop of hierarchy is easier to comprehend and to predict.

Of course administrative appraisal does not only arise in the taking of top-level decisions; it is also frequently involved in the interpretation or application of those decisions, and in decision-taking at lower levels. This chapter is not concerned with minor decisions.

The way in which any official approaches an issue will depend both upon his institutional position, and upon his knowledge, training and experience. All these factors will influence his appreciative judgement, which includes, as Sir Geoffrey Vickers points out, both a view of the relevant facts of the situation (a reality judgement) and also a view of the significance of those facts for the official's responsibilities or aims (a value judgement). Sir Geoffrey rightly stresses that:

> The relation between judgements of fact and of value is close and mutual; for facts are relevant only in relation to some judgement of value and judgements of value are operative only in relation to some configuration of fact.[1]

This means that an official will normally disregard any facts which do not seem relevant to his organisational or professional duties. Conversely he will be attentive to those facts which seem helpful or relevant for the discharge of his duties as he understands them. These points are of course familiar features of all human behaviour, which reflect the need to economise mental energies and to respect the institutional and intellectual roles assigned to others. At the same time, the kind of relevant facts and values which are recognised by an official will turn to some extent upon his personal interests and ambitions, and more fundamentally upon the pattern of roles which is established within the system.

ADMINISTRATIVE STRUCTURE AND SPECIALISATION

Frequently, problems of administrative appraisal are discussed in terms of the relationship which should hold between 'generalists' and 'specialists'. A pure distinction of this kind exists in few countries besides Britain and governments shaped or influenced by British traditions, and the distinction is in any case a very crude one. Still it is rooted to some extent in the historical development of civil services, particularly European ones.

Traditionally, the work of central public administration was largely concerned with the formulation and implementation of general regulations within a framework of law. This work corresponds to the Weberian notion of bureaucracy and was the province of generalists, who needed competence and reliability in the handling of public business but did not require special technical qualifications. The senior generalists in most European countries were experts in public law, for which in Britain was substituted an acquired knowledge of political connections and administrative procedures. However, they were experts in a strictly administrative or legal sense, and the 'power of the expert' which Weber stressed referred to the advantages of continuous administrative experience, as compared with the intermittent knowledge of government acquired by legislative politicians or 'political notables'.[2]

Specialised experts entered government service in a variety of ways. Some came as advisers on public policy, others as members of technical inspectorates, and the majority as providers of specific services of various kinds. The numbers and influence of these experts depended very much on the scope of government. For example, engineers have for a long time been a more potent force in French than British government, because in France central government has been directly responsible for a much larger share of public works and physical developments. The same expert will frequently function both as controller of a public service and as a policy adviser, and the more important the service the stronger as a rule will be his status as an adviser.

The policy responsibilities of central government have grown more rapidly everywhere than has its direct provision of services. Also many services have become more closely related to policy goals, and consequently less capable of being operated in a routinised way or according to primarily technical criteria. For example, a meteorological office is or ought to be insulated from any policy influences, except for the size of its budget; but a host of technical services offered to industries, agriculture and local authorities are justified partly by their contributions to various governmental policies, and for this reason are often linked with regulatory controls or public subsidies. This situation produces an interpenetration of policy and technical issues, thus broadening the range both of specialised factors which the ultimate decision-makers must consider and also of policy question which concern or impinge upon technical experts.

It is still fruitful to make some distinction between 'bureaucracy' and 'technocracy', despite the mixture of civil service staffs. Jean

Meynaud's book, *Technocracy*, after some useful initial definitions, appears to equate technocracy with the power exercised by all senior officials.[3] This is unsatisfactory, because technocracy should refer to the excessive power or influence of technical experts resulting either from an exaggerated weight being put upon some technical factor in a policy decision, or from the aggrandisement of the function with which the expert is particularly concerned. By contrast, the pathology of bureaucracy is ritualism in the form of excessive attention to rules and procedures at the expense of substantive goals. These pathologies are considered later.

In Britain, the traditional system of administrative appraisal can be seen as a series of Chinese boxes. In theory, a departmental minister remains omnicompetent in the centre of the stage. The minister is advised confidentially on policy issues by administrators, who in turn collect any necessary advice from relevant specialists. This system was designed at and for a time when the functions of government were very limited, the number of relevant specialists was small, and ministers could in fact (if they chose) make all important decisions. The system has responded to modern pressures through increasing the discretionary authority of administrators, and through increasing the dependence of administrators upon various forms of expert advice. Additionally, top specialist advisers have gained easier access to ministers, and a number of policy posts have become filled by specialists.

The essential principle of the system is the distinction between policy and finance as the concern of generalists, and technical and scientific matters as belonging to appropriate specialists. In their evidence to the Fulton Committee, the Association of First Division Civil Servants (the administrative class) notes that ministers who are non-specialists need the support of a 'body of staff who can bring to bear on the work of the Department the same type of considerations that the minister would himself bring. . . .'

> The essential function of this group of staff is to bring together the disparate issues involved in taking major decisions of policy, to advise on what these decisions should be and subsequently to put them into effect. The Administrative Class is uniquely able to perform this function because of its broad background, intellectual capacity and experience of operating in government.[4]

The structure of the British civil service is strongly based upon this generalist-specialist dichotomy, and the principal specialist classes (the scientific civil service, the 'works group') are service-wide, although many smaller specialist classes are departmental.

The Fulton reforms are aggregating the various classes into still larger blocks, but the distinction between generalist and specialist classes has been retained at lower levels although all senior posts at under-secretary level and above have been formally integrated into a single policy and management group.[5]

The dominant position of the generalist has turned upon his capacity to interchange staff and line functions in a flexible way often through the different uses of separate or parallel hierarchies. In departments or divisions providing policy outputs, a hierarchy of specialists may serve as staff to the hierarchy of generalists, whereas in departments providing technical services, a substantial technical hierarchy may be flanked at the top only by a nest of senior generalists controlling the specialists through their advice to the minister on policy and finance. The variable and pragmatic structures of British departments can be seen as adaptations of the generalist-specialist division to different types of work.

The dissatisfaction of specialists has been one cause for the creation of 'integrated hierarchies' in many departments, such as the erstwhile Ministry of Transport which had difficulties over recruiting enough good engineers. Consequently engineers and administrators were merged in some of the divisions and placed under either joint heads or (later) under a head selected according to the nature of the work.[6] A similar system operated in the giant Department of Trade and Industry, where about half the controlling posts at under-secretary level were held by generalists and half by specialists. On the whole, the divisions selected for specialist leadership do work which has a fairly high technical content.

Despite these developments in the departments, and the Fulton integration of senior management posts, the basic division between generalists and specialists remains firmly rooted in civil service methods of recruitment, training and function. The system continues to select the same sized group of generalists for rapid promotion, and the new Civil Service College has accorded its highest priority to the training of generalists and particularly of the abler ones who will receive more prolonged training. The effect of adopting more conventional notions of line management ('integrated hierarchies') will certainly be to increase competition for senior posts. At present, career prospects are poorer for specialist classes than for generalists at higher levels because of the large proportion of posts concerned with policy and finance at this level.[7] Some gradual change in this balance of top posts may be expected to come about, but the separate systems of recruitment and training will presumably ensure that most posts with an appreciable policy content remain with the generalists.

The British system has not created any very strong or cohesive cadres of specialists. This is the result of the policy dominance of the generalist, the service-wide recruitment of the broad specialist classes, and the lack of in-service training or indoctrination for specialist groups. This deflation of *esprit de corps* helps to retain and perhaps strengthen the intellectual objectivity of the individual specialist, but means that specialists often have an aloof attitude to policy issues. The rejection of the Fulton proposal that each department should have a senior policy adviser, in charge of planning and research and with direct access to the minister, is a setback for the idea of creating expert teams under specialist control.

In France, the British distinction between generalists and specialists is replaced to some extent by that between administrative and technical corps. However, the pattern of roles and relationships is very different. As already noted, the general administrators do not form a single group but are divided into separate corps of varying prestige. Conversely, some of the technical corps are educated to play a much broader role than do any specialist groups in Britain. While the highest administrative corps specialise in tasks of financial control, administrative justice, and field co-ordination, many of the top executive positions in French ministries are held by technicians. Between one-third and one-half of the 120 directorships of divisions, which constitute the key posts in French ministries, are held by members of technical corps among whom engineers predominate.[8]

Thus a British-type polarisation between co-ordinators and advisers does not occur, and members of both leading types of corps receive broad training in general management, as well as in particularised skills. Moreover, for the higher echelons, the learning of special skills is intellectually related to their use within government. Thus the various corps of engineers receive both a general scientific training and also training in relevant aspects of administration. The differentiation between the various technical corps of engineers turns more upon the nature of their 'mission' than their particular brand of engineering skill.

The effect of this system is to stress the integration and interpretation of expert knowledge in the service of public purposes, rather than the British approach of accepting independent contributions from separate specialisms which must ultimately be subordinated, to some extent, to 'administrative' considerations. The French system, however, tends to deflate the contributions of experts who are not members of some prestigious corps: for example, the strongly entrenched position of the engineers has inhibited the contributions of architects and town planners, although a separate corps for the latter now exists. These specialist groups who are recruited in the general market are inevitably less effective than those who have received high-quality pre-entry training – a situation which does not arise in Britain or the U.S.A.

The American civil service system encourages a high degree of occupational specialisation, and does not produce any broad categories of either generalists or specialists. Although the whole service is formally integrated for pay purposes, albeit with many exceptions, it is divided into 435 occupational series. The character of each series is determined primarily by departmental rather than service-wide tests, and the workings of the position-classification system encourage tasks and qualifications to be defined in a particularist and specialised manner. It is generally in the interest of the individual civil servant to stress the technical aspects and differentiated nature of his work, and to add to his specialised qualifications through training courses and private study.[9]

The advantage of the system is to achieve a better balance and greater diversity of intellectual skills within the civil service than is the case with other systems. These qualities carry through to the higher grades of the service, whose members were found by David Stanley to have the following basic qualifications; 24 per cent engineering, 21 per cent social services, 14 per cent law, 13 per cent physical sciences, with the remainder broadly spread among agriculture, biology, medicine, etc. A study of 63 bureau chiefs showed that 26 had been trained as engineers, scientists or technicians, 9 as economists, 8 as lawyers, while 20 had had business or administrative careers. In most cases, the chief's education and experience seemed highly relevant to the work of the bureau.[10]

In the American system the 'generalists', for example administrative experts, have poorer career prospects than do scientific experts. Congress, for instance, has excluded top scientists and doctors from the staff ceilings which apply to the top grades, and these and some other specialists are paid at special rates. This is in sharp contrast to the British situation, the explanation being of course the central role of career generalists in Britain as opposed to their auxiliary role to political executives in the U.S.A., together with the higher cultural prestige of scientific experts in that country. A visiting British team commented on 'the vigour, enthusiasm and contentment of senior scientific and professional staff', and noted that it was difficult for the administrator 'to play his proper role in matters of finance, personnel and grading' where such staff was concerned.[11]

The great problem of the American system is how to bridge the wide gap between the strong specialisation of the career civil service and the broad requirements of executive management. Since there is little systematic career planning for the service as a whole, the line managers of the agencies emerge by proving their capacities within a particular organisational and political setting. These executives have considerable respect for specialised knowledge, but the policy framework within which they elicit information is often a narrow one and they have little opportunity for learning broader skills of policy analysis.

The distinction between 'generalists' and 'specialists' is plainly outmoded at higher organisational levels. In all systems, the problem is to secure officials who can perform creditably either as a specialised generalist or as a generalised specialist. The former individual must move from a broad educational background to detailed knowledge of some administrative process or activity, while the latter individual must move from specialised intellectual knowledge to proficiency in the skills of organisation and policy-making.

But this generalised convergence of roles at the top occurs in ways that are very much influenced by the starting posts of the system. In the British system, the dominance of the generalist is rooted in methods of recruitment and career planning which operate whether or not it is easier for administrators to understand scientists than for scientists to learn administration. The American system starts with both generalist and specialist forms of recruitment, but the civil service is organised by specialisms until the higher line positions are reached for which intellectual qualifications (while needing to be broadly relevant) count for little in comparison with the right mix of political and managerial skills. In the French system, however, a broad differentiation of specialised generalists and generalised specialists is set right from the beginning, is buttressed by appropriate training, and carries through in separate but interweaving streams to the higher positions of the service.

Against this background of different systems can be considered some theories about administrative appraisal, starting with the problems and dysfunctions of different systems, and proceeding to intellectual problems of administrative appraisal and the contributions which training can make.

CONTROLLERS AND SPECIALISTS

The problems of administrative appraisal are very considerable indeed. It is hard to discover or invent any system which can satisfactorily weld together the contributions of numerous experts on a basis which is also realistic in political and administrative terms. All methods of organisation turn out to have some dysfunctions. However, we can reasonably start by considering two opposite but well-entrenched types of cultural belief. One is that the appropriate controller of specialists should himself be a specialist. The other is that the controller should be an administrator who is well versed in public policy needs and administrative 'feasibility', but has no other relevant qualifications.

The first belief contains some obvious sense, but is subject to severe qualifications. In the first place, the controlling specialist must inevitably be a 'generalised specialist' who is directly familiar with only a part (sometimes a very small part) of the disciplines which are relevant to the work of his agency. Government has to draw upon many experts who are highly proficient in subjects which are tangential to administrative decisions, or which while being of basic importance to some decision, represent only one of many factors which must be taken into account. The controlling specialist cannot be expected to know all these fields at all intimately.

In Britain, these comments are plainly true of such top-level specialists as the chief planner in the Ministry of Housing and Local Government or (much more so) the chief scientific adviser to the Ministry of Defence. For example, in advising on the location of a new town, the former individual has to consider factors relating to topography, soil conditions, water supplies, transportation, agriculture, industrial location, etc., all of which are the province of other specialists. His skill must therefore lie in evaluating other specialists' contributions (often done by consultant teams) within a framework of certain accepted techniques and objectives. In the same way, a 'polyvalent' engineer will not be particularly well-versed even in some branches of engineering, and will be fairly ignorant of many other specialisms which he should take into account.

Secondly, the specialist turned controller is subject to severe administrative and political pressures. The time which must be devoted to these duties both deters many experts from seeking such posts, and ensures that those who do have appropriate organisational and political talents. The same factors apply in part to an expert who functions as a chief adviser and not an executive.

An effective adviser needs the ability to draw conclusions from complex masses of data in terms which seem intelligible and realistic to the ultimate decision-makers. It does not follow, though, that this gift of translation is coupled with high intellectual capacity in the sphere of knowledge which is being translated, for these two kinds of ability are logically and psychologically separable. Again, the chief adviser has his own executive responsibilities for controlling the work of his professional juniors, and a conflict is not unlikely between the goal of successful influence with colleagues or superiors, and that of efficient direction. The top executive must of course give still more attention to direction, but he is also less liable to be frustrated by problems of making his advice effective.

It is very difficult for scientists or technologists or other experts to keep up with their specialisms, particularly in subjects that are growing rapidly. Thus the specialist controller's stock of knowledge may become obsolete, which can be more dangerous than having no stock at all. To the extent that administrative positions also attract second-rate experts, the danger is compounded. Out of touch with his intellectual peers, the controlling or advising expert may become prone to lay undue stress upon the administrative aspects of his role and to copy these from the dominant style of the system which he inhabits. It is a frequent reproach against White-hall scientists that they are excessively 'Whitehall-minded', although evidence is lacking. At all events, these problems increase the advantages of recruiting expert advisers on a temporary basis from such sources as universities. This method ensures that the expert is more genuinely in touch with intellectual developments in his field, a factor which may be more valuable than close familiarity with the governmental machine. However, this solution is hardly a feasible way of producing executives who have adequate specialist qualifications, and its application to advisory cadres is limited by its deterrent effects upon the recruitment and promotion of junior specialists.

The doctrine of purely administrative forms of appraisal has its traditional home in Britain, where however this system has come under increasingly withering attacks.[12] As Vickers' theories underlined, any appraiser will be guided by a given set of values and he will not willingly seek out facts or opinions which do not fit within this framework. The general administrator's set of values include political realism (or what he takes to be such); simplification and tidiness of decision-fnaking; clear allocations of duties and responsibilities; and attention to administrative precedents and experience.

Lord Bridges, a former official head of the British civil service, puts the four most important qualities of an administrator as (i) the power of rapid analysis; (ii) the capacity to recognise the essential points in the situation; (iii) the sense of timing; and (iv) the capacity to think of likely developments up to a year ahead. His analysis gives strong weight to timing and limited foresight (political realism) and to the simplification of a situation such that a decision can be reached.[13]

An administrative view-point, such as that sketched by Lord Bridges, is not necessarily inimical to the influence of specialists. On the contrary, it is, or at any rate was, a cardinal part of this *credo* to trust to the opinions of the relevant expert on matters outside the competence of the administrator. There are, however, two qualifications to this maxim. One is that purely administrative considerations (tidiness, economy, ease of decision-making) create a bias for consulting only one official (or officially approved) expert wherever possible. The co-ordinative style of British administration will then ensure strong backing for the beliefs of the most relevant expert within the most interested department.* Of course counter-views may be produced by expert advisory bodies, which sometimes indeed serve as the administrator's source of expert advice, but the interventions of such bodies on detailed or complex issues are necessarily limited. There is also always the possibility, which is far from welcome to officials, that ministers will seek private expert advice, but the efficacy of this advice is limited by its sporadic character and by the administrator's preference for official channels.

The second qualification to the administrator's trust in specialists is his tendency to view the social sciences as inferior or unnecessary forms of specialism, inasmuch as their findings are more debatable than those of pure science and touch more directly upon the administrator's own area of competence. These suspicions may indeed have some justification (we return to this point). However, if the administrator has himself no special skills in economic or social appraisal, this function may simply be omitted or erratically performed.

As noted in an earlier chapter, the style of Treasury appraisal

---

* An example of this situation was the Stansted airport case, where the Ministry of Aviation's choice for the third London airport was heavily influenced by technical factors of air control and air safety, which proved in the end to be much less decisive or important. *Report of the Commission on the Third London Airport*, 1.8–1.23 and Chapter 8 (London, 1971).

is particularly concerned with injecting a sense of financial responsibility into departments, and with the smooth reconciliation of divergent claims. These can be seen as specifically administrative objectives. On the other hand, the Treasury's methods of economic appraisal used to be extremely superficial, and only since the Plowden Report of 1961 has it made much use of professional economic skills and techniques. Similar defects have been alleged against those departments responsible for the control and co-ordination of the vast development programmes of the nationalised industries. These deficiencies of administrative appraisal have been well-documented by Select Committee inquiries into such matters as the railway electrification programme, the Concorde supersonic airplane, the Ferranti affair, and other matters.[14] While some of these apparent blunders partly reflect (as the last chapter also showed) the methods of political decision-making, administrative methods have certainly supported these political tendencies. Resting content with 'political realism', administrators failed to provide adequate or independent standards of appraisal.

Some of the strongest critics of British administrative methods of appraisal have in fact been economists,[15] while there has been little explicit criticism from scientists and technologists. The economists' criticism should, however, be treated with reserve because economic forms of appraisal also tend to be somewhat shallow and organisationally biased (see below). Policy appraisal in British government does not appear to have become noticeably more penetrating or successful since more professional economists were hired, and since administrators themselves studied economics. Also gross mis-estimation of the costs of weapon systems and aviation projects has occurred equally in the U.S.A. and to some extent in France, despite different systems of appraisal. For example, the more detailed studies of the economics of Concorde undertaken by the French government made no difference to the decision, and indeed France has been more willing than Britain to prefer technological glory to economic realism where supersonic airplanes are concerned.

The qualifications of policy appraisers cannot really be considered in isolation from the system which they inhabit; for the system largely settles the kind of policy framework to which expert evidence of various kinds must be related. Thus in the American system, policy issues tend to be articulated within a more limited organisational framework than in Britain, and governmental executives have greater dedication to particular goals. This means that expert advice can be used intensively within a limited but periodically changed statement of relevant issues. In Britain, the administrative appraisers handle expert evidence within a less partisan type of policy framework, but without having much capacity to specify goals or define issues themselves. One system leans more towards partisan definitions and uses of expert advice, the other system towards inadequate or ineffective use of some experts, although both these criticisms can be alleged against most administrative systems.

The limitations of the general administrator concern his capacity to apply his assets of independent broad experience to particular policy fields. This calls for a more deeply questioning and penetrating approach to specific issues than has been usual in British administration, together with greater analytic capacity over policy issues. It raises the question of how far some degree of goal commitment is necessary for effective inquiring into particular policy problems, and as to whether the detached objectivity which is the administrator's *forte* can achieve satisfactory results without support of greater social knowledge and perhaps also wider social experience.

'BUREAUPATHOLOGY' AND TECHNOCRACY

The analysis of administrative behaviour offered in the last section can be considered in the light or more general theories and concepts. Some theorists see these problems as essentially deriving from the general conflict between hierarchy and specialisation. Victor Thompson, for example, traces most forms of 'bureaupathology' to the inadequate qualifications of executives or administrators to control the specialists who work under their control. These men possess the formal rights of authority (to review, to veto, to affirm), but more and more they lack the specialised competence which alone can provide a satisfactory basis for decision-making. The results, according to Thompson, are the use of all sorts of devices for propping up the intellectually weak foundations of hierarchical authority. These include an obsessional stress upon the tasks of control and co-ordination and an often arbitrary use of these methods, so as to justify and display the executive's power in fields where he cannot be challenged: together with a cultivation of falsely romantic theories of the executive's role and unnecessarily dramatic exercises of authority (dramaturgy).[16]

The general difficulty with Thompson's thesis is plain. There is no adequate evidence that a specialist occupying an executive position will act less hierarchically than a non-specialist. Thus his general argument turns into a criticism or refutation of hierarchy itself. He wishes in effect to substitute the 'authority of knowledge' for the 'authority of status'. This is in principle a desirable substitution. Its practical implication is that there should be the maximum freedom of communication among different specialists, and the maximum consultation of all those experts who have something relevant to contribute. Thus the argument is in favour of a greater informality and flexibility of administrative organisation, along lines that were noted earlier in this book.

Unfortunately, these precepts are inadequate to remove the problems of hierarchy. Authoritative decisions have still to be reached by someone, and the greater the number of individuals who have a claim to participate in these decisions, the harder does it become to weigh all these contributions fairly in reaching an ultimate decision. One can accept the need for a team style in administrative appraisal, and the consequent broadening of the decision-making process. At the same time, there are limits (both practical and intellectual) to the possibilities of joint decision-making, especially when the participants are very numerous. The logic of formal authority, which must reside somewhere, compels the harder issues to be shifted upwards to groups of decreasing size.

There is also the fact that no amount of expert evidence will (as a rule) point logically and unambiguously to a given conclusion; on the contrary, the views of different specialists will frequently point in different directions, even if the basic aims of policy are clearly established – which is rarely the case. Doubtless, fuller communication among specialists should reduce misunderstandings and the areas of disagreement; but it would be Utopian to suppose that this process will ever be complete, quite apart from its time costs.

However, it is also interesting to consider the relevance of Thompson's thesis to different systems. One would expect his description of 'bureaupathology' to apply to general administrators, particularly perhaps British ones, because of their lack of specialised qualifications. In some ways this seems true. It can be said, for example, that these administrators put excessive value upon co-ordination for its own sake, rather than for its substantive achievements; that they make an undue mystery of the machinery of government; and that they practise mild forms of dramaturgy to support their own status and prestige. Thus, a permanent secretary will usually think it necessary to express his ministry's views in person to an investigating committee, even when there are specialists in his department capable of doing the job much better; and to lay great stress upon his control of communications between the minister and his department. However, in a sense such acts merely reflect the conventions of responsible government, since a chief official is always expected by his political superiors to appear fully knowledgeable and competent, whether he really can be so or not.

On the whole, however, British administrators are singularly free from the ritualism which is a main feature of 'bureaupathology'. The nature of their training on the job breeds flexible and pragmatic attitudes. The 1,000 or so principals who represent the first posts of real responsibility within the administrative class carry out a diverse range of tasks which necessitate prompt reactions to sundry political, financial and administrative requests. Their style of administrative co-ordination may be shallow but it is reasonably prompt and flexible, and a competent administrator has little use for unnecessary formalities; he has not the time for them. However, it is true that this ease of communication is more prevalent among administrators themselves than in their relations with specialists. At this level, the weaknesses of the dual system become evident, and some of Thompson's strictures are applicable.

If one seeks clear examples of administrative ritualism, they are more likely to be found in France or the U.S.A. In France, the division of administrators into separate corps, combined with a formalistic rather than a pragmatic training, produces an elaboration of separate forms of control and communication, especially at lower levels. An example is the division of financial control into processes performed by three separate administrative corps. In the U.S.A., the great diversity of procedures for approving grants-in-aid that are laid down by numerous Federal agencies, and the barriers to their simplification, represent a clear case of ritualism. We may conclude that 'bureaupathology' does not simply or even primarily arise out of conflicts between hierarchical controllers and specialists. It is often a product of excessive fragmentation of administrative action among separate corps or agencies, and is especially likely to arise when some administrative group seeks to protect a unique or distinctive role when this no longer properly exists.

The converse of 'bureaupathology' is technocracy. The sources of technocracy lie in the different qualifications of experts, and in the limitations of all forms of expertise. Some forms of expert knowledge are highly scientific and objective in their methods, but have only limited relevance to policy judgements. At the other end of the spectrum are skills whose methods are less scientific but whose policy contributions are much broader. The former category includes pure scientists and (to a lesser extent) engineers and technologists, the latter includes such experts as town planners, management experts and economic advisers.

Scientific training often makes an expert scrupulously objective about the policy implications of his knowledge, and it is not unusual for pure scientists to take an aloof attitude towards administrative decision-making. On the other hand, a few scientists and many technologists are prone to policy judgements which considerably exceed the relevance of their skills. Familiar examples are the narrow expert who exaggerates one technical factor in relation to a complex decision; the technologist who is keen to get an invention adopted irrespective of costs; or the engineer who wants to build roads without bothering much about their environmental effects.

One can contrast the skills of a highway engineer and a town planner. The former has fairly precise objective knowledge about the load-bearing capacities of various structures, but his knowledge is instrumental and does not logically entitle him to say what structures shall be built; but professional status enables him to exercise much influence over policy decisions. The town planner has no comparable store of scientific knowledge. There is no scientific procedure for blending together the diverse skills (engineering, architectural, economic, sociological, etc.) which are relevant to urban design, so that the planner must be guided throughout by policy judgements (unlike the engineer, for whom knowledge and policy are logically distinct); but the value of the planner is or should reside in his ability to utilise a variety of skills within a given policy field. His knowledge is shallow and piecemeal, but its application is broad.

Thus a 'broad but shallow' expert is liable to misuse his status if he makes excessive scientific pretensions, and sometimes if his knowledge is too heavily tied to one relevant discipline; for example, a town planner who is primarily an engineer is in a position to import technocratic attitudes into a broader policy field than the latter. On the other hand, an administration which utilised only purely scientific forms of knowledge would secure only instrumental contributions from its experts, thus producing an unbridgeable gulf between experts and policy-makers. Since experts must be allowed (for both sociological and practical reasons) to make contributions which extend beyond their expertise, it is wiser to recognise this fact and to seek an appropriate balance between the 'narrow but deep' and 'broad but shallow' types of expert contribution.

Technocracy affects administrative systems in two main ways.

207

First, technocracy may refer to a way of reaching decisions, and in particular to ascribing excessive weight to the views of individual experts. As already noted, this may occur not through the efforts of the expert himself, but through rigid or superficial methods of administrative appraisal. Alternatively, an energetic or dogmatic expert may be able to acquire great influence, especially under conditions which favour centralised decision-making.

An example is Lord Snow's account of the activities of Lord Cherwell before and during the Second World War. This is not in fact an example of administrative technocracy, inasmuch as Cherwell advanced his opinions primarily through political channels, especially his friendship with Sir Winston Churchill. Moreover, Cherwell was not a specialised expert but a scientist who had opinions on a variety of subjects. The point is that his ability to make some of his opinions prevail, against those of the official scientific adviser (Sir Henry Tizzard), was partly due to the lack of sufficiently diffused awareness, throughout the system, of the nature and significance of the issues at stake. One cannot draw the conclusion that bureaucratic sources of advice are always to be preferred to political sources, since the character and abilities of the two protagonists (Cherwell and Tizzard) might have been quite different. One can note, however, that an administrative system can permit technocracy through having weak resources of scientific knowledge.[17]

Secondly, a more obvious and potent type of technocracy can result from the executive power of a group of experts. The cohesion and morale of such groups is likely to be highest when *esprit de corps* is combined with *esprit de service*; in other words, when a distinctive cadre of experts based upon specialised training is also closely identified with a particular agency. However, technocracy itself will not necessarily result from this circumstance, since it is a product of *excessive* influence of some skill in relation to a given set of problems.

For example, the forestry service is notable, in the U.S.A. and in France and even to some extent in Britain, for its strong combination of *esprit de corps* and *esprit de service*. *Eaux et Forêts* represents the only purely professional service in France which contains no civil administrators, and has its special forestry school at Nancy. Herbert Kaufman's account of the U.S. forest rangers gives a fascinating account of the power of specialised training in creating shared attitudes and work methods among lonely, dispersed field workers. Yet the forestry service is not technocratic inasmuch as it favours a broad approach to the problems of forestry conservation and development. In contrast may be placed Charles Hardin's critique of the attitudes of the engineers in the soil conservation service of the Department of Agriculture. The 'soil doctors' have an exaggerated faith in the capacity of contour engineering to solve farm problems.[18]

A frequent form of technocracy is the exaltation of technical factors at the expense of broader economic considerations. This is often alleged against French engineering corps such as the *Ponts et Chaussées*, but the technical bias of this corps is offset by the financial bias of the *Inspecteurs des Finances*.[19] It could of course also be claimed that some financial methods are as functionally lopsided as technical methods, without the justification of achieving concrete results. A clearer example of complete technical disregard of economic factors is provided by the U.S. Army Corps of Engineers. This Corps is prodigal in its willingness to provide services cheaply or free to local interests in order to get their support for local public work projects. Its technocratic policies contrast with the more rationally economic approach to water resources development of the Bureau of Reclamation.[20]

Specialised corps quite often engage in mutual conflicts. Examples are the disputes between the general purpose corps of rural engineers and other technical corps in France, and between different cadres of agricultural specialists in both France and America. Such rivalries tend towards the exaggeration of technocratic view-points. This type of technocracy is much less evident in Britain. It is significant, though a pity, that no studies of the characteristics of technical field corps have been done for Britain. Some *esprit de corps* is certainly to be found, for example in the national agricultural advisory service or in the agricultural land service, but its expressions are apparently much milder than in American or French equivalents.

THE PROBLEMS OF ECONOMIC APPRAISAL

Administrative appraisal occurs at several levels. In general terms, we can think of a level of economic and social appraisal which lies midway between more technical types of judgement and ultimate policy decisions. Economic and social appraisal is more value-oriented and more closely linked to political decisions than are technical judgements. Moreover, these forms of appraisal become more important and dominant at the higher levels of policy-making. This is because they provide the basis on which technical possibilities are appraised, and relevant questions are asked of more specialised experts. Satisfactory processes of administrative appraisal require the posing of relevant questions at the right time and at the appropriate level of the administrative system.

Our lives are continually being changed by technological innovations. However, unless one adopts a view-point of technological determinism, the development and uses of these inventions must logically depend upon appraisal of their social benefits. Not only do the effects of innovation have to be traced and assessed, but the possibilities of guiding innovation so as to achieve more beneficial or acceptable results have continuously to be explored.

The technical feasibility of a project can often only be judged by experts who are closely involved with its development. The policy-maker or adviser, however, must attend closely to the project's probable economic and social consequences. Administrative appraisers of the Concorde supersonic airplane could say little of value about whether the plane would actually fly, but they could consider how far sales of the plane might recoup public expenditure on its development, what benefits the plane might bring to the British air corporations or to other industries, and how far the noise levels produced would be acceptable to the public. Investigation of these questions would have required that market, industrial, technical and social surveys were initiated at an early stage, and that their findings were then used to pose further questions to the plane's developers (for example, about the feasibility and cost of design modifications).

The centralising tendencies of modern government produce a necessity for exceedingly difficult and complex forms of appraisal. Administrative appraisal is easiest within a bounded institutional context which includes firm objective standards that must be satisfied. It is obviously easier for a nationalised electricity industry controlled by financial targets to settle its investment programme, than it is for a Ministry of Power to co-ordinate the combined investments of the electricity, gas, coal and atomic power corporations. In both cases, complex forecasts and judgements have to be attempted about future markets and supplies, the rate of technical progress, trends in productivity, etc.; but in the latter case, the variables are more numerous and their interactions considerably more complex, important additional factors such as the balance of payments play a large part, and the final judgement is controlled less by specific calculations and more by general considerations about the 'health of the economy'.

At the same time, the higher levels of administrative appraisal contain a larger economic content and a smaller technical one. This point does not of course apply to the appraisal of a large individual project, but to the successive co-ordination of projects and programmes. This result comes about for several reasons. One is that the nature of technical appraisal does not vary with administrative levels, whereas economic appraisal does depend upon whether one is adopting a 'micro' or 'macro' view-point. At the same time, however, economics provides certain yardsticks of comparison with which to aid policy decisions, which technical appraisals cannot furnish. Finally, it is easier to undertake economic appraisal than it is to find scientific experts who are really capable of reviewing the judgement of colleagues working in an advanced technological field.

The impact of centralised co-ordination upon forms of appraisal is clear in the case of nationalised industries. In Britain, the public corporations still possess almost complete technical autonomy and some financial autonomy, but are controlled by successive or joint economic appraisals made by the controlling ministry and by the Treasury. In France, the nationalised industries are controlled even on technical matters by supervising departments, notably the Ministry for Industry, while economic appraisal and policy-making is largely exercised by the Ministry of Finance.[21]

These developments have increased the importance of economists in administration. In principle, economic techniques offer methods for comparing all projects in terms of their net yields or benefits. The economist's style also makes him sensitive to the inter-relations of different policies and programmes, E. A. G. Robinson, for example, claims that:

> ... the most valuable contribution of the economist to policy-making comes from the fact that he is by training sensitive to the interrelations of different things – that he refuses to accept the tacit assumption of the administrator that, because the administrative hierarchy is so architectured, this thing is separate from that.[22]

However, the economist's general contribution to administration is of the 'broad but shallow' kind. As Ely Devons notes, an awareness of elementary economic principles such as of supply-demand relationships can illuminate many administrative problems, but does not necessitate much special knowledge. Moreover, the 'optimising' approach favoured by economists does not constitute their exclusive property, but corresponds to the model of the rational administrator sketched by Herbert Simon. This approach corresponds to one logic model of decision-making. It requires that all important or relevant consequences of a decision should be traced and evaluated, if possible through the use of quantitative methods.

The economist's skill consists in the conversion of these consequences into common denominators of gain and loss expressed in monetary terms. As economic appraisal seeks (or is forced) to become more comprehensive, the number of factors to be valued increases, and the assumptions behind their quantification in monetary terms become more complex and questionable. The rational appraisal of complex issues turns primarily upon the identification and analysis of relevant factors rather than upon their conversion into necessarily arbitrary monetary equations, although quantification of particular items in both economic and non-economic terms will often be helpful.

The theoretical limitations of cost-benefit analysis were briefly discussed in Chapter 1. The impossibility of arbitrating a complete policy issue through such techniques was strikingly illustrated in Britain by the experience of the Roskill Commission. This body spent over £1 million upon a cost-benefit analysis which was supposed to demonstrate the relative costs and benefits in monetary terms of four alternative airport locations. However, there was heated and inconclusive argument about the figures to be attached to those items which were quantified, while the Commission accepted that some important items could not be quantified at all. The main effect of the exercise was to translate policy issues into complicated technical analysis without thereby elucidating or resolving those issues. The main use of cost-benefit analysis appears to be as a supporting argument for particular organisational or policy view-points.[23]

Cost-benefit analysis may stimulate administrators to look more closely into the consequences of some decision; but the conversion of the results into monetary terms adds no new facts and is too arbitrary to provide an acceptable answer for policy problems. What such methods can do, however, is to provide *one* type of independent check upon the arguments of specialised bodies or of interest groups, through comparing the effects of a decision as estimated by a specialised body with the effects as quantified by a cost-benefit analysis. However, the use of such comparisons requires administrators to have a sophisticated understanding of the relationship of techniques to theories of policy-making.

The economist in administration can function in two capacities. One role is as a technical auxiliary to policy-makers – to provide the quantification which can make their decisions more precise.

This is the position of economic statisticians engaged in national accounting, whose calculations are indispensable to modern budgetary decisions, but who do not decide what those decisions shall be. This is also the potential function of econometricians whose work may enable various types of relationships (between monetary flows and employment levels, for example) to be controlled more precisely. The same auxiliary role can be assigned to those cost-benefit analysts who clearly recognise the limitations of their assumptions. Their contribution is more objective and helpful in fields where the importance of social side-effects is limited, and where technical and economic judgements can be closely correlated; for example, in the evaluation of alternative patterns of investment in power generation or in the development of water resources.[24]

Alternatively, the economist can function as a policy adviser who makes (explicitly or not) certain value assumptions. Administrative experience enables an economist to marry his techniques with practical judgements, and to gain utility at the expense of purity. Sir Alec Cairncross, head of the government economic service in Britain, noted that he gained more insight into economic administration through his three and a half years in the planning of aircraft production than from any academic learning, and Devons has noted that the administrative opinions of economists often have little relationship to their special knowledge. This of course is a common circumstance with all types of expert advisers.[25]

The difficulty with economic advice is that of disentangling predictions which are necessarily subject to wide errors from the values assigned to various possible outcomes. In situations where (for example) the policy-maker is concerned with the balance between inflation and unemployment, his choice between the range of possible predictions is naturally influenced by his valuations of marginal changes in the two parameters. The economist's own normative beliefs or theories are likely subtly to affect this type of judgement; for example, 'growth' economists are prone to believe that measures to expand production and productivity are the best way to tackle a balance of payments problem, while 'equilibrium' economists prefer measures for reducing effective demand. Subtly linked with these judgements are different valuations of the relative desirability of full employment, stable currencies, etc., and behind these valuations still lurk the normative models of the functioning of the economy which can be traced either to classical economics (with its self-regulating mechanisms and stress on harmonious adjustments) or to modern growth theories (with their stress upon positive interventions and a full use of resources). Economic advisers who start by stressing the objectivity of their methods often seem to end up by introducing, almost unconsciously, a number of normative assumptions.[26]

Even if the economic adviser seeks to be fully neutral, his association with economic politicians and economic administrators or managers will rarely permit it. These participants differ of course in their knowledge and use of specifically economic techniques; but their relations are certainly influenced by the extent to which they put the same valuations on possible outcomes. A growth-minded politician will prefer to work with a similarly oriented administrator, who in turn will prefer the assistance of an economist of similar predilections. Policy-making thus becomes a joint product, embodying three varying contributions; that of the economist has the highest technical content and probably (though not certainly) the lowest policy one. If the economist attempts to be completely neutral in his approach, he will probably be an unacceptable member of the team; but to the extent that he introduces some value assumptions, his judgements have in fact a lower claim to authority than have those of his colleagues, one of whom has the title of popular election and the other that of being an appointed co-ordinator. It is interesting that nonetheless disgruntled professional economists are apt to blame administrators for rejecting not their techniques, but their policy advice. This position is only tenable if it be assumed that there is some certain road to a desired goal (economic growth, for example) which only the perversity of administrators, and perhaps of other economists, is obstructing. The credibility which is accorded to such critiques in Britain arises, presumably, from the naïve belief that an economist is the best person to make a nation rich. Curiously the same view is less likely to be held about a firm – presumably because the economist is supposed to do for government through his art what the market does for firms through competition.

Conversely, an economist can guard the purity of his research by eschewing all contact with policy-making, which is the view of the increasing proportion of economists and other social scientists who remain permanently in universities. In this way, their attention is directed to the more logically rigorous aspects of their subject, free from awkward institutional complications. However, the practical utility of their work also dwindles, unless formal and abstract methods of reasoning provide more insight into social behaviour than seems probable. This again is an illustration of an earlier thesis; fully scientific techniques offer much narrower contributions to administrative appraisal than do more versatile but more suspect forms of knowledge. Economics tends to become polarised between the limits of fruitless science and very debatable art, although a useful but under-cultivated middle ground certainly exists.

THE QUALIFICATIONS OF ADMINISTRATORS

This chapter has made it plain that there is no ideal set of qualifications for administrators. The diversities of intellectual knowledge and institutional experience which are relevant to their work are so numerous and complex that, even setting aside cultural differences, no universal prescription can reasonably be offered. There is also the point that no administrator in the modern world can hope to know more than a small fraction of what ideally might be desirable.

The matter need not be left there, however. The previous analysis has brought out the importance of economic and social forms of appraisal for administrative co-ordinators operating integrated systems of decision-making. This point is expressed in the French description of the higher civil servant as 'the social scientist in action', and justifies the special training which general administrators receive in France. It is worth asking in what ways 'social science' can provide a satisfactory basis for the training of administrators.

'Social science' is a broad conception which comprises, in terms of administrative relevance, two main branches. Historical and institutional studies, such as political and economic history, social and economic structure, comparative administrative systems, etc., provide insight into the problems of policy-making and administration in the modern world, without furnishing any specific techniques for administrative action. Statistics, quantitative economics, management studies, and methods of social analysis provide techniques of direct service to administrators. Thus, within the framework of the 'social sciences', and cutting across academic distinctions to a considerable extent, there exists the age-old dichotomy between cultural and instrumental forms of learning.

The traditional image of the general administrator is of a cultured and cultivated man, whose knowledge of society is historical and institutional or legal, and until recent times the main arguments about his education revolved around the significance of law, and the claims of modern as against ancient history or philosophy. An extension of his education to take in modern social structure or economic institutions can be accommodated within this tradition, but instrumental techniques fall outside it. This exclusion has rested upon a subtle distinction between 'administration', as concerned with high affairs of state, and 'management' as concerned with the routine management of public services, a distinction for long expressed in the relationship between the administrative and executive class in Britain.

The exclusion of quantitative and managerial techniques from administrative education is no longer practicable. Although these techniques must primarily be performed by various specialists, the administrator must at least understand their relevance for his own tasks of analysis and appraisal. Conversely of course, a heavy concentration upon the study of quantitative techniques, to the exclusion of institutional and historical studies, would turn the administrator into a technician who was uninformed about the structural and historical setting of the problems with which he must wrestle. Thus one concludes that the administrator needs knowledge of both main branches of 'social science'.

Empirical social studies are useful for the administrator because they throw light upon the multiple causations and interactions of human behaviour. These studies are also mutually linked and mutually corrective. For example, studies of the results of the administration of rent controls or of guaranteed farm prices show how fallacious are economic theories about supply and demand unless accompanied by sociological understanding of the reactions of housing tenants or farmers. Again, the administrator who tried to decide how many residents of a congested urban area should move to a new town on the basis of economic costs would be too limited; for he must consider equally the effects of the move upon community structure. These points support a conclusion that the administrator's education in social sciences should be broadly based, and not dominated by one specialism such as economics.[27]

Granted the relevance of 'social science' for administrators, one can still question whether an exclusive diet of these subjects is in fact appropriate for a whole administrative class. The administrator will in any case occupy the opposite pole of an intellectual spectrum from the pure scientist. As Lord Snow has pointed out, the scientist must think deeply and obsessively about one subject, whereas the administrator must think briefly and rapidly about many subjects and their interconnections. The administrator's view of all decisions as limited and conditional leads easily to an overconcentration upon immediate problems, and to difficulty in stepping outside the pressure of circumstances and using a real exercise in foresight. Snow's contention that science helps to instil a more imaginative insight into the shape of things to come, and thus to rescue administrators from the tyranny of the present has plausibility.[28]

The study of social sciences has its negative aspects. Understanding of social behaviour provides a vital corrective against the excesses of 'technocracy', but plunges the student into a complex world of multiple and uncertain effects, wherein the deeper exercises of scientific imagination find little place. A critical treatment of technical innovation in terms of social and economic effects is always useful to public policy, but often too negative since it is the innovators who change life. One not infrequently, for example, sees the rational planner making belated criticisms from the sidelines while the forceful engineer changes the shape of the city. This is not all the engineer's fault.

All administrative systems have to cope with two related problems of education and training. These are: how to secure that the disciplines studied are effectively related to administrative needs without loss of intellectual integrity?; and how to secure an adequate diversification of intellectual backgrounds without impeding communication among senior officials? If administrators must study a variety of subjects in a rapid and relevant way, the obvious method of doing so is in a special training institute, rather than through the much more diverse and academically specialised methods of university education, the danger being that the institute will become intellectually conformist and inbred, once its initial inspiration has ceased to operate. Secondly, the penetration of administration by a cross-section of modern specialised knowledge can best be achieved by recruiting administrators from diverse intellectual backgrounds, but it will then prove harder to establish a common language of administrative appraisal.

The French system leans very heavily towards specialised forms of administrative education, for not only does it include lengthy training courses specially designed for the main groups of administrators, but their prior university education is also heavily dominated by the requirements of the system. Through their study of law, modern history, economics, politics and international relations, the French corps of general administrators emerge with a broad understanding of the characteristics and functioning of modern societies. The counterpoise to the general administrators' education is provided by the mathematical and scientific education of the principal technical corps, and communication between these two main groups is facilitated by the fact that some study of management and of quantitative techniques is included in both forms of training. This system ensures that administrators study relevant subjects in a relevant way, and forges a common administrative language.

The weakness of the French system is the somewhat procrustean and conformist view which it takes of the intellectual equipment necessary for administrators. Moreover, it is an open question in France as to how far this equipment really corresponds to the requirements of modern administration, and how far it is shaped by exclusive pedagogic traditions. The teaching provided at the *École Nationale d'Administration* (E.N.A.) has been much influenced by the geographic and intellectual proximity of the Paris *Institut d'Études Politiques*. The latter institution was the intellectual precursor of the former, and has provided at least three-quarters of the E.N.A.'s direct intake of university students since its creation in 1945. Administrative training in France has consequently been criticised for producing officials who are schooled only in a particular social science tradition, which is too abstract and inadequately managerial and which unduly favours certain subjects, for example politics over sociology. E.N.A. has introduced greater attention to mathematics and quantitative techniques, and has tried to broaden its recruitment, but its academic foundations remain somewhat inbred and idiosyncratic whatever their intellectual merits.[29]

In Britain, French ideas of administrative training have acquired some attraction for administrators themselves as well as for their critics, as a possible answer to the charge of 'amateurism'. A traditional strength of the British system is its intellectual catholicity of recruitment. The fact that botany or zoology seems a strange preparation for a specifically administrative career need not be reckoned a criticism at all, if a diversity of intellectual backgrounds has intrinsic value and if appropriate post-entry training is also provided. In practice, though, administrators have largely been recruited from historians, classicists and students of literature, with few scientists or mathematicians and not many economists; and post-entry training only started to much purpose in the 1960s and has encountered the obvious problem that (in contrast with the French situation) administrators lack any common intellectual background on which the training can build.

Not surprisingly, economics and statistics were the first subjects to be studied briefly by administrators at the Treasury Centre for Administrative Studies (C.A.S.) founded in 1963. Although administrators may think in compartments which economists ignore, both are much concerned with alternative use of resources. Acquaintance with economic theories of resource allocation, in so far as these can be applied to government, offered the easiest apparent way of making administration more 'scientific'. While this acquisition of

218

greater numeracy had obvious worth for administrators, it represented a somewhat one-sided inculcation of the social sciences, a criticism which was formally met by the addition of courses in government and organisation and in social administration. The absorption of the C.A.S. in 1970 into the much larger Civil Service College represented the merging of a small programme for an élite group of young administrators into a large organisation concerned with many types of training. Although training for generalists continued to occupy a high priority, the problems of teaching a greater miscellany of subjects to a larger annual intake of students within a large institution were considerable.[30]

The concept of teaching social science to administrators, while possessing a certain general utility, does not provide an adequate basis for the design of training. In academic terms, the social sciences divide into a diversity of subjects between which the theoretical links are fairly weak. In administrative terms, it is important and indeed essential to relate the study of techniques to broader forms of theoretical and institutional analysis, yet no academic discipline offers a satisfactory means of doing this. The time available for post-entry training is thirteen months in France, excluding field assignments, and at the most will be one year in Britain for the 'fast-stream' of young administrators. Without the moulding effect of a common pedagogic experience, such as occurs in France, it is difficult for the British course to offer more than a brief miscellany of rather unrelated subjects.

A further central question is the relationship of training to forms of specialisation. A possible criticism of both French and British training is that it is largely unspecialised in terms both of subject areas and of processes. The E.N.A. was originally intended to train administrators in various subject areas (economic, financial, social, general and foreign affairs) to which they could then be assigned; but the preference of both the *corps* and the abler students for unfettered selection based upon general performance defeated the concept. A similar fate met the cruder Fulton distinction between training in economic and in social administration. Courses at both E.N.A. and C.S.C. make some use of optional subjects, but the basic principle in both cases remains that of acquiring knowledge which can be useful in all departments or agencies.

To some extent, methods of policy analysis and planning or the treatment of organisational problems can be taught in a general way. However, administrative issues as a rule only acquire much force and interest within a specific setting. This setting may be a broad one, such as governmental relations with private enterprise, nationalised industries, the planning of the environment, welfare services, etc. Policy and organisational issues in any of these fields require considerable background study or experience to become really interesting and intelligible, so that their use as illustrations in a general course is necessarily superficial. However, there is obvious value in a course which tries to harness all relevant forms of knowledge and analysis to the exploration in depth of some defined set of governmental problems. A course of this kind represents specialisation to the general-purpose administrators, but it amounts to generalisation and a broadening of perspectives for most specialists and for others working in the relevant sections of government.

A distinction can be drawn between preparatory training which is necessarily formal and somewhat academic in character, and training at later stages which builds upon and enlarges the official's experience. Courses dealing with particular areas of government would seem to be more suitable for administrators with experience, although it can be argued that the young entrant would benefit from a full survey of the issues of government that are relevant to the agency which he will join.

Administrative systems vary a great deal over the attention which they give to initial training, as well as over its form. In France, as noted already, considerable stress is laid upon the 'formation' of young administrators. This arises not primarily from any academic theories but from the existence of a distinctive administrative philosophy which can be passed on to new entrants, changes only slowly, and reflects established beliefs about the roles and prerogatives of administrative cadres and about the functions of government itself. In Britain, the considerable attention now given to initial training is primarily concerned with the dissemination of managerial skills and techniques, and there is not much sign of the creation of any administrative philosophy. In the U.S.A., the notion of any 'formation' of administrators in the French sense is wholly out of line with the traditions of the civil service, although the 'management intern' programme establishes some relationship between academic studies and practical apprenticeship with an agency.

Training at senior levels is primarily concerned with helping administrators to tackle increasingly broad policy and organisational issues. The pluralist and specialised character of American government makes this kind of training especially necessary in the U.S.A. A Federal Executive Institute has been created in order to provide initially eight-week courses for senior executives in the top three grades (16–18). These courses assume basic knowledge of management and techniques, and concentrate upon discussion of the central machinery of government, national policies and administrative strategy. While similar courses can be found in Britain or France, there is less need to improve communication among senior administrators where they have received a similar initial 'formation'. This kind of policy-oriented approach is rare in Britain, presumably because administrative traditions are wary of policy discussions.

Whilst one may doubt the desirability of a strong administrative formation and philosophy, training should relate information, theories and techniques to policy and organisational issues. Unless the connection is made, training becomes merely a 'catch-up' programme in certain academic subjects or else an assimilation of techniques whose relevance to governmental action is poorly considered and which may soon get out of date. Thus a training institute has to achieve forms of intellectual synthesis which are less necessary in universities, and it must cultivate practical relevance without losing intellectual objectivity. The worst enemy of this task is political or administrative dogmas, but in addition neither a primarily academic nor a primarily technical approach assist its realisation.

The education of administrators or executives will inevitably become a longer process. The ability to undertake more systematic forms of economic and social appraisal is of growing importance, and this implies the capacity to ask relevant questions of a growing army of experts, and to understand the significance of their answers for administrative decisions. There can be little doubt of the value of specific forms of administrative training, which can develop a common administrative language, and relate the findings of academic disciplines (especially in the social sciences) to administrative needs. The difficulty, however, is to develop forms of training which preserve intellectual integrity while achieving administrative relevance. The danger that the training will be dominated by the special interests of a government or of an administrative class are obvious enough, but at the same time training that is too detached from policy problems is likely to have limited value. The challenge is to develop effective training programmes without sacrificing the intellectual diversity and capacity for creative thought upon which the quality of administrators will continue to depend.

REFERENCES

1 Sir Geoffrey Vickers, *The Art of Judgement* (London, 1965), p. 40.
2 H. H. Gerth and C. W. Mills (eds.), *From Max Weber, Essays in Sociology* (London, 1947), p. 232.
3 Jean Meynaud, *Technocracy* (London, 1968).
4 Quoted in F. F. Ridley (ed.), *Specialists and Generalists* (London, 1968), p. 18.
5 For the traditional structure of the service, see W. J. M. Mackenzie and J. W. Grove, *Central Administration in Britain* (London, 1957), Chaps. 1, 3 and 7.
6 David Regan, 'The Expert and the Administrator', *Public Administration* (Summer 1966).
7 See the analysis by T. H. Profitt pp. 13–57 of *Specialists and Generalists*.
8 See p. 125 of *Specialists and Generalists* ('France' by F. F. Ridley, which is the main source for this section).
9 *The Civil Services of North America*, Report by the Civil Service Department (London, H.M.S.O., 1969) has a good summary of the American system.
10 For sources, see R. H. Pear, pp. 174–87 of *Specialists and Generalists*.
11 *The Civil Services of North America*, p. 44.
12 For the best of these attacks, directed primarily at Treasury attitudes, see Max Nicholson, *The System, the Misgovernment of Modern Britain* (London, 1967). For shallower assaults, see Brian Chapman, *British Government Observed* (London, 1962); H. Thomas (ed.), *Crisis in the Civil Service* (London, 1968).
13 Sir Edward Bridges in A. Dunsire (ed.), *The Making of an Administrator* (Manchester University Press, 1956), pp. 12–13.
14 For review of Treasury methods, see Estimates Committee 1957-8, Sixth Report: *Treasury Control of Expenditure*, H.C. 254-I; for appraisal of public corporations, see Select Committee on Nationalised Industries, 1967-8, First Report: *Ministerial Control of the Nationalised Industries*, Vols 1–3.
15 See contributions to H. Thomas (ed.), op. cit., and S. Brittan, *The Treasury under the Tories 1951–64* (London, 1964).
16 Victor A. Thompson, *Modern Organisation* (New York, 1961).
17 C. P. Snow, *Science and Government* (Oxford, 1961).
18 Herbert Kaufman, *The Forest Ranger* (Baltimore, 1967); Charles M. Hardin, *The Politics of Agriculture* (Glencoe, Illinois, 1952), Chaps. 4, 6, 14 and 15.
19 F. Ridley and J. Blondel, *Public Administration in France* (London, 1969), pp. 211–13.
20 Arthur Maass, *Muddy Waters* (Cambridge, Mass., 1951).
21 *Ministerial Control of the Nationalised Industries* and Ridley and Blondel, op. cit., Chap. 17.
22 Introduction (p. vi) to W. A. Johr and H. W. Singer, *The Role of the Economist as Official Adviser* (London, 1955).
23 P. Self, 'Nonsense on Stilts: Cost-Benefit Analysis and the Roskill Commission', *Political Quarterly* (July 1970); *Report of the Commission on the Third London Airport* (London, 1971), especially Chap. 12.

24 For sources, see Martin S. Feldstein, 'Cost-Benefit Analysis and Investment in the Public Sector', *Public Administration* (Winter 1964).

25 Sir Alec Cairncross, 'The Work of an Economic Adviser', *Public Administration* (Spring 1968); Eli Devons, 'Economics and Administration', in *Essays in Economics* (London, 1961). See also David Henderson, *The Use of Economists in Whitehall*, Oxford Economic Papers (1961).

26 A good example is Johr and Singer, op. cit. In the second half of this book, value judgements continually intrude although they are at least fairly explicit, as the value judgements of economists frequently are not. For a full critique, see Terence W. Hutchison, *Economists and Economic Policy in Britain 1946–66* (London, 1968).

27 Peter Self, 'The Education of Administrators', *Political Quarterly* (July-September 1967).

28 Snow, op. cit.

29 For the French system of training, see Henry Parris, 'Twenty Years of *l'École Nationale d'Administration*', *Public Administration* (Winter 1965), and *Rapport de la Commission d'Étude des Problems de l'E.N.A.* (Paris, April 1969).

30 For British developments see Desmond Keeling 'The Development of Central Training in the Civil Service, 1963–70', *Public Administration* (Spring 1971). For the stress on techniques in British training, see Civil Service Department, First Report, Chap. 4 (London, 1970).

Chapter 7

ADMINISTRATIVE MOTIVATION
AND PERFORMANCE

INTRODUCTION

In contrast with the Weberian portrait of a rational bureaucracy, maintained by objective standards, impersonal rules, and expert skills, modern theorists have increasingly concentrated upon the 'dysfunctions' of bureaucracy. These 'dysfunctions' are often seen as the unwanted by-products of methods which are in themselves rational, but which are exaggerated in their execution or fail to adjust to new requirements because of their intrinsic rigidity.

Several sociologists have detected a series of vicious circles in administrative behaviour. Robert Merton suggests that the bureaucratic stress upon reliability and predictability leads easily to inflexible behaviour. The consequent difficulties with clients strengthen the administrator's need to make his actions fully defensible, which leads to more rigid rules, and so on. Philip Selznick contends that the delegation of tasks to specialised agencies can result in an undue dependency of the agency upon outside interests, which leads to pressure for further delegation of power. Michel Crozier (following Alvin Gouldner) notes the use of impersonal rules as a means of making power relations less visible and less offensive to subordinates: one result is a reduction of performance levels, which leads to pressure for more rules. Harry Cohen reports that the use of quantitative performance tests in social service agencies results in the staff skimping clients' needs in pursuit of a high numerical score of tasks done; this may be followed by stiffer performance tests.[1]

One has only to inspect a series of vicious circles of this kind to note that the posited ill effects need not necessarily occur; corrective action might be taken in an opposite direction. Some of these conclusions are of course based upon particular field studies, but again the 'dysfunction' found within one administrative system is not necessarily present within another.

This leads to a second general point. Weber offered a generalised model of bureaucracy, but modern studies pay attention to cultural variations in administrative behaviour. These variations are certainly considerable, and the question arises as to how far the 'dysfunctions' of a particular system are necessarily related to the virtues or merits which may be claimed for that system.

This chapter is concerned with the problems of motivation and performance, as these concern the higher levels of bureaucracy. The subject is an important, indeed vital one, because of the great tasks and broad discretion now entrusted to senior officials. High performance is expected and required from them, yet some of the intrinsic conditions of administrative action offer little incentive to high levels of personal endeavour. These conditions include:

a) Very elaborate requirements of consultation and accountability. The senior administrator works within three interlocking circles which comprise his own agency and its special public, other public agencies, and the general organs of political control. Consultative and co-ordinative needs have steadily expanded because of the proliferation of agencies and interest groups, the increasing interdependence of public programmes, and the widening range of special skills that can be utilised in public decisions. The emphasis upon the team style and the slow accumulation of relevant material before final decisions are reached inevitably tends to diminish personal decisiveness and responsibility. The individual administrator's share in the final result is hard to estimate, either for blame or praise.

b) Senior administrators within central government operate at a level that is remote from the final consequences of their decisions. Many of their acts are concerned with setting limits to or exerting influence upon the decisions of others. An elaborate and sometimes contradictory pattern of controls and inducements descends the governmental system and affects the acts of operating agencies, private firms and individuals. It is hard for a senior official to know the consequences of his recommendations and decisions, or for anyone else to discover what these have been.

c) Political conditions, even where they do not impose anonymity upon the official, inhibit a just evaluation of his work. Such administrative achievements as the saving of public money, the improvement of internal procedures, or the simplification of regulations often receive little recognition from political leaders. The results of administrative decisions are subject to partisan political judgements, often made in ignorance of the

225

circumstances in which the decision was made. An official may willingly work to enhance his minister's reputation, and the latter may be duly grateful in return, but political recognition of administrative worth is uncertain and erratic. The official is protected from this situation by the high degree of self-regulation which occurs in modern bureaucracies, and which enhances his security. An official's career is mainly dependent upon the opinions of his peers and the judgements of senior officials. However, this collective peer judgement cannot but be influenced by the absence of external tests of performance, and by the advantages of a cautious pooling of responsibilities.

It is often said that administrative performance suffers from the fact that it is not subject to objective market tests. In fact, much behaviour in private firms is not subject to market tests either, and is also qualified by the existence of monopoly and oligopoly. It remains true that administration is not usually subject to the tests of solvency and profit which must still be met by private firms, and which provide one type of test of individual performance.

In the modern world, market tests are increasingly supplemented or replaced by the tests of professional standards and forms of self-regulation. Many professions are in general demand, and their practitioners are guided by standards which are not peculiar to public administration (for example, medicine, physics, engineering, architecture), although sometimes the skill is learned with special reference to its administrative usage, as in the case of engineers in the French public service. There is also a growing number of professions or skills which are only or mainly practised in public service; examples are public health, town planning, forestry and many forms of social welfare. The development of professional or vocational training in these fields has permeated public administration with special tests of proficiency and accomplishment, although some of these tests are vague and debatable in comparison with those offered by more scientific disciplines.

A critical question is how far administration itself can be regarded as a self-regulating profession which has its own distinctive standards. Certainly administrators may share a professional code of ethics which in some systems has importance for guiding their behaviour. They can also make use of a growing battery of specialised and quantitative techniques, and utilise the whole range of social sciences. However, compliance with an ethical code or knowledge of relevant disciplines does not itself provide an adequate test of administrative performance. Administrative evaluation by superiors still turns upon the recognition of attitudes and qualities which cannot be closely specified or impartially tested.

Because of this situation, and the absence of ultimate market tests of solvency or profit, administrative promotion still leans heavily upon the only fully objective factor which can be introduced, that of seniority. The weight placed upon seniority varies somewhat between systems, but all bureaucracies face the problem that seniority itself (being automatic) is a weak incentive to hard work and exceptional effort. The supplementary methods which are used to modify the application of seniority rules thus have much importance, and vary considerably between systems.

Until recently, little attention was paid to questions of motivation and morale in the public service. Rationalist theories assumed that officials were adequately inspired by their sense of public duty, while hierarchical theories put their trust in the efficacy of formal controls and discipline. Investigations of the actual attitudes of civil servants ran counter to both rationalist and authoritarian beliefs, and were not judged necessary or desirable. However, Nigel Walker's study of civil service attitudes in Britain has shown the error of these assumptions.

Job satisfaction in the British civil service appears to be lower than among equivalent executive and clerical groups working for private firms. The causes of satisfaction or discontent also differ between public and private sectors. Civil servants as a whole regard their greatest benefits as being job security and pensions, while the private sector workers are relatively more impressed with the interest of their work and with promotion prospects. The civil servants varied considerably in the extent to which they believed their work to be important or useful, and curiously enough some of those who most believed in its importance had the lowest efficiency ratings from their superiors, and vice versa. However, the civil servants did generally believe that their work was unfairly and disparagingly viewed by the public and press, and the 'thankless' nature of their work was seen as one of its drawbacks. According to Gournay's account, it seems that the French civil service is regarded by the general public with still greater hostility and incomprehension, although its critics often favour a civil service career for their children for reasons of security and prestige.[2]

To some extent, all societies can draw on certain motivations to public service which are less evident in other occupations. Attachment to some view of social welfare or general interest is certainly one reason for entry into the civil service, in contrast to the pull of more commercial or competitive types of career. While an abstract

227

commitment to public duty can provide only a limited spur to effective performance or personal endeavour, its importance as a regulative ideal for public service remains considerable. Public service motivations are generally harnessed more fully and effectively by systems which attach high personal prestige and status to a successful administrative career. As already noted, such prestige can exist even where the public service is subject to much hostile criticism. By contrast, other systems lay less or little weight upon the distinctive motivations of public service, and seek instead a public service which is as closely assimilated as possible to the work of the rest of society. This chapter will explore the effect of different systems of administrative recruitment and promotion upon the attitudes and performance of public officials.

OPEN AND CLOSED CAREER SYSTEMS

The most striking and familiar contrast in administrative careers is that between the 'open' American system and the 'closed' European ones; American administrative practice minimises the differences between public and private agencies. Government is seen as performing a variegated collection of jobs which require a cross-section of the skills that are possessed and needed by the whole society. The dominant conception is thus that of a 'service state' which is fully open to general social influences, and which reflects as far as possible the attitudes and values of the general population.

These conceptions cannot fully be applied of course to the classic governmental functions of foreign policy, defence and justice. However, even in these realms, government is permeated by the values and techniques of American society. The American air force uses advertising techniques to reveal its services to peace, and the Defence Department under the leadership of secretaries drawn typically from the motor industry attempts to deploy the same techniques of production and costing as private industry to weirdly different types of problem.

The belief that American bureaucracy should be 'socially representative' has a long history. The Jacksonian revolt which brought wholesale political patronage into the Federal system was inspired by hostility to a closed and somewhat aristocratic administrative élite, for which was substituted a broad cross-section of party adherents. When political patronage ceased to attune with the standards expected elsewhere in society, it was replaced gradually by a merit system which filled government with a diversified cross-

228

section of averagely skilled men and women. The opposition which greeted the Hoover Commission proposal for a senior civil service reveals the continued hostility to any suspected form of administrative élitism.

The personnel system of position-classification accords well with these basic values. The duties of every post in the public service (save for political appointees) are classified, and the position can be filled by anyone with the requisite skills. These skills are learned through the general educational system, not in institutes dedicated to government service. Recruitment into the public service can occur at any age or level, although an agency inclines strongly towards the promotion of its own employees. Until recently, there was little systematic planning of careers within the Federal service, although bureaux and departments pay increasing attention to the subject and an executive career programme is now operated by the Civil Service Commission. Typically, however, this plan is concerned with widening the range of competitors for top posts, drawing from both inside and outside government, not with the deliberate planning of individual careers. It is indeed extremely difficult to combine a position-classification system with career planning, because either the latter system applies only to a selected group (in which case it cuts across the general values of the service) or else it theoretically applies to everyone, in which case it dissolves into a pattern of more flexible competition for specified positions.[3]

It follows that in the American system no specially trained and recruited cadres of public officials exist, if one excepts those dedicated professional groups (such as foresters) who are necessarily identified with a particular public programme. The closest resemblance to a European general administrator is a specialist in programming or budgeting, who will often have attended a graduate school of business and public administration.

The obvious dysfunction of an open career system, which can be set against its social representativeness, is its inability to cultivate or reward a general ethos of public service. Organisational loyalty or *esprit de service* will certainly exist, but it will be confined to the social or professional goals pursued by particular agencies; no group will exist to stress the values of service to government as a whole. If the general values of society are competitive and egoistic, these will be reflected within the public service, where, however, career conditions are likely to prove less favourable to their realisation. Compared with private firms, the public service offers smaller financial rewards for achievement, a stress on seniority is inimical to egoistic ambition, and top positions are largely held by political appointees. For these reasons, the incentives to public service may be weak, and the rewards of success will often accrue to aggressive action on behalf of particular agencies.

By contrast, the European systems have always viewed public administration as a special vocation, carrying particular rights and privileges and requiring a period of training or induction into the mysteries of public action. Certainly, these ancient concepts have been much modified by the growth of public welfare functions, and the assimilation into public service of numerous skills and professions of a more specific kind. However, the citadels of these systems have so far remained intact. General administration remains a largely closed and well-defined career, marked by recruitment at an early age from somewhat narrow social and educational groups, and by a systematic pattern of promotion in which a person's rank and pay depends not upon a definition of job content but upon the position which he has reached within a regulated hierarchy.

The advantage of a closed career system, based upon high standards of entry and a strong public ethos, is that it inspires administrators to work hard in the service of the State. General administrators themselves frequently testify to the exacting demands of their occupation. For example, Robert Catherine talks of the almost monkish sense of vocation which a French administrator requires, while C. H. Sisson, in a somewhat different British context, stresses the need for self-abnegation, claiming that the British administrator is most useful when an absolute nonentity. While Sisson certainly exaggerates one particular quality, it is impossible to doubt the devotion to public service of senior officials in these two countries. They work hard for long hours, and they are reluctant to dilute the quality of their cadres in order to lighten their load. For example, the British administrative class has for years numbered less than its specified complement but administrators themselves have shown no wish to lower standards of recruitment.[4]

The converse dysfunction alleged against the closed administrative system is of course its tendency to the production of a socially unrepresentative élite. To some extent this result is inevitable. If high entry standards are fixed, and if a specialised ethos of public service is built up, administrators cannot be expected or intended to mirror the composition or attitudes of the general population; and the converse of their sense of duty is likely to be a sense of their importance which can become arrogance. However, the extent to which administrators constitute a narrow or closed group, and assume arrogant or élitist attitudes, cannot be known *a priori*.

In this brief discussion, open and closed career systems have been presented somewhat as ideal types. The actual situation is always a good deal more complex. The extent to which a system is closed depends primarily upon the opportunities and conditions of entry. If entry qualifications are laid down which can only be learned in governmental training schools or institutes, the system can be regarded as more 'closed' than if general educational attainments suffice for entry. In this sense, the French system is more closed than the British, and produces a more distinctive and inbred type of official. Again, no system excludes possibilities of late entry into public posts, and none genuinely offers completely open competition for higher positions. Thus it is possible to enter scientific or technical grades in the British civil service at any level, and even the administrative class now recruits a small proportion of its senior members from outside sources, although this arrangement is largely due to staff shortages and consequently does not injure internal prospects for promotion. Conversely the theoretical 'openness' of the American system is heavily qualified in practice by the inbred character of many agencies and by the very limited mobility between agencies. In contrast with the British situation, the parts of the American system are less open to lateral entry than is the system as a whole to entry from outside.

The relationship between open career patterns and position-classification methods is also not an exact one. In theory, the specification of the precise duties of a post facilitates the appointment of the best qualified person and discounts claims of status or seniority save as these reflect relevant experience. In practice, agencies have considerable discretion over the specification of posts subject to general standards, and the job requirements are often listed so as to facilitate or favour the promotion of an established official. Moreover, the detailed listing of job requirements can tend towards a very particularist view of requisite qualifications, at the expense of broader standards of competence, and in this sense is not necessarily favourable to competitive conditions of entry. Conversely, the 'rank-in-the-man' system has to be combined with some use of position classification as a means of settling the duties and numbers of each grade or category of staff. This system is also obviously more applicable to general administrators than to scientific or technical cadres.[5]

The purpose of classification systems is often misunderstood. The main use of a fully integrated structure, such as exists in the U.S.A. and is now being introduced in Britain by stages, is to co-ordinate the pay of all civil servants according to a general set of grades. The case for a common pay scale is in conflict with the case

231

for relating the pay of each occupational group to its nearest equivalent group outside the civil service. The diverse tasks of civil servants justify the latter arrangement, although the large number of civil servants and their dominant position in some professions are arguments for internal harmonisation. Internal harmonisation of pay in the U.S.A. appears as somewhat contradictory to the 'service state' principle, and the system exists largely because it is the prerogative of Congress to determine pay scales. To meet the claims of those groups who command scarce skills, like scientists and doctors, many exceptions are allowed to the general grading system.

The notion of a harmonised pay structure has only a very limited relationship to the Fulton notion of a 'classless' civil service in which both horizontal and vertical barriers to mobility are minimised. Such barriers must necessarily exist, and the question is which ones are least undesirable. Because of specialisation, any integrated classification system must be assembled from a number of occupational groups or 'series' of which (as noted earlier) there are 435 in the U.S. civil service. If there are a lot of such groups, as is the American situation, mobility is impeded by the proliferation of specialised qualifications at the expense of generalised competence. If the number is too small, the large professional groups which then exist should have considerable internal mobility but will dominate smaller specialist groups as occurs in France. A satisfactory system must strike some balance between these tendencies, without being able to avoid some undesirable obstacles to mobility arising from either professional prerogatives or excessive specialisation.

Vertical mobility appears to be blocked by the existence of separate classes performing similar or related work at different hierarchical levels. However, the real obstacles to promotion consist in methods of recruitment to higher level positions, rather than in the existence of a separate class as such. For example, in Britain considerable movement occurred from the executive to the administrative class before their merger in 1971, and such movement will still be restricted by the entry qualifications fixed for what used to be 'administrative class' positions. But it is true that the existence of separate vertical classes has usually been linked with a sharp differentiation of job opportunities based upon initial educational qualifications. The replacement of separate classes by an integrated structure is at the least a symbol of intention to improve opportunities, even though it does not guarantee this result.

Political expectations about civil service reform tend to be very naïve. The Fulton Committee's advocacy of a 'classless' civil service was represented by itself, and was generally believed to imply the elimination of all barriers to movement within the service except those which derive from the capacity of an individual to do a particular job. But in practice the listing of jobs, and the matching of jobs with qualifications, is not an objective science but depends upon how the tasks of government are viewed. Any reform must contend with the strong and often unconscious assumptions which the officials of each system hold about the nature of their work and about its appropriate qualifications. For example, the British distinction between 'generalist' and 'specialist' which is alien to most countries comes so naturally to British administrators that post-Fulton analysis of job requirements simply continues to assume the need for this differentiation.

Thus civil service structure depends considerably upon the interpretations put upon their tasks by occupational groups and by administrative agencies. Systems vary considerably as to *which* influences upon structure are the stronger, the British and French systems favouring the influence of broad occupational groups, the American one that of agencies and of narrower specialists. Each system is policed by a Civil Service Commission whose task is to control the claims of special interests and to uphold certain general notions of competence and equity. The Commission will itself express beliefs about administrative efficiency which reflect the values and traditions of the system – negatively if the Commission sees itself primarily as a watchdog against patronage, positively if it seeks to sustain some tradition of administration which is dear to its members.

Unless patronage is involved, politicians usually have little interest in the details of administrative reform, which are elaborate, tiresome and win few votes. Moreover, officials will generally prefer, however much they disagree among themselves, for the bureaucracy to be as self-regulating as possible. Therefore reforms such as the Fulton one are handed over for implementation to the very officials whose jobs need to be reconsidered and redefined as a first step in the reform. Of course, these officials must contend with rival groups inside the bureaucracy who want reform and have provided much of its impetus. For example, the application of Fulton depended upon the Whitley council machinery of consultation which, for all its much admired moderation, reflects the interests of contending occupational groups.

233

ADMINISTRATIVE EGOISM

It is always tempting to explain social behaviour in terms of laws of human nature, and bureaucracy is becoming a subject for such exercises. Starting from simple egoistic assumptions of a Benthamite kind, American economists such as Gordon Tullock and Anthony Downs have developed quite elaborate hypotheses about administrative behaviour. These hypotheses are supported with examples, but they cannot of course be proved unless one accepts their basic assumptions. However, the assumptions and illustrations seem plausible enough for these portraits of bureaucracy to have at least some initial credibility. In a cruder but wittier manner, the bureaucratic 'laws' of C. Northcote Parkinson derive their force from a similar mixture of behavioural assumptions with some telling factual illustrations.[6]

These writings prompt the reflection that classical Utilitarianism is not dead. It has been harnessed to explain apparently irrational features of bureaucracy, which are not socially or politically desired but nonetheless occur, such as wasteful forms of administrative competition and empire-building.

Anthony Downs's model of bureaucracy, for example, rests upon the three hypotheses that every official is significantly motivated by his own self-interest even when acting in an official capacity; that he will pursue his personal goals rationally; and that some kind of reciprocal relation exists between an organisation and its social function. Starting from these axioms, he produces 200 'laws' and propositions, many of which supposedly demonstrate the inevitability of high competitive behaviour.[7]

Officials have direct personal interest (in terms of power, income and prestige) in the survival and growth of the agency to which they belong. Expansion of the agency will reduce internal conflicts, through giving greater scope for all its members, and will overcome the hazard of absorption or destruction by rival agencies, which is said to be a serious possibility only in the early stages of an agency's growth. Further growth will increase the control of the agency over its environment, and its certainty of survival. Since for officials the benefits nearly always exceed the costs of growth, an agency will try to go on growing regardless of other factors (such as difficulties of internal co-ordination). Downs accepts that the rise and fall of agencies is primarily to be explained by the external value placed on their social functions, but argues that an agency will vigorously look for new functions if its original base disappears. These propositions echo Parkinson's two 'laws' of work expanding

234

to fill the time available, and the multiplication of subordinates.

Downs also produces five 'ideal types' of officials, labelled conservers, climbers, zealots, advocates and statesmen. The first two types are wholly self-interested, while the other three types combine self-interest with attachment to successively broader policies or entities. He can then deduce that a new agency will be dominated by advocates or zealots, that a rapidly expanding one will attract climbers, that a mature old agency will contain many conservers, etc.; and he can postulate various phases of agency development as these groups enter and retire.[8]

Gordon Tullock applies the same kind of reasoning to problems of administrative control. He assumes that an official will usually attempt to adjust the orders of his superior to suit his own interest. Moreover, an unscrupulous egoist will probably rise faster than a scrupulous one, because of his greater flexibility in deciding when to conform or disobey. For example, members of the State Department in foreign embassies are much more likely to rise in their careers if they devote themselves to influencing Americans instead of influencing foreigners.[9] To the old Benthamite riddle of how to combine egoism with general utility, Tullock can find no adequate answers. Methods such as performance tests and sample analysis of subordinates' decisions produce their own distortions and possibilities of evasion, although some checks have limited usefulness. Indeed, the only real cure for the deficiencies of control seems to be less government. (In contrast, Downs ends by assuming that voters must value the specific benefits which they receive from certain agencies above the general cost of government – or they would vote less taxes!)

It is hard not to smile at these Swiftian demonstrations of the inevitability of 'bureaucratic free enterprise'. If intended as universal demonstrations (as they are), many of the propositions are clearly false. For example, even conceding the egoism of officials, in many systems this is not bound up with the survival of a particular agency. In Britain, an administrator will move between departments without loss of pay or prestige. However Downs's suggestion that the boundaries of an organisation depend upon who is the effective employer and paymaster meets this point. British government now becomes a single 'bureau', prone to expansion, although interdepartmental conflicts now become harder to explain. Again the general tendency of officials to favour growth (which is possibly true) has to contend everywhere with institutional controls upon growth, which sometimes include, in France for example, the training of highly qualified and prestigious officials for the special task of preventing administrative waste and aggrandisement.

In any case, egoistic axioms should not be assumed. It is true that almost all men, officials included, are interested in personal rewards, but these rewards are pursued within socially prescribed codes of conduct. It is always a question of degree as to how far an individual makes separate, private calculations of his interest, and how far he identifies his interest (consciously or not) with the realisation of socially prescribed goals or standards. In this sense, American society is more egoistic than is British or French society, and for reasons already given this difference is more marked in relation to administrative behaviour. Much American administrative theory is concerned with problems of reconciling individual desires with organisational objectives, and with the tendencies to organisational disintegration which egoistic behaviour produces. A well-known textbook on public administration starts by explaining how group values must be laboriously constructed ('building blocks of organisation') before administration can proceed.[10] No European writing assumes such a weak public ethic.

One is therefore tempted to conclude that such theories as those of Downs and Tullock reflect pathological tendencies of American administration, which result from the infusion of competitive and egoistic values into a system which cannot offer corresponding economic rewards or incentives, especially since a majority of its top posts are filled with temporary executives drawn from the private sector. It would nonetheless be wrong to conclude that American administrative behaviour is so egoistic. The influence of professional standards, public service codes, and some degree of general dedication to the service of government are too considerable for such a crude belief. It also seems to be the case that in all Western societies, choice of career is partly guided by personal or temperamental preferences as between the social values of government service and the economic values of private enterprise; to that extent, all bureaucracies contain a self-correcting device against purely egoistic behaviour.

Moreover, the explanation of administrative competition and aggrandisement within American government can be traced to institutional and political factors, rather than to the egoistic ambitions of officials. Deductive theories of bureaucratic behaviour, based upon supposedly self-evident axioms, have a spurious explanatory appeal. Such hypotheses ought not to be mistaken for sociological study of any bureaucracy, even when accompanied by enough supportive data to suggest that some tendencies of the system are being accurately portrayed.

ADMINISTRATIVE ÉLITISM

If the pathology of an American-style open career system is egoism, that of élitist administrative systems consists in stratification and stagnation. These conditions will arise if bureaucracy is hierarchically divided into groups between whom little movement occurs, combined with a strong concentration of power at the highest levels. Conflict between individuals over organisational goals will be partly replaced by conflict between groups. The power and privileges of the highest group may be associated with a high ethic of public service together with personal initiative and responsibility. At lower levels, one is more likely to encounter defensive and negative attitudes towards the organisation, marked by a legalistic interpretation of duties, indifference to organisational aims, and lack of individual ambition.

Conditions of bureaucratic stagnation still exist in most States. They occur, for example, in the two French public agencies described by Michel Crozier, one of which is a clerical agency dealing with financial credit under the control of the Ministry of Finance, and the other a tobacco monopoly. Both organisations display all the depressing features popularly assigned to bureaucracy: routine and monotonous work, few opportunities for innovation, strong external control of policy, heavily impersonal rules and routines, and rigid stratification of occupational groups in accordance with the predetermined output of the French educational system.

Under these conditions of minimum mobility and scope for ambition, the various groups (managers included) appear to engage in an almost static war of position. Much of group behaviour is defensive, concerned with the avoidance of personal dependence upon superiors, with the protection of private rights, but not with the co-operative fulfilment of organisational objectives. The *grève du zèle* (work to rule) is said to be the workers' way of maintaining a zone of unpredictability so as to enhance their poor bargaining power, just as the technical engineers and maintenance men in the industrial monopoly keep their skills secret so as to try to maintain their indispensability. There is little effective communication even between the technical engineers and the managers of the industrial monopoly (who are also engineers), and if a manager fails to obtain one of the rare opportunities for setting up a new factory, he is inclined to relapse into ritualism.[11]

237

Clearly some features of behaviour within these two agencies are to be expected in the case of any highly routinised and large-scale type of operation. However, this behaviour also reflects the existence of a stratified hierarchy and a heavy centralisation of power. There is little effective delegation of responsibilities to the agencies or within them. The stagnant bureaucracies described by Crozier are in a sense the counterparts of the managerial élite whose direction of the *économie concertée* has won such acclaim in France and abroad.

In both Britain and France, recruitment of the general classes in the civil service is based upon levels of achievement within the educational system. The French categories of A, B, C and D, established by the law of 1946, corresponded broadly to the British administrative, executive, clerical and typist classes. In both countries, the top class has been reserved for university graduates of high quality, the second class has drawn its recruits from good secondary schools (grammar schools or *lycées*), and the third has required no more than an adequate school-leaving certificate. Recruitment problems have shifted somewhat with changes in the educational system – for example, university graduates increasingly entered the British executive class – but on the whole the differential opportunities offered by the educational system are built into the administrative structure, and closely limit the careers open to entrants.

However the administrative pyramid is much steeper and harder to climb in France than in Britain. This is largely because in France administrative grading is based much more closely and competitively upon levels of educational achievement. At the highest levels, it is the results of the E.N.A. examinations which settle whether a candidate joins one of the *grands corps* or becomes merely an *administrateur civil*; moreover, the most prestigious corps, starting with the *Inspecteurs des Finances* and *Conseillers d'État*, draw their recruits in descending order from the top of the examination lists. In a similar way, the highest technical corps recruit their members from the brightest students at the *École Polytechnique*, which itself takes the best mathematicians produced by the *lycées*.[12] By contrast, British administrators all enter at the same level.

Movement between classes has been much more difficult in France, partly because of the stress upon formal examinations for promotion as opposed to the more pragmatic tests applied in Britain. To facilitate such promotion, it was originally intended that half the students of the E.N.A. should be drawn from serving officials in grades below the administrative class, but in fact only about 25 per cent of entrants came from this source in the years 1961–3; while over a ten-year period, only 13 per cent of serving officials won admission into the *grands corps*.[13] Moreover, many of the officials who do get into the E.N.A. consist of graduates who failed their original entrance examination and spend a few years in the civil service awaiting a second chance.

The relative flexibility of the British career structure can be seen from the results of Walker's questionnaire. Over half the members of the administrative class in his sample had started their careers in other classes, including 16·3 per cent who began as clerical officers and thus rose by two levels of general class. Of the senior executive grades in his sample, 41 per cent had risen from the clerical class, and 40·1 per cent from other grades, including postmen, messenger boys, etc. Altogether in 1966, 38 per cent of the total administrative class and 31 per cent of its higher ranks had been promoted from other ranks. These relatively high proportions owed a good deal to the after-effects of wartime expansion and post-war shortages in direct administrative recruitment.[14]

In both countries, senior officials show greater satisfaction with their jobs and interest in their work than do the members of lower grades, which in itself is hardly surprising. The differences appear greater in France, where the lower grades value public service primarily for its security while the top officials stress its intrinsic value and interest. This situation also corresponds to the reputation of different classes in the two countries. While the reputation of the British administrative class declined somewhat in relation to its French counterparts, that of the British executive class remained relatively untarnished and was certainly superior to its French equivalent.[15]

It is inevitable that some hereditary traditions will permeate the selection process in any society where certain distinctive qualities and attitudes are expected of administrators. Candidates with an authoritative air, a diplomatic manner, and the right sort of cultural versatility will start with advantages.

In both Britain and France, certain schools and universities have very well-established reputations as educators of administrators, and thus transmit appropriate attitudes and traditions. Indeed, educational factors are much more significant than the income of parents (once a minimum is passed) in shaping administrative recruitment. Civil service selectors are guided to some extent by these same traditions. This need not imply conscious bias, but merely that the image of the good administrator has some self-perpetuating quality.

The considerable dominance of Oxford and Cambridge as the sources of administrative recruitment has been due to two related factors; the tradition of these universities in preparing students for the civil service, and their production of a high proportion of graduates in the arts and humanities who are the group most attracted to an administrative career. It is also significant that Oxbridge accounts for a much higher proportion of successful than of total candidates. Oxbridge dominance is declining, accounting for 58·7 per cent of successful candidates in 1968 compared with the high figure of 88·1 per cent in 1957–63 (average).[16]

The much greater pre-eminence of the Paris *Institut d'Études Politiques* in supplying successful entrants into the E.N.A. is due to its very close intellectual and social links with the latter institution. This tradition is sustained by teaching provided at the *Institut* by eminent figures in the *grands corps* themselves. Such monopolies can only be broken or modified if other universities are encouraged to improve and specialise their teaching in similar directions, and if the intellectual basis of administrative recruitment is broadened. The Civil Service Commission in Britain has been pursuing these aims with some limited success, but the French situation is more claustrophobic.

In order to broaden the basis of administrative recruitment, two methods are available. One is to maintain existing levels and standards of entry, but to achieve greater educational equality of opportunities. From this standpoint, the broadening of educational opportunities in modern democracies assists the democratisation of administrative élites. Some social diversification of the administrative class in Britain has for long occurred through the attractions of this career to poor but able scholars at Oxford and Cambridge. The 'Method One' system of entry enabled these scholars to gain admission primarily through purely academic brilliance in subjects of their own choosing, whereas 'Method Two' depends primarily upon group and individual tests for which cultural advantages are more helpful. The abolition in 1970 of 'Method One' was based upon the superior results claimed for the second method of entry, but the change was socially acceptable only because cultural advantages have become more diffused among the university population. In France, the continuing stress upon written examinations as a basis for administrative selection and promotion has also widened the social range of entrants, but the existence of a strong educational monopoly very much reduces the theoretical equality of objective academic tests.

The second method of broadening recruitment would be to modify standards of entry, and to lay greater weight upon subsequent performance. However, the guardians of any élite are invariably opposed to any dilution or alteration of established standards. The French attempt to equalise recruitment into higher administration through the common courses provided at the E.N.A. ran aground upon the insistence of the *grands corps* in taking only the cream of the school's output. In a society which greatly values formal educational achievement, a high élite can maintain its status and powers only by outdoing all others in entry conditions.

In Britain, the merger of the administrative, executive and clerical classes will theoretically terminate the existence of an administrative élite altogether. In practice, as noted earlier, the results will depend upon the methods of selection and promotion used within the new integrated class. The pooling of all generalist graduates into a single entry stream, in place of their separate recruitment to administrative and executive positions, is itself simply a recognition of the enlargement of university education. More significant is the decision to continue to select, from this enlarged entry, a 'fast stream' destined for rapid promotion. The selection of these 'high fliers' will now depend upon post-entry performance within the service, instead of simply upon the entry competition itself. However, this apprenticeship period has been kept to a maximum of three years so as not to discourage able applicants; and the entry marks awarded by the Civil Service Commission still seem likely to influence considerably the eventual selection, especially as the French method of awarding marks for the various stages of training will not be followed.[17]

Administrative élitism in its purest form involves the conjunction of narrow and privileged channels of recruitment with the maintenance of the duties and privileges of a small administrative group. The exclusiveness of the members' origins helps to sustain that of the administrative group. It seems clear that élitism in this sense is steadily diminishing in European governments. Channels of recruitment are steadily being broadened, and the structure of administrative organisation is becoming less stratified. The democratisation of administration mirrors that of education and of society generally. Nonetheless, administrative élites possess considerable capacity for survival. The traditions of the British administrative class have clearly had a very considerable influence upon the implementation of the Fulton Report.

This analysis has shown that administrative élitism is considerably more limited in Britain than in France, and is likely to be further modified. It is by no means easy, however, to balance the dysfunctions against the advantages of élitism; or to put the same point pragmatically, to know what is the optimum mixture between open and closed career systems within any society.

The American notion of a 'representative bureaucracy' implies that senior officials ought to be drawn from as broad a social spectrum as possible. This ideal cannot overcome the fact that, as with virtually all professional occupations, the senior posts of all public services are disproportionately filled from the offspring of the wealthiest classes. In so far as comparisons can be made, it seems that the French senior civil service is much more nearly a monopoly of the upper middle class than is the British. In the U.K., the top 3·3 per cent of the population as occupationally classified provided 37·2 per cent of successful candidates for the administrative class in 1949–52; in France, the top 3·1 per cent of the population provided 67·4 per cent of direct entrants into the E.N.A. in 1959 – a considerably higher proportion. In the U.S.A., representation of the middle and lower middle classes in the senior civil service was considerably stronger, but not of the working class.[18] In all three countries, very few children of the lowest income groups attain the higher civil service. These results accord broadly with the social structure of these three States, and more particularly with the access of social classes to educational facilities.

'Representative bureaucracy' can be more broadly understood as the inculcation of the bureaucracy with the ideas and values of society as a whole. From this view-point, while the senior bureaucracy cannot be representative in social class terms, at least it can be claimed that officials ought not to be drawn from narrow social and educational traditions. British administrators have often been criticised for the narrowness and 'remoteness' of their social backgrounds and experience; for example, Reginald Bevins (an ex-minister) condemns the 'academic and wholly unworldly' attitudes of senior civil servants, as revealed by their lack of practical familiarity with the problems of housing, industry and education experienced by the mass of the population.[19]

The difficulty with such criticisms is to disentangle the respective effects of social background and occupational experience. The attitudes of British administrators seem primarily to derive from the circumstances that their careers are geographically restricted (being confined largely to the capital), administratively remote (being removed from the operating activities of local government and public corporations), and politically emasculated. Social backgrounds are a secondary influence, as well as becoming increasingly diverse.

In a social system which is already stratified and deferential, the circulation of élites has more effect in introducing new vigour and talent into the bureaucracy than in increasing its representative character. In the last century, the British civil service has on balance broadened rather than narrowed the range of career opportunities. At the same time, it is questionable whether those senior civil servants who have risen from humble origins display a more effective sympathy with working-class problems than do colleagues who have never experienced those problems. This result is only to be expected in any society which complies with Burke's dictum that it should always be possible but never easy to climb the social ladder. Doubtless this situation is changing as the values of British society become more egalitarian.

The defence of specialised sources of recruitment for senior administrators is the sense of public vocation and duty which may thereby be sustained and transmitted. The question of when 'vocation' becomes 'arrogance' or 'privilege' depends upon the view-point of the observer, and upon the characteristics of the institution and tradition under examination. However, the conflict between a vocational and a representative view of the qualifications of public servants is related also to political values.

In its political sense, 'representative bureaucracy' suggests the permeation of administration by pluralist interests. In its extreme form, this concept would imply that each agency should be manned by the kind of people with whom it mainly deals. An agricultural agency dealing with mid-Western, mainly Protestant wheat-growers would be recruited from this section of society. This 'service' view of the functions of the State is in conflict with the traditional European view which sees administrators not as the servants of particular groups, but as controllers and arbitrators. An arbitrative role implies a certain detachment and even aloofness from the groups with whom administrators must deal. This requirement certainly does not imply a narrow social basis for administrative recruitment, but it may possibly support the value of a certain heritage of administrative education and style.

The case for some degree of élitism has also to be related to the changing functions of modern bureaucracies. The justification for maintaining at an early stage a cadre of administrators who are intended to reach high positions (the 'high fliers' approach of the British Civil Service Commission) is that it secures for the public service able and ambitious people who might not otherwise enter it. The dysfunction of this method is that the headstart given to the able few will depress the efforts of a larger number of moderately able people whose services may consequently be lost or under-used. Supporters of élitism stress the value of good ability as shown by initial intellectual and character tests, while critics doubt the validity of such tests and emphasise the value of developing and rewarding individual capacities through a variety of post-entry training facilities and a more open-ended structure of career opportunities. On the whole, it would seem that the critics have a more realistic view of administrative requirements. The need for a much greater diversity of skills and aptitudes in modern administration, and the opportunities for developing such qualities after entry, suggests that too much priority for 'high fliers' may be mistaken – especially as the quick identification of this group is bound to be culturally guided. From this standpoint, the failure to equalise opportunities open to graduates in the British civil service would seem mistaken.

The complete abolition of élites can be regarded as Utopian: effective questions concern the extent, character and direction of élitism. In the U.S.A., business and military élites certainly exist. Indeed the self-conscious élitism of the 'organisation men' of large private corporations is in some ways an American equivalent of the attitudes of European senior administrators. It can be plausibly contended that élitism is at least more justifiable and necessary in government than in business, in so far as government has greater need of dedicated and impartial action that is only indirectly linked to personal gain. The price for securing such men may be the award of high social status and the fortifying recognition of their special importance. It is not without significance that the U.S. Government is now investigating what special honours could be conferred upon meritorious civil servants.

We may be tempted to conclude that any society gets the bureaucracy it deserves, and that the virtues and vices of any system are inextricably mingled. This is too simple. Bureaucratic pathologies are capable of being reduced by corrective action, and even by the adoption of methods drawn from other societies within certain cultural limits. Strong élitism is undoubtedly harmful to the exercise of personal initiative and responsibility and to the diffusion of skills and abilities. It need not therefore be regretted if the older bastions of bureaucratic authority become less exclusive and less dominant. Yet it remains important that modern States should be able to call upon persons of high integrity and competence who are attached to a generalised view of public purposes. The value of a bureaucracy of this type has been demonstrated in many newly independent States such as Pakistan, where the general administrative class formed a bulwark against divisive forces in a way which would have been impossible for a bureaucracy recruited simply according to functional skills and lacking any élitist element.[20]

Even should the nation State melt away in favour of international groupings, the same skills have to be brought into play on a still broader scale. A highly egoistic society is unlikely to produce the motivations which these duties require. To that extent a need will remain for the vocational motivations that some administrative élites manage to inspire.

REFERENCES

1 Robert Merton, 'Bureaucratic Structure and Personality', in R. Merton, et al., Reader in Bureaucracy (Glencoe, Illinois, 1952); Philip Selznick, T.V.A. and the Grass Roots (Berkeley, California, 1949); Michael Crozier, The Bureaucratic Phenomenon (London, 1964); Harry Cohen, The Demonics of Bureaucracy (Iowa State University Press, 1965).

2 Nigel Walker, Morale in the Civil Service (Edinburgh University Press, 1961), pp. 170–8 on job satisfaction, pp. 192–3 on image, pp. 231–4 on criticism. B. Gournay, Introduction à la Science Administrative (Paris, 1966) p. 191.

3 Paul Van Riper, 'The Senior Civil Service and the Career System', Public Administration Review (Summer 1958), pp. 189–200.

4 C. H. Sisson, The Spirit of British Administration (London, 1959), p. 127.

5 For details of U.S. system, see Glenn Stahl, Personnel Administration, 6th ed. (New York, 1971).

6 Anthony Downs, Inside Bureaucracy (Boston, 1967); Gordon Tullock, The Politics of Bureaucracy (Washington D.C., 1965); C. Northcote Parkinson, Parkinson's Law or The Pursuit of Progress (London, 1958).

7 Downs, op. cit., Chap. 1.

8 Downs, op. cit., Chaps. 2 to 9.

9 Tullock, op. cit., p. 43.

10 H. A. Simon, D. W. Smithburg and V. A. Thompson, Public Administration (New York, 1950).

11 Crozier, op. cit.

12 G. K. Fry, Statesmen in Disguise (London, 1969) p. 130.

13 Henry Parris, 'Twenty Years of l'École Nationale Administration' Public Administration (Winter 1965), tables, pp. 401, 402.

14 Walker, op. cit., p. 166; Fry, op. cit., p. 429, table 2.

15 For the quality of the British executive class, see Frank Dunnill, The Civil Service, Some Human Aspects (London, 1956).

16 The Method Two System of Selection, Report of the Committee of Inquiry (London, 1969), p. 21. See also Fry, op. cit., p. 435.

17 For proposed new plans for recruitment and promotion, see Fulton: a Framework for the Future and Fulton: The Reshaping of the Civil Service (London, National Whitley Council, 1970 and 1971).

18 R. K. Kelsall, Higher Civil Servants in Britain (London 1955), p. 157.

F. Ridley and J. Blondel, *Public Administration in France* (London, 1969), p. 38. R. Bendix, *Higher Civil Servants in American Society* (Boulder University of Colorado Press, 1949).

19 Reginald Bevins, *The Greasy Pole* (London, 1965), p. 68. Earlier criticisms of the social attitudes of civil servants are summarised in R. K. Kelsall, *Higher Civil Servants in Britain* (London, 1955), Chap. 10.

20 Ralph Braibanti, 'The Higher Bureaucracy of Pakistan', in R. Braibanti (ed.), *Asian Bureaucratic Systems Emergent from the British Imperial Tradition* (Durham, North Carolina, 1966).

Chapter 8

THE DILEMMAS OF
ADMINISTRATION

INTRODUCTION

This book has covered a wide range of topics, and each chapter is to some extent self-contained. The last chapter is not designed to summarise the contents and conclusions of the other chapters, since in my opinion that would be not only difficult but unrewarding. This decision follows from the fact that the book as a whole does not attempt to construct a new system of administrative theories or to develop a grand plan of administrative reform.

My aim has been no higher than to discuss certain key issues of public administration in terms of a relationship between theory and practice. Many of these issues can be viewed as dilemmas, in the sense that the theoretical pros and cons of different models of organisation are nicely balanced, and also in the sense that the vices of particular systems are usually entangled to some extent with their virtues.

Nonetheless, attempted objectivity has not prevented me from inclining to some conclusions. Chapter 1 suggested that better tests can be found for judging the desirability of governmental planning than the theories usually advanced. Chapter 2 showed the fallacies of the functional and other principles as a basis for government organisation, but accepted the desirability of integrating policies across broad 'functional fields'. Chapter 3 analysed the losses of administrative competition and conflicts, but noted also that co-ordinative machinery can achieve little and become a fetish, unless effectively linked with policy-planning. The same chapter showed the limits of formal measures of reorganisation unless accompanied by an integration of professional skills and by popular acceptance of integrated policy goals. Chapter 4 suggested that there are strict limits to the amount of staff assistance which any government leader can effectively use, and indicated the desirability of reducing the volume of issues referred for top-level co-ordination.

Some of the questions about political-administrative relations which were discussed in Chapter 5 get further attention in this chapter. Chapter 6 tried to demonstrate some of the meanings of technocracy, and the kinds of bias in administrative appraisal revealed by different types of experts. It suggested the shallowness of economic forms of appraisal within government, and stressed the importance of giving administrators a broad-based but critical education in the social sciences. Chapter 7 indicated the need for balance between egoistic and élitist types of motivation in administrative systems, and showed how broader ladders of opportunity should be introduced into systems that are too élitist.

It seemed appropriate in this last chapter to deal with a number of key issues or problems which have occupied a latent place within the earlier chapters. These issues serve to some extent to integrate the previous discussions, although covering only a part of the ground. Also they appear in a sequence which hopefully offers some cumulative perspective upon the nature and problems of modern administration, and thereby perhaps helps to justify an increasing recourse to the author's own opinions.

The first section on Administrative Organisation tries to resolve some of the puzzles about this subject implicit in Chapters 1–4. The special features of administrative organisation assist the discussion in the second section about Administrative Efficiency which shows the complexity of this notion and its considerable divergence from tests of business efficiency. The discussion of efficiency leads on fairly naturally to the tensions between administrative responsibility and effectiveness, which are considered in the last two sections. Administrative Responsibility considers the place of the administrator within the context of modern democratic theories, and Administrative Professionalism returns to questions about the structure of the public service and the relations between officials and politicians that were discussed in Chapters 5–7.

ADMINISTRATIVE ORGANISATION RECONSIDERED

The fashionable subject of organisation theory is always liable to fall into the fallacy of 'misplaced concreteness'. Are organisations properly regarded as separate entities, having lives and histories of their own, and subject to ascertainable laws of growth or decay? Or do they consist rather of fluctuating and overlapping systems of co-operative action possessing only a small degree of autonomous behaviour and intelligible mainly in terms of wider systems of social behaviour? While both concepts may be valid within limits, the choice of the first approach easily leads into dubious beliefs about the solidity and autonomy of particular organisations. This may be reflected in a tendency to believe that all the intellectual descriptions that can be offered of the functioning of an organisation are practically significant or meaningful.

It is generally agreed that an organisation does not consist of a set of persons and equipment, but of a system of co-operative action governed by rules and by actual or presumed objectives. An individual often belongs to many organisations. Not only do organisations extensively overlap in membership but they also often form cumulative pyramidal systems or linked horizontal systems. The most usual definition of formal organisation is a juristic one, expressive of legal status, rights and liabilities. However, a legally-defined organisation is sometimes a relatively weak centre of decision-making and may be controlled to a large extent from other centres. The definition and enumeration of organisations poses considerable problems.

The most usual prototype of modern organisation theory is the large business corporation, particularly American ones. It is possible to study business firms in terms of their competitive and symbiotic relations with each other, and also to inquire what factors limit the growth of a business corporation and affect its capacity for cohesive action. However, this interesting field of investigation is an inadequate guide to administrative behaviour, save to the extent that cultural and institutional factors encourage public agencies to emulate the behaviour of business firms, as happens in the U.S.A., but very much less so in the majority of countries.

Organisation theory is prone to the fallacy of 'misplaced concreteness' when it supposes that organisations possess clearer boundaries, greater autonomy and stronger loyalties than they do. The theory that the first aim of an organisation is survival is in a sense a tautology. A particular organisation cannot continue with its work if it ceases to exist. The theory that the second organisational aim is growth is not a tautology, and is often, but not universally, true. Growth frequently enables an organisation to pursue its goals more effectively, to enjoy greater stability in relations with its environment, and to offer greater satisfactions to its members. Thus it is natural to hypothesise that most organisations possess intrinsic tendencies towards growth, if circumstances permit.

However, every organisation is composed of individuals, each of whom has his or her personal aims which will frequently be different from those pursued by the organisation as a whole. The willing support of most members is contingent upon some agreement between personal and organisational aims, and their support is also related to the possibilities of pursuing personal aims more effectively by switching to some other organisation; this is so whether personal aims are material or ideal, selfish or altruistic.

It is perfectly true that some organisations command very strong loyalties which can be counted on almost irrespective of the organisation's actual behaviour. This is particularly true of 'messianic' and totalitarian forms of organisation, such as some Churches, some States, and some political parties. However this hypostasisation of very powerful or comprehensive types of organisation is not highly relevant to the study of administrative behaviour in democratic societies, although it is always a latent factor. A feature of such societies is organisational flexibility and pluralism, and the absence of rigid or over-riding loyalties save on some points to a Church or a State.

At a much lower level, it is also true that many, indeed most organisations command a greater degree of personal loyalties than rational support for their goals would justify. This is a natural enough reflection of the values attaching to social co-operation and fellowship in almost any form. The famous Hawthorne experiment and other studies have illustrated how strongly valued by workers are satisfactory patterns of social co-operation, so that individual support for an organisation may often have little relation to rational appreciation of its goals. At the other extreme, many voluntary organisations can draw upon the appeal and comradeship of altruistic service in ways which enable them to survive the disappearance of their original goals, and to substitute new ones in order to keep the organisation alive. This 'succession of goals' is a frequent feature of organisations.[1]

It is often claimed that management at least has a special commitment to organisational survival and growth. This is certainly true to the extent that the jobs, incomes, status and prestige of the managers are directly involved. If, however, managers can secure equal satisfactions by changing jobs, their allegiance is far from sure. In business organisations, much of the apparent zeal and commitment of senior staff derives from competitive rules rather than specific loyalties. If a business corporation should disappear or be absorbed, its managers are usually quite happy to shift their loyalties promptly to another corporation; indeed fervour devoted towards propping the losing party is often a recommendation for service with the winner. The cult of organisational loyalty in big business is partly a charade, as can be seen from its more curious and artificial features.[2]

In public administration, the loyalty of executives to particular agencies depends very much upon the nature and conventions of

250

the governmental systems. It was noted earlier that American officials appear to be more committed to the survival and growth of particular agencies than do British officials, a prime reason being the different consequences for personal careers and status. But in any country, officials will usually have some loyalty to their agency, partly because of co-operative satisfactions and partly through commitment to the agency's goals. The loyalty may be particularly marked when the agency stands for some new and admired objective which must be pursued initially in a hostile environment (the Department of Economic Affairs or the Office of Economic Opportunity might be examples). Still the agency is usually valued instrumentally in a rational sense, despite its accumulation of sentiment. The frequent zeal of officials for the development of some particular *service*, like health or education, does not usually imply attachment to a particular agency. Loyalty to an agency is like a glove which can be taken on and off as the interest of the official (whether a personal or ideal interest, and usually a mixture of the two) suggests. In government, it is usually politicians who have the strongest commitment to particular organisations, because as ultimate controllers and legitimators of the organisation their status and prestige is closely involved. But of course a goal-oriented, as opposed to a status-oriented, politician will again have a more instrumental approach.

Modern life is highly organised, but commitment or loyalty to particular organisations is a very variable phenomenon depending upon such factors as social culture, career systems, and (in public administration) political and professional allegiances. Organisations are frequently valued instrumentally rather than intrinsically, so that their survival or growth depends upon their capacity to serve the goals of their members and sponsors.

How are we to view organisation *within* public administration? This question is rarely asked, because it is usually assumed that government consists of a congeries of organisations that can be listed and classified. But the administrative system is so interconnected that it is just as possible to view it as a unity ('macro' approach) as to view it as the interaction of separate organisations ('micro' approach).

The macro concept, although rarely put in these terms, is implicitly held by those who believe that the whole of administration should be organised so as to realise an orderly hierarchy of public goals. A macro view is encouraged by the growth of comprehensive economic planning and resource allocation. This macro approach is least tenable of large Federations, particularly the

U.S.A., but more applicable to the relatively small and homogeneous States of Western Europe, including Britain.

A micro view of the administrative system divides it into numerous separate public organisations, guided by separate goals and linked together by various forms of mutual interaction. While this is just as valid and in many ways a more realistic picture of the system than the macro approach, there are considerable problems over identifying the components of the system. This is particularly so if we attend not to legal forms, but to the realities of administrative decision-making. For example, one could apply the following tests for identifying administrative organisations in Britain.

1 *Legal tests.* This would give us a list of the Crown, numerous public corporations and boards which are separate legal entities, and a large number of individual local authorities. This test is a poor guide to the differentiation of separate centres of decision-making. Some boards established by Parliament are independent legal corporations and others are not. The choice depends upon special considerations, such as whether it is necessary for a board to enter into contractual relations over property, and whether its staff should or should not be liable for actions under the Crown Proceedings Act. These questions have very limited relevance to the capacity of the board to act as an independent focus of decisions. There is something very artificial about a classification which recognises a parish council as a separate organisation, but which treats a central ministry as merely part of a larger organisation called Her Majesty's Government.

2 *Political tests.* These tests have considerable importance for establishing the democratic status and authority of particular bodies. It is a political convention in Britain that all effective power must be democratically legitimised; while legitimation is never completely absent, its extent will affect the power which any body or official possesses. A good example is the difficulty of establishing effective regional boards of civil servants in Britain. Each regional official possesses legitimacy as the servant of a minister, but a board of such officials lacks legitimacy and hence is ineffective. Consequently, when the Labour Government in 1964 established regional economic planning boards, it created a parallel system of regional planning councils. While these councils were only appointed by a minister, and formally were to act as advisers to the boards of civil servants, their existence certainly imparted more

legitimacy and hence more power to the boards. Indeed, legitimising conventions in Britain are such that the relationship between board officials and regional councils has tended to copy that between local government officials and local elected councils, as can be seen from the fact that the issue of a regional plan, formally the duty of the board, has been tacitly passed to the regional council.

Tests of political status are a better guide to the location of effective authority than are legal forms, but they are still rather vague and shifting guides. For example, one would expect an elected local authority to be a more autonomous type of organisation than a public corporation which is only appointed. In practice, the reverse is perhaps as likely to be true. This situation can be traced to the increasing centralisation of political authority, which makes it possible for a ministry official, acting often on his own discretion, to give what amounts to orders to the elected local councillors. The official partakes of the democratic legitimacy of his minister, which is a great deal stronger than that of a local council. The notion of legitimacy is therefore a vague concept, more capable of exciting attention for its absence than of being closely weighed or calculated.

3 *Financial tests.* The possession of an independent source of revenue certainly increases the autonomy of any organisation. The relative independence of some user-supported public corporations can partly be traced to this situation, and corporations in Britain that have become dependent on subsidies have had less autonomy and been subjected to more frequent enforced reorganisations. Still one cannot make too much of this financial test or prefer it above political tests of status. Even the most financially viable corporation is liable to considerable ministerial interventions, and controls over local government services are shaped much more by the national political interest in each service than by the extent to which it is nationally rather than locally financed.

4 *Sociological tests.* These would investigate the attitudes and loyalties of officials. For example, what are the organisational loyalties of a local education officer? His immediate commitment is to an education department working under a committee of local councillors. Formally and legally, he is an official working for *x* county council and a servant of the county. However, he receives considerable guidance and directions from the Ministry of Education, and undoubtedly sees himself as a member also of a national

education service. Complex organisational loyalties of this kind are a normal feature of public administration.

This analysis is a way of pointing out that administrative structure in Britain is a continuum which can be subdivided in different ways. Administration can be thought of as comprising sets of decision-making chains which follow different patterns. *Organisational* chains bind together the decisions of a body which possesses some degree of legal and political autonomy. *Functional* chains bind together decisions which are concerned with the performance of some general service or function. The organisational chains can be more precisely described because they operate within more determinate boundaries, and correspond to conventional classifications of legal or political authority. The functional chains are more fluid because the definition of function, as we have seen, is never easy, and because they must also be mediated through formal organisational channels.

One point about this distinction is that a functional chain often embraces many legally distinct organisations; while an organisational chain often links a number of diverse functional activities. For example, the National Health Service comprises a set of related functions which are discharged through a number of legally separate organisations. Conversely, a local authority provides an organisational framework for linking together a number of functions which have limited relevance or relationship to each other, such as police, parks, health clinics, water supply, etc. This organisational chain of decisions is concerned basically and primarily with the choice of priorities, the allocation of funds, and the provision of general management services. Functional co-ordination, which is also of course necessary for a multi-purpose local authority, arises as the consequence rather than the cause of its general organisational duties. By contrast, in the case of the National Health Service, functional requirements explain the development of administrative structure.

Thus we can see that the frameworks required for functional and organisational co-ordination are differently conceived. The former correspond to the frequently changing needs of particular functions or sets of related functions. The latter correspond to the rather more durable requirements of general-purpose governments, of which the most important and complex is central government itself. The tensions between functional and general organisational needs lead to frequent conflicts of interest, and to continuous re-adjustments of structure to function and function to structure, which were discussed in an earlier chapter. These tensions underlie many of the problems relating to co-ordination, decentralisation, and central management.

254

This distinction can also be related to administrative efficiency. Functional efficiency is primarily goal-oriented, being directed towards the achievement of tasks or standards. General organisational efficiency is more concerned with 'metabolic' factors, for example the balancing of administrative inputs and outputs, and the optimum allocation of available resources among competing demands. Of course, each concept of efficiency implies its alternate. There are competing uses and resource constraints *within* each functional field, while general metabolic efficiency cannot be pursued *without* functional guidelines.

The question of efficiency is explored in the next section. Here our interest is in the tensions between 'macro' and 'micro' aspects of administrative organisation. The political system provides the formal framework, design and subdivisions of administrative structure, and political parties, pressure groups, etc., provide the demands to which administration responds. The administrative system is knit together formally through the unitary character of political sovereignty, and pragmatically through the fluid play of political forces which concern themselves with different parts of the system as occasion requires. Political opportunity costs are linked throughout the system so that the aim of one agency may sometimes only be realisable through a sacrifice by some other agency which is functionally unrelated to the first one.

Politics also settles the subdivisions or grants of legitimacy and power among parts of the system. This occurs in two principal ways. First, certain organisations – particularly State and local governments – possess an independent constitutional basis and a separately defined constituency. Under some conditions such governments can operate as genuinely rival centres to central government in respect of legitimacy and power, but the general trend is for increasing linkage between central and local politics, with national parties and issues dominant. Simultaneously, leaving aside perhaps 'problem' regions, central government appears to have acquired greater legitimacy for the exercise of authority over territorial subdivisions.

Secondly, a delicate balance of legitimacy exists everywhere between political and professional authority. In Britain this relationship is very well-established and routinised by conventions which always respect the ultimate rights of review and control exercised by the political element, but which concede strong advisory and discretionary rights on a *de facto* basis to the professional element. This relationship incorporates a rather special view of the 'political' function, which is often exercised by part-time, unpaid elected members (local councillors) or very part-time appointed ones; and which still incorporates the 'non-political' notion of control by Benthamite 'lay gents'. (The only fully professional political control is that exercised by ministers. Parliament is not really a professional political body in the American sense, and Edward Heath is said to be the first Balliol man who admitted to wanting to become a 'professional politician'.)[2]

These rather special British conventions should not disguise the importance, in any system, of the subtle gradations of professional authority which politicians recognise. The authority of career officials is at its strongest when linked with operationally vital knowledge (for example doctors, scientists) or when supported or tested by some kind of market discipline (for example the managers of user-supported public enterprises). There are of course considerable cultural differences in the legitimacy of authority accorded to various professions and skills, and major differences too in the extent to which political-professional relations are routinised (as in Britain) or subject to specialised and personalised forms of politics. Lawyers and economists often function as quasi-politicians, particularly in more politicised systems (the U.S.A.).

The significance of these points for the administrative system is that the subdivision of power or decision-making rights is very much related to various articulations of legitimate authority. The articulations are much too subtle to be expressed adequately in any system of public law, especially of course where public law has been simplified by a heritage of Crown authority or blurred through unresolved tensions in a basic constitution. But if one tries to understand (to take an earlier example) the degree of autonomy possessed by a local education department, this can only be done by inspection of the subtle degrees and relationships of authority spread among various politicians and officials, both local and central. Even within a fairly conventionalised system, these relationships are continually changing, giving a musty look to formal textbooks. The difficulty of identifying organisation within the administrative system can be ascribed a good deal to this shifting continuum of authority relationships.

Our earlier discussion of administrative structure and functions (Chapter 2) was not related to any theories of the social system; but it is interesting to suggest some connections. Structural-functional theories derive originally from biological analogies, and attempt to show how the parts of any system contribute to the survival, stability, growth or other requirements of the system as a whole. Following this approach, it is clear that governmental functions make their various contributions directly to the social system, and not to the controlling administrative system. This latter system should be viewed as a transmission belt for conveying political demands to functional units and carrying back counter-proposals based upon experience; and in accordance with the flow of this political dialogue, for steering the distribution of resources (legal powers, money and staff) among the various functional units.

In Parsonian terms, government agencies are primarily concerned with goal achievements of various kinds, which support the requirements of the social system as a whole. Of course, if one borrows also from Robert Merton, one can see these agencies as performing latent as well as manifest functions. A town planning agency may have the manifest goal of improving accessibility between homes and work-places, and the latent function of maintaining a separation of classes through the lay-out of the town. But in any event, the goal-directed functions of the agencies can be contrasted with the integrative functions of the administrative system as a whole. On the Parsonian model, the administrative system would seem to be an auxiliary or supportive device for integrating the parts of the social system and for maintaining cultural patterns.[3]

Theories of the social system provide a 'macro' perspective upon administration, whereas much organisation theory offers a 'micro' perspective. However, both approaches seem to require some notion of 'system needs' whereby the operation of some system is at least partly explained. If the social system is taken as the unit of analysis, then these needs are more typically concerned with the harmonisation of the parts according to some equilibrium notion. If the organisation is taken as the unit, while internal harmonisation is again important, the needs of competition with other organisations bulk large. Of course, the same point might be made about social systems through reference to the international competition between States; but, though equally logical perhaps, this view of the social system does not occupy the shop window of contemporary sociological analysis.[4]

Again theories of the social system are slippery and elusive, whereas since A. F. Bentley, pluralist models of bargaining between organisations have claimed to be grounded in harder facts.[5] One can talk plausibly of the needs of 'organisational maintenance and enhancement', and view the political system (seen as that part of the social system concerned with the exercise of power) as explicable in terms of the efforts of organisations to achieve their diverse and often conflicting goals through appropriate means. This book has already suggested the grave inadequacies of such theorising when applied to the behaviour of government organisations, however these be defined; but it is worth restating the position in terms of general social theories.

First and most basically, motives and values can be ascribed directly only to individuals and not to organisations. We can sometimes plausibly explain the behaviour of an organisation in purely situational terms, for example by consideration of its tasks, resources and the nature of its environment; but on inspection, these explanations tend to be particular and partial, and to require reference to individual valuations as well as to organisational needs. For example, Philip Selznick's famous case study of the Tennessee Valley Authority claimed to show the necessity for the T.V.A. to co-opt locally hostile elements into its organisation in order to function effectively. Some dilution of its goals or ideals was the necessary price for achieving certain specific results. But while Selznick may have correctly portrayed the situational dilemma of T.V.A., there was no organisational determinism which compelled a particular course of action. The T.V.A.'s goals were interpreted (in this case largely forged) by its leaders and staff; if these had been more idealistic, they might have preferred the symbolic and demonstration effects of a slower, harder course of action to one that compromised their ends; if they had been more pragmatic, their compromises would have been still greater. Further, any course of action had to make assumptions (necessarily very speculative) about the behaviour of other groups. T.V.A. acted as it did because of the particular blend of idealism and pragmatism held by its leaders, who in this case – because of the novelty of the organisation – had in fact an unusual plasticity over charting their course.[6]

Secondly, the behaviour of a government agency can usually only be understood in terms of the aims and values of other social groups. These groups will often be formally organised also, for example as a pressure group or as a professional body; and this body may be strong or weak, and specific or diffuse in its influence upon the agency (a diffuse approach occurs if a professional body gives weak guidance to its members, although individual members express strong views). Other relevant social groups are organised only weakly or not at all in a formal sense, but influence the agency through the interpretations of their needs made by politicians or professional workers. Finally, the social groups in question may be external to the agency or occupy an internal position of either a political or professional character or sometimes both.

As Chapter 3 showed, the behaviour of government agencies

258

varies greatly according to the nature of their staff resources and clientele, and of the political and professional groups concerned with their operations. The survival or growth of an agency will be judged by its usefulness to the aims of these various groups. The behaviour of an agency can be partly understood (as was mentioned before) from knowledge of its constitutional status and jurisdiction, and its formal relationship with other agencies; but further explanations must bring in social groups whose aims and values can have a decisive effect upon the policy and survival of the agency. Although certain generalisations can be risked, the possible patterns of agency behaviour are many and varied. Where a strong 'agency philosophy' is encountered, explanation involves not only the nature of the ·agency's task and resources but the accumulated values of its leaders; which returns us to the relevance of individual motivations as worked out within a given (sometimes very restrictive) situational context.

Thirdly, the behaviour of every agency is balanced between the special requirements of its particular task and the general ones of the governmental system. Even in highly pluralistic systems, the latter requirements are important and cannot just be reduced (as some theorists would have it) to 'rules of the game'.[7] Public interest, as standing for the presumed welfare of society as interpreted through the State, can be contrasted with special interest, as playing the same part for some particular social group. In each case, interest is a normative, hence infinitely debatable, concept. Public interest in its turn can be divided into its more generalised and more specialised manifestations, the latter being expressed through the activities of particular agencies or local authorities.

Government as a general system of organisation is more durable and pervasive than a particular administrative organisation, but it is equally reducible to or dependent upon individual valuations. Thus we cannot remove the excesses of organisation theory through substitution of the needs of political or social systems since these are equally questionable as causal or determinative factors. Whether a social system will remain in equilibrium or will change direction cannot be decided by any inspection of its 'needs', but depends upon complex accumulated pressures and impulses which are conveyed through an enormous variety of organisational forms. But administrative organisation has the special feature of being balanced between impulses transmitted through the general machinery of government and those conveyed through the special environment within which each agency operates.

This discussion helps to illuminate some of the familiar tensions or 'dilemmas' of administrative organisation. Let us briefly reconsider the large issue of centralisation versus decentralisation, which has been covered at several points in this book.

Viewed as a general conflict of values, one can have a temperamental or humanitarian bias towards one side of the argument, but one cannot escape the need for a balance of some kind between opposing considerations. Should there be more uniformity or more experiment? More technical specialisation or greater authority for the line manager? More overhead control or more discretion for the field official? More sophistication or more accessibility of service? While one can draw up a schema of abstract values, this discussion lacks bite and interest. The issues, like most administrative ones, only become alive when applied to actual situations; and the problem for administrative analysis is to develop generalisations which rise above the passions engendered by a single case without soaring to the empyrean level of abstract values. Administrative discussion is continually polarised between the heat of highly specific controversy and the cold of 'academic' theorising. What is needed is cultivation of the middle ground, of middle-level theories.

Chapter 4 gave explanations for the general growth of administrative centralisation, and suggested that the same causes were at work within the administrative system as a whole as within any of its subdivisions. These causes cannot be written off as a kind of technological or organisational determinism. The basic *functional* cause of centralisation is the increasing specialisation of skills and work processes linked with the lateral subdivision of clientele groups. The basic *political* cause is the increased power and legitimacy of centralised executive leadership linked with and supported by pressures for centralisation put forward by professional groups. The two kinds of causation support each other, sometimes probably unintentionally. The *effects* of administrative centralisation are the growth of overhead controls; the creation of larger administrative units; and the strengthening of 'vertical' forms of control and co-ordination.

But if this analysis be accepted, what can or should be done about administrative centralisation? One point this book has amply illustrated. There seems little point in sighing for a simpler administrative system. Counter-measures to centralisation can be taken, and some of these were sketched earlier in the book; but these measures do not cancel the previous processes, rather do they sophisticate the system further through introducing additional devices for consultation and co-ordination into the already complex structure. For example, the answer to more vertical co-ordination (for example the increased linkages between different levels of government covering the same service or group of services) appears to be the addition of more horizontal co-ordination as well (for example stronger links between the various services provided at the same geographical level). Or again, the answer to the fragmentation of welfare services seems to be not a reversal of specialisation, but the use of an *additional* general-purpose service to deal with awkward cases and 'pick up the pieces'.

What then is the justification for a modern belief in 'decentralisation'? Clearly not an abstract system of values (although these have their place), nor yet a mere preference for simpler times or smaller groupings (although the preference may have validity). The justification, in so far as it can be based upon administrative analysis, must rest upon a diagnosis that the system has moved undesirably far in certain directions, under a mixture of causes whose full effects were not anticipated or wanted, and that remedial action is necessary. Evidence for this diagnosis can be found less within the administrative system itself (although some problems of morale are certainly relevant) than in social discontents which are related to its functioning. These include the failure of administrative specialisation and centralisation to cope with the mounting problems of large cities; the reduction of civic spirit and community interest; the *anomie* of individuals confronted with a sophisticated machine that lacks sufficient channels of accessible, unspecialised two-way communication.

But if one asks precisely what remedies should be chosen, the discussion moves beyond the limits of a primarily analytic book. One moves to the frontiers of administrative reform and innovation, and the most relevant point here is that reform should be based upon an understanding of the development and strains of administrative organisation.

THE MEANINGS OF ADMINISTRATIVE EFFICIENCY

In this section we will consider tests of efficiency in public administration, and specifically the differences between public and business administration in this respect. The question of *how* different public is from business administration depends in the first instance upon our perspective. If we concentrate upon the *input* side of the account, we see that the administrative system responds to a complex set of demands articulated through the political system which have no parallel in business administration.

It is true enough that modern firms, especially large ones, must be sensitive to political influences and pressures, because of their frequent need for governmental support and their liability to governmental regulation. However, these influences impinge usually as extraneous factors of which the firm must take account or which it must seek to modify or manipulate. Political influences do not in any way acquit firms of the need to observe market tests of efficiency, unless a firm is prepared and is able to rely indefinitely upon public subsidies, in which case nationalisation may be around the corner. Business firms are not directly integrated with the political system in the way that all administrative agencies (including even most public corporations) necessarily are. Administrative agencies inhabit a political instead of a market environment, and the political system articulates demands and monitors results in quite different ways from the market system.

However, if we concentrate upon the *outputs* of administrative organisation, the resemblance to business management is somewhat greater. This is because all organisation is shaped to an appreciable extent by the technical nature of the work being done (see the discussion in Chapter 2 on work units), and the final products of administration have some, though very varying, resemblance to those of business firms. Administrative outputs can be briefly classified as follows:

a) *Public utilities*, for example roads, railways, airports, electricity, etc.
b) *Social services*, for example health, education, welfare, etc.
c) *Scientific and technical services*, for example scientific and technological research, agricultural development and advisory services, etc.
d) *Military and paramilitary services*, for example defence, police, prisons, etc.
e) *Basic powers of regulation and assistance*, for example protective regulations concerned with the safety, health and welfare of workers, consumers and the general public; regulation of competition: forms of assistance to agriculture or industries.
f) *Overall planning* of the economy, the environment and social welfare.

This necessarily crude list contains many points of overlap and interconnection. For example, remand homes might come under (b) or (d), depending upon the view taken of their primary purpose, and many of the technical services under (c) are linked with powers of regulation or aid (*e*). However, the list should suffice for our immediate needs.

The first three items on the list represent services which have similar technical requirements of organisation, whoever runs them. The organisation of a gas grid, an airport, a hospital, an old people's home, and a scientific research station is in each case closely conditioned by the nature of the work being done. The most obvious difference due to public provision is that the organisational framework is usually much broader and more complex. Thus a public hospital, unlike a private hospital, must be fitted into a regional or national hospital service, thus entailing not only elaborate lines of managerial or policy control but also frequently forms of service specialisation which affect considerably the organisation of the hospital. Of course, large private organisations may produce similar problems of control, scale and specialisation, but particularly in relation to social services (*b*), comprehensive provision is frequently a feature of public action but is rarely attempted in the private sphere.

Another aspect of public organisation is the frequent need to attend to indirect social costs and benefits, for example over the provision of roads. Of course, the action of private firms can have similar effects, for example industrial pollution, and in both cases steps are necessary to make the providers of the service in question more socially responsible or accountable. But whereas the steps taken (if any) appear to the private firm as external constraints upon its freedom, or as educational exhortation, in the public case social accountability of this kind may be built more directly into the organisational structure for providing the service. Thus the organisation of a highways department may be considerably affected by the workload involved in considering the social, as opposed to technical, aspects of highway construction with the consequence (for example) that engineers occupy a less basic place in the structure than they would in a private road construction firm. This result can be seen as another facet of the interplay between political inputs and technical outputs.

The last three items on the list are fairly rare outside government, and have few true parallels in business organisation. Military etc. services (*d*) are confined to government because of their close dependence upon the coercive authority of the State. Powers of regulation and assistance (*e*) also depend closely upon government's unique rights of coercion and taxation, and the scope and variety of public activities provided under this head has absolutely no parallel in business management. Overall planning (*e*) may be thought to have some similarity to the planning of operations by the headquarters of a giant business concern, but while some techniques of research and planning are similar, the kind of operations being planned are very dissimilar. Public planning entails the coordination of a much broader range of agencies and powers, and is directed to much broader (and frequently vaguer) ends, than can be posited of even the largest business organisation.

We have now reviewed briefly the nature of the *political* inputs and the *technical* outputs of the administrative system. The missing element so far in this discussion is the *economics* of public organisation. Economic tests provide the most usual definition of efficiency, and it is desirable to see how these tests differ as between business and public administration.

For the purpose of this discussion, 'efficiency' should be distinguished from 'effectiveness'. Effectiveness may be said to refer to the achievement of some policy goal, if possible at minimum cost but above all successfully. Efficiency refers to an input-output relationship, whose models are provided either by physics or economics. In physics or engineering, efficiency refers to a maximum of work achieved for a minimum input of energy. In economics, the notion is one of 'optimisation', for example obtaining maximum satisfaction for a given outlay of resources. The economic sense of efficiency is comprehensive to the extent that it can reduce all relevant values to common monetary terms. In business management, this necessary process of reduction is achieved through market mechanisms. In public administration, however, a large question-mark hangs over the meaning and significance of 'economic efficiency'.

In business management the achievement of policy goals (effectiveness) is closely related to and dependent upon tests of efficiency over the use of resources. These tests can be crudely summarised by the word 'profit', if we include therein all relevant business indicators about the firm's use of resources. The profit test, in this broad sense, is not of course unambiguous and deterministic. It leaves plenty of room for debate about stability versus growth, about quick profits versus gradual accumulation, or about the respective interests of shareholders, managers and workers. All these issues can be settled in different ways by different firms, within a framework of market disciplines. The argument does not assume either that 'profit' or market indicators are a satisfactory test of the firm's contribution to general social welfare, since the financial efficiency of the firm may be gained at the expense of indirect burdens upon the community or perhaps hardship for its

264

own workers. This is a subject for theories about the general value of the market system.

The immediate point is simply that profit in this broad sense provides a basic and ineluctable test of any business firm's efficiency. Moreover the growth, decline and aggregation of business firms is largely a function of the flow and use of financial resources. If, for example, a family firm puts 'sentiment' (towards its workers, customers or locality) before market tests, it will stagnate and eventually die. If the same firm fails to exploit the latent value of its assets, it becomes vulnerable to takeover by some financially more aggressive firm. Financial tests of efficiency control the flow of resources to and among firms, and produce a kaleidoscopic pattern of frequently shifting patterns of business organisation.

It is a familiar point that profit tests are lacking in government. But what replaces these tests as a determinant of the flow of resources? As already noted the governmental system is supplied primarily from a central resource tank, where the proceeds of taxation are pooled, and from whence an elaborate system of pipes carries the flow of resources in an orderly way throughout the whole of government. The flow from the tank passes through successive control points (Treasury, departmental, local authority, etc.), which successively allocate and sometimes recombine the flow of resources. By contrast, resources flow to business firms from a great variety of sources, do not follow orderly channels and control points, and are quickly diverted according to indices of resource efficiency shown by individual firms.

The closest analogy to market competition for resources among business firms is political competition for resources among public agencies. 'Political' must of course be understood in a wide sense. It includes all pressures for increasing expenditure upon services or objectives that are put forward by political parties and leaders, client groups or other beneficiaries, officials, experts and advisers, etc. The interplay of all these pressures need not detain us here but some of the effects of competition for resources under the conditions of the administrative system can be summarised.

a) The administrative system is a slow-moving re-allocator of resources. This is because virtually every division of expenditure has its 'lobby' of supporters, and no market tests exist to demonstrate inefficiency or force bankruptcy (that the whole government should go bankrupt is a remote possibility). Also resources are channelled through administrative controllers who, lacking any sharper tests to apply, naturally develop considerable regard for precedents and commence their investigations from a well-established base line.

b) Increases of expenditure tend to be more selective and erratic than do curtailments. If a budget must be cut, it will be politically easiest and fairest to make all-round reductions rather than to concentrate upon particular services. On the other hand, especially if the economy is favourable, a sudden burst of expenditure upon some object can occur. The most likely immediate causes are an upsurge of political concern over some social problem (a British example would be the sudden bursts of expenditure upon public housing) or political alarm about some external threat or competition; for example, the first Russian sputnik enabled a large appropriation to be successfully claimed for the American space programme. These manifestations of political concern are often responses to objective shifts of social conditions – for example, education or old people's welfare have to be stepped up when there are more children or old people; but additionally, new expenditure may be demanded because the public 'conscience' refuses to tolerate any longer some state of affairs which may have existed for a long time. John Gaus has testified to the importance of sudden, unforeseen disasters for stimulating administrative action.[8]

c) Despite occasional bursts of expenditure, the whole system works under continual pressure for economy. The total of demands for public spending, as politically expressed, continually exceed the maximum amount which the taxable capacity of the system (once again politically determined) can sustain. It follows that prestigious controllers must be appointed to enforce what economies they can upon public agencies. This leads to the familiar budgetary 'game', with divisions or departments often overstating their requirements by varying amounts (depending upon their perception of the best strategy) and controllers trying to cut back demands to comply with political guidelines. This situation also leads to frequent search for small economies, and makes the system unresponsive to forms of administrative innovation which lack distinctive political appeal.

The last point suggests an important difference of public from business administration. An imperative requirement of business efficiency – some would say its first rule[9] – is market *innovation*. New products must be developed which consumers want sufficiently to yield a profit. But in government the problem is more one of market *compression*. Administrative controllers must somehow weed out the surplus of political demands for expenditure as best they may. It is true that governments often and increasingly need to innovate, but innovation is guided by political not by market tests and must make its way against a sluggish headstream of numerous existing commitments.

An illustration is to compare a social security agency with a large insurance company. The technical aspects of the work are fairly similar, for example the handling of vast numbers of payments and claims. The policy aspects are very different. The social security agency produces an output which is legally fixed in quantity and quality, whereas the insurance company must bid competitively for new business against other firms. Rule-making at a high governmental level plays in the first agency the part which underwriting and policy over insurance risks plays in the second case. In the first case, economic efficiency is a question of achieving the greatest economies over providing a fixed service, in the second case, a matter of expanding business in profitable directions. Technical innovation is facilitated in the first case by the fact that the job is fixed, whereas in the second case it is subsidiary to market innovation.

Some critics may complain that this account has given a traditional 'political' view of the budgeting process, without consideration of 'economic' tests of efficiency which have been introduced particularly over the last decade. This complex subject cannot be treated adequately here. However, it is possible to indicate briefly the contributions and limitations of these new economic techniques, so as to see what differences they make to general tests of administrative efficiency.

Some of these techniques are concerned essentially with clarifying budgetary choices. The idea of programme budgeting is to organise the budget according to a list of final outputs or programmes instead of according to the traditional basis of inputs of staff, equipment, etc. Backed up by improvements in management accounting and in functional costings, it becomes possible to list the cost of each part of a programme (the programme 'elements') and to know more precisely what must be paid for alternative programmes and combinations of programmes. These techniques do not necessarily imply any attempt to value the outputs of government in monetary terms, nor is their utility dependent upon such efforts. It is enough that they can demonstrate what kinds and mixtures of outputs, for example in terms of education or health or defence programmes, can be purchased for different money costs. These techniques therefore do not affect the general characteristics of resource allocation in government which have been described, but they should facilitate a more explicit and penetrating selection of priorities by political leaders and parliaments – although the actual difficulties of using these methods effectively are very considerable, particularly for parliaments.

Secondly, and much more dubiously, some new techniques try to value the outputs of government in monetary terms. These techniques are most plausible where 'shadow prices' can be reasonably imputed to some output of government from observation of market behaviour. For example, one might measure the price which water from a public irrigation scheme would probably fetch in a free market, and compare this with costs of production. Such devices enable government, for example, to estimate more precisely the subsidy being paid to some group of farmers, and to compare this with other ways of assisting farmers or with saving the money. Whatever happens to the irrigation subsidy, this is another example of choice clarification.[10]

In most cases, however, monetary valuation of the outputs of government (other than in tautological terms of the costs of inputs) is a dubious and esoteric art, whose main use is to provide ammunition for some policy view-point. Let us take the example of education. Education can be valued as an individual capital good, for example the possession of some qualification increases a man's earning power at a rate which can be capitalised notionally; or as a social capital good, for example the training of more engineers will have a monetary value for industrial efficiency and possibly for the balance of payments; or as an individual consumption good, for example an ability to appreciate classical music is worth something to a cultivated person; or finally as a social consumption good, for example well-educated individuals may make better citizens and some monetary value may be placed by society upon the maintenance of a stable democracy.

Ingenious methods of some type can be found for estimating each of these 'outputs' of education in monetary terms, but their plausibility is mostly very low, and no adequate theoretical basis exists for choosing how to measure each item or how to bring the various items into a consistent equation. Nor is it to be expected that such a theoretical basis will be found, because these dilemmas of calculation simply mirror age-old value conflicts about the *qualitative* value and purposes of different kinds of education.

Any monetary figure assigned to the total value of education or of any part thereof carries little conviction. What might be done is to demonstrate that certain kinds of education will probably confer certain types of economic benefit upon the individuals who receive it and upon society generally. Such arguments are always partial and debatable, and (if they are understood) will certainly be opposed by persons who have a different view of the good of society and the point of education. Nonetheless, such analysis may sometimes be worthwhile, so long as it is understood as a contribution to policy analysis and not as a measurement of the value of educational output. Similar conclusions would apply to attempted measurements of the outputs of health, welfare, police, defence, and a host of other administrative programmes.

Any concept of governmental efficiency must certainly take account of the indirect social costs and benefits produced by public programmes. The difficulty is that these indirect effects are legion and there is no logical framework available for bringing them into a consistent system of accounting. Once again one is caught inevitably in the elaborate toils of policy analysis, which can be illuminated by empirical investigations and calculations but which cannot be effectively brought within the framework of a monetary equation, because any figures quoted will vary so enormously in terms of their logical status and plausibility and their degree of 'hardness' or 'softness'. It is useful for economists to draw attention to significant 'externalities' which conventional financial accounting ignores; but it does not follow that there is any valid method of bringing these externalities into a common system of accounting.*

Where does this discussion leave the subject of administrative efficiency? Business management is guided by specific but socially narrow tests of resource efficiency, which can be confined to the firm in question. The equivalent tests for government must refer ultimately to the welfare of the whole society, as politically articulated. Tests of resource efficiency therefore dissolve into a seamless web of the interacting benefits and costs of the whole set of public policies, and the internal costs of any public programme must theoretically be weighed against its net social benefits. The latter factor can never be objectively measured, and the function of resource analysis is to follow the contours of policy analysis, making partial calculations where possible or (much more dubiously)

* Theoretically welfare economics provides the logical framework for this operation. However, welfare economics is a purely notional set of concepts which provides a platform for criticising the 'narrowness' of the market or of financial accounting, but can offer no positive basis for the arbitration of conflicting social claims. See P. Self, *Econocrats and the Policy Process* (Macmillan, 1975).

expressing different values and opinions in hypothecated monetary alternatives.

Given this lack of any adequate *positive* tests of resource efficiency in government, it is natural enough for stress to be laid upon separate tests of goal achievement or goal effectiveness. An individual agency cannot possibly calculate its impact upon the welfare of the whole society in resource terms or any other terms, but it can strive to accomplish its particular mission as understood by itself. The agency will appreciate, indeed will be compelled to appreciate, the need for public economy, and it will pursue its goals subject to the constraint of trying to minimise costs. But whereas in business, goals are subordinate to (or incorporated in) tests of resource efficiency, in an administrative agency resource efficiency primarily operates as a constraint upon tests of goal achievement.

What is true for the agency is also broadly true for government as a whole. Government is judged in the main, both externally and internally, not by any sophisticated tests of input-output efficiency or of 'value for money', but by its mix of social achievements subject to some overall limitation upon its total demands for taxation and investment. It is true that the reduction of taxation is sometimes made a principal test of the success of some government, but the test is crudely applied without much delving into factors of resource efficiency. To a large extent, also, acceptable levels of taxation seem to be set by political habits and psychology,[11] and analysis of overall resource efficiency is beyond the capacity of any investigation, however expert. Such investigations have to concentrate upon discovering particular wastes or arguable diseconomies.

The relationship between goal and resource tests of efficiency in public administration is complex and interesting. We can look briefly at two aspects of this relationship – first over the procedures of governmental planning, secondly over the arrangements for delegation or devolution of particular tasks.

The ideal of a more rational system of resource allocation has taken a strong hold of many governments and parliaments. In Britain, the presentation of budgetary estimates has been redesigned so as to enable Parliament to discuss, in advance, alternative patterns of expenditure, and so as to drive home the necessity for matching increases in one direction with savings in another. Parliamentary select committees have been overhauled to give pride of place to a new Committee on Public Expenditure, with subcommittees concerned with particular estimates. The P.E.S.C. exercise (public expenditure survey committee) occupies a central place in government financial planning, and is the method for revising annually the five-year projection of government expenditure. As noted in Chapter 2, a major reason for the reorganisation of 1970 was the desire to facilitate central resource planning. Thus both parliamentary and government organisation have been extensively overhauled for the sake of resource planning.

The problem, however, in any system is to relate resource planning meaningfully to policy analysis. Policy analysis builds upwards from particular goals or problems into broader functional fields. Its efficiency tests are related to the desirability and feasibility of particular goals, subject to resource constraints. General resource planning has to absorb and order this diversity of policy goals. It is the aim of P.P.B.S. (planning, programming, budgeting systems) to establish an effective connection between these two approaches.

Theoretically this connection might be established in two ways. One method would be a hierarchical ordering of relevant policy goals (a goals matrix) to which resource analysis could be subordinated. This is the 'goals first' approach, which is sometimes possible in a particular field (for example defence) but rarely so for government as a whole. Even if some general goal, such as economic growth, could be given a notional pride of place in the system, the position is subject to severe qualifications; for example, the need to maintain an acceptable distribution of wealth between different social classes and geographic regions. In any modern democracy the diversity of political and administrative demands is such that a systematic goals matrix is virtually impossible to construct for government as a whole, although the attempt to do so may provide a useful therapeutic exercise for an incoming government.

The alternative approach of 'resources first' returns us to attempted measurements of the value of governmental programmes or outputs. Accepting that this usually cannot be done directly through imputed money values, it may still be possible to establish indirect tests of the value of programmes through the use of social indicators of various kinds as well as of limited forms of cost-benefit analysis. The aim would then be to review the order of resource priorities on the basis of evidence afforded by these tests. It is accepted, however, even by P.P.B.S. enthusiasts that this evidence about resource efficiency is limited and dubious, and that superficial reviews of programmes are of little use. Analysis of the value of programmes, from a general resources standpoint, must therefore be cautious and selective.

271

In the U.S.A., excessive faith in the possibilities of P.P.B.S. led to strain upon administrative machinery and to a good deal of rather shallow and formalistic analysis. A more selective approach is now favoured. In Britain P.A.R. (program analysis review) is the intended technique for examining the value of particular programmes from a central reviewing point, and in theory P.A.R. will function as an indispensable adjunct to P.E.S.C. The actual prospects for achieving this integration, or even for pursuing P.A.R. systematically, appear somewhat dubious.*

Secondly, we can look at the relation between policy tests and resource tests in terms of the mandates that are given (or could be given) to semi-independent public agencies. Such an agency can either be instructed to achieve certain goals, subject to specific resource constraints, or it can be told to comply with certain tests of resource efficiency as qualified by certain policy constraints. Both elements will be involved in the mandate, but the balance and mixture of the two criteria is instructive. Resource tests are appropriately applied to semi-commercial types of service which are mainly user-supported, but the tests can of course be different from those applied to business firms. This is the position of public corporations operating nationalised industries. But there is also a large twilight area of government, where resource tests can be introduced to varying degrees although policy goals usually dominate.

An example would be a new town development corporation. This body is lent capital by the Treasury which it must repay together with interest; it is assisted by certain housing subsidies and initial financial concessions. The new town corporation is also handed certain policy objectives, which typically include the development of an economically balanced town (that is one with employment roughly proportionate to the resident population); the provision of housing for all social classes and of adequate social facilities; and a contribution to the relief of congestion in some large city through drawing-off industries and through rehousing lower-income workers.

Thus the new town corporation is subject to both goal and resource tests of efficiency. There seems little doubt, however, that the success of the new town will primarily be judged by its social achievements rather than by the state of its accounts. The resource tests will work essentially as constraints (more or less vexatious)

* All the more so since P.A.R. must be handled by the Treasury if it is to be related effectively to P.E.S.C., but this arrangement has not been clearly established. See Sir Richard Clarke, *New Trends in Government* (London, 1971), Chapters 3 and 4.

upon its policy objectives, rather than as an end in themselves. Moreover, the variety of goals entrusted to the new town corporation, and the large number of yardsticks to which their success might be judged, point to the difficulties of establishing acceptable objective tests of 'goal effectiveness' (which in turn might be fed back into decisions about resource priorities). The rationality of policy analysis is improved by selective investigations and data collection, but ultimate judgements remain crudely qualitative.

Possible balances of resource and goal tests can be seen from other examples. If a government's aim were to make its official printing operations more 'commercial', the Stationery Office could be set financial targets subject to the constraint that it must publish official documents. However, this would generally be regarded as a curious reversal of the proper position of such an agency. On the other hand, the efficiency of a forestry commission might be primarily judged by resource tests of a semi-commercial kind, subject to policy constraints of aiding the conservation of woodland resources, assisting agriculture and tourism, and protecting the beauty of the countryside. A mixed set of tests would in this case appear more appropriate.

Few efforts have actually been made to unravel the meanings of efficiency in public administration. Desmond Keeling draws a distinction between three types of activity within the government service, with which are associated quite different tests of success or efficiency. Administrative tasks require quasi-judicial attitudes and methods; 'diplomatic' tasks entail the balancing of diverse policy goals; while management requires the most efficient use of resources. It would seem to follow from this analysis that very different organisational patterns and personnel policies would be appropriate to different areas of government service, and that economic tests can be applied to the managerial tasks in a way that is impossible for the other activities.[12]

One difficulty, as Keeling fully recognises, is that government organisation is a continuum from 'administration' to 'management' as here defined, and it is hard to cut the cake satisfactorily. Nonetheless, concepts of 'accountable management' and 'management by objectives' must make distinctions of this kind, and the general effectiveness of public administration may be thereby increased. But a greater difficulty with this definition is the treatment of efficiency tests. It would be a counsel of despair to assume that no resource tests at all can be applied to 'administration', even though these are bound to be partial and inconclusive. Conversely, the idea that 'management' can be subjected to economic tests that bear

273

some resemblance to business management is false. The products of government operations are not usually sold, and it is impracticable to judge the performance of a government 'manager' by the kind of market tests which can be applied to the branch manager of a business firm. One has only to compare the behaviour of the business line managers described by Dalton[13] with that of public officials in any country, to observe a great gulf between the two.

At the same time, the idea of giving the 'line managers' of the administrative system a greater discretion over the use of resources has much to commend it. It is important to be clear, however, as to when and why such a policy may be desirable. The performance of the line manager cannot as a rule be satisfactorily judged by economic tests, and often not by quantitative tests of any kind. Essentially he is being armed with greater managerial or professional discretion to achieve his assigned function. The test that must be applied to the result is 'goal effectiveness': has he used the resources under his command to better effect? This will always be a matter of judgement, since the output of his unit cannot be satisfactorily measured. But greater managerial discretion of this kind will be desirable where the task is intrinsically discretionary, and where the manager has professional knowledge which is lacking among the administrators who control his supply of resources.

A government research station is one example. The director of such a station, if he is competent as both scientist and manager, will be the best judge of the equipment and of the kinds and levels of staff that will yield the best results within a specified budget. This situation will make him more 'accountable' only in the sense that he now has greater freedom to run the station well or badly. In either case, the only possible judgement upon the performance of the research station will be a broad qualitative one, which must be made periodically by the controlling authority or by an investigating committee. In this case, purely managerial tests, such as the keeping of proper records and accounts and good staff relations, while important, are secondary to judgements about the output of the research station.

Where, on the other hand, a line manager has little or no discretion over the nature of his agency's output, his say over the use of resources must be based upon purely managerial factors. For example, managers in a social security organisation have no say at all over what final services to provide; these are statutorily fixed, and even marginal cases are arbitrated. The tests of efficiency for this organisation are fairly clear; they are good service (especially promptness and courtesy over meeting claims) and economy.

Managerial tasks are strongly oriented towards the training and supervision of staff, and towards the use of techniques and equipment (such as computers) which will minimise costs for the pre-specified workload. The efficiency of such an agency clearly depends upon good working and consultative relations between management and staff, and upon the ability of managers to propose and operate new working methods. On the other hand, the size and cost of the agency, the basic nature of its statutory responsibilities, and the comparative ease (when compared with the research station) of defining and checking its degree of efficiency, all suggest that basic decisions about the use of resources and methods of work within the agency must be approved at a high governmental level, even though changes often derive from the experience of line management.

These two examples show how different (and more debatable) is the meaning of efficiency in a research station than in a social security agency. They also indicate how greatly delegations of managerial authority need to vary with the nature of the work and final output. But additionally, delegation of authority in government is universally impeded by the existence of overhead controls over finance and personnel, which are much less evident in the case of business management.

The conventional explanation of this difference is that the line manager in business can be objectively tested for efficiency, and it is often assumed that delegation in government must therefore depend upon somehow devising similar tests of an economic or quantitative kind to apply to line managers. Enough has already been said to question this conclusion. In fact, in large business firms the discretion of line managers is often limited considerably by overhead controls, even though these controls are more flexibly applied than in government. But the major differences are due to the special financial and staffing conditions of government.

Meticulous financial control in government derives from the requirements of parliamentary and political accountability, operating under conditions of highly centralised resource procurement. Detailed control was once justified as a means of checking the probity and the frugality of officials. In modern government, the traditional techniques of financial control have become a cumbrous and rusty instrument for these purposes. More flexible and decentralised systems of financial management work better, especially if supplemented periodically by broad-ranging 'efficiency audits' carried out by a watchdog authority.[14] However, the administrative system has become entwined in its own over-centralised procedures for controlling and allocating resources, and with a series of formal check-points, none of which penetrate deeply into broader issues of resource efficiency, but still delay eventual decisions. Lord Bridges, once head of the British Treasury, concludes that more decentralisation of financial control is essential, but admits that the Treasury has not known how to achieve it.[15] This aim requires the dropping of all assumptions about the propriety or necessity of long-standing procedures.

Personnel controls represent a different type of issue. The employees of a modern civil service tend to prefer procedures of selection, grading and promotion which are clear, uniform and standardised. Conversely, they tend to oppose the idea of giving to line managers greater discretion over personnel matters. This preference for collegiate authority and egalitarian methods of management, and this distrust of personal authority and competitive methods, are part of the ethos of the public service. The introduction of a more directly discretionary and competitive climate into the public service could therefore have a depressing effect on morale and motivation,[16] which must be set against its beneficial effects over aiding delegation of authority and stimulating personal responsibility. Thus, while some loosening of central personnel management is no doubt possible as well as desirable, the process would necessarily be slow and cautious.

The discussion in this section has been far-ranging. We will briefly summarise certain conclusions about efficiency in public administration.

a) The only ultimate test is the welfare of society, which is usually vague and debatable.

b) The clearest tests of efficiency arise when a goal or task can be defined and allocated in a fairly precise way. Effectiveness (as it should be called) then consists of maximum achievement of the task at minimum cost.

c) However, even in these cases, effectiveness is necessarily a matter of opinion or judgement. Various indices, tests and empirical investigations can be devised to test the results of a programme, but they yield only partial conclusions.

d) Goal effectiveness is also in conflict with the test of goal co-ordination. How one strikes the balance depends upon one's preference between the less fettered pursuit of particular goals (which may be inconsistent or contradictory) as against more co-ordinated planning (which may inhibit particular goals and be unsuccessful). Temperamental preferences apart, the choice must depend upon circumstances which include the importance

276

and self-containment of the individual goals, and the methods and techniques available for their reconciliation (see Chapters 2 and 3).

e) Goal co-ordination is a political skill or art, but it also depends upon detailed understanding of the interactions between related programmes and their demands upon resources. Goal co-ordination works best within functional fields and becomes artificial and ineffective if extended too broadly.

f) Resource allocation is primarily settled by political pressures. However, budgetary techniques can clarify the range of expenditure alternatives, state financial costs with precision, and suggest some of the resource consequences and implications of each main option.

g) Clear and coherent tests of resource efficiency in government are unavailable. Governmental conditions create a perennial need for economy, and it is also very much easier to calculate savings of cost than it is to estimate the benefits of almost any public expenditure. Ultimately these benefits must be weighed through policy analysis, within which any findings about resource costs and benefits need to be incorporated.

h) Co-ordination of resources and of goals poses unresolved problems in government. Government organisation faces a choice between facilitating one or other of these types of co-ordination.

i) Delegation of authority to agencies can be assisted through specifying an appropriate mix of policy and resource objectives. Greater delegation of authority to line managers must vary with the nature of their tasks, and its extension requires greater acceptance of the value of professional authority in appropriate circumstances. Delegation is restrained by traditional forms of financial control which have outlived their utility.

Contemplating this list, the student of administration may recoil from its complexity, while the efficiency expert may dislike or disbelieve that the subject is so intractable. However, in government it is as dangerous and possibly futile to make an idol of 'efficiency' as it is to give up the subject as a bad job.

ADMINISTRATIVE RESPONSIBILITY

The tensions between the requirements of responsibility or 'accountability' and those of effective executive action can reasonably be described as *the* classic dilemma of public administration. It is a dilemma which has grown no less onerous, but considerably more complex, with the passage of time. If one were to draw up an agenda of the most urgent and difficult current problems of high-level administration, it might read like this:

a) The demands for public consultation and participation in administrative decisions have grown rapidly, reflecting an increase in the number of groups and individuals who expect to be consulted and also reflecting subtle changes in general notions about the meaning of democracy. Some of the more traditional and formal requirements of administrative accountability have been lightened, for example in relation to legislative and financial authorisation of administrative acts, but older duties of accountability continue to exist alongside newer, more flexible notions of consultation and participation. The meaning of administrative accountability has become broader and vaguer, its requirements more exacting, and the exact weight that should be given to these requirements more puzzling and uncertain. In a sense, administrators have more discretion, as their active members have long requested, yet the use of this discretion is bounded by formidable if pragmatic political imperatives and constraints, and the administrator himself lacks an adequate 'philosophy' for coping with this situation.

b) Secondly, high-level administrative decisions have become more complex for technical as well as political reasons. A growing range of experts and specialist opinion must be injected into the decision, as well as the widened range of organisational or institutional view-points. Theories of rational decision-making have been developed in part as a response to these difficulties; but whilst such theories may help to structure problems, they cannot solve them, and they run into mere formalism and ritualism when they demand more clarification of objectives and fuller measurement and evaluation of consequences than is practical or sensible. Still, real or pretended, the administrator must devise a framework of rational and expert analysis that can be fitted in somehow with the framework of consultation. How is this to be done?

c) Finally, the intended output of the whole process is the effective execution of a public decision, policy or law. Plainly, the number of public measures to be implemented has vastly grown, and the problems of implementation and enforcement

278

(especially the latter) have increased because of shortage of resources, pressures for measures which are intrinsically hard to prosecute successfully, and probably reduced popular willingness to comply with administrative edicts. However, administrators are also strongly exhorted to achieve positive and prompt results. Hence tension between the demands for more participation and more rational decision-making, on the one hand, and greater effectiveness, on the other. The pressures pull strongly in opposite ways.

This tentative agenda confirms a familiar point – the close connection of political and administrative issues. It is true that in theory, questions of implementation can be divorced from those of policy-making, and assigned to an independent 'management science'. This discipline may provide certain general theories of relevance for the large-scale management of men and resources under a diversity of conditions, yet the efficiency of the management process cannot be adequately investigated or judged save in terms of policy objectives. These objectives are also very numerous and diverse, so that managerial efficiency in public administration requires numerous specific studies which can come to grips with policies and operating conditions in many different fields.

To regard politics as primarily a 'constraint' upon managerial efficiency in the public services is to throw any meaningful test of efficiency out of the window. Observation of attempts to implement the Hoover Commission Reports in the U.S.A. or the Fulton Committee Report in Britain reveal the shallowness and ritualism of scientific management in a governmental context. For example, reorganisation plans are regularly submitted to Congress on the premise that they will save x millions of dollars (Congress prefers the actual figure to be specified), when plainly they will do nothing of the kind, and are introduced in pursuit of policy objectives which are often not stated.[17] In Britain, the Civil Service Department works hard to spread managerial techniques through research and training, but pays little attention to the relation of these techniques to policy-making and analysis. This is because techniques can be regarded as 'neutral' and policy studies seem 'political', but the two activities make little sense in mutual isolation, and the use of techniques is in fact heavily loaded with policy implications.

Of course, it is not meaningless – far from it – to demand that more effort should be put into administrative implementation and less into consultation and accountability, but many who urge this course ignore its difficulties. For example, it is not just whim or

279

inefficiency on the part of British administrators which causes motorways and airports to take far longer to plan than they do to construct, but the requirements of consultation and consensus-building over routes and locations done according to both statutory and informal procedures. Quite possibly these procedures could be streamlined and expedited without serious loss to anyone, and the experience of ministers, M.P.s and top administrators certainly inculcates a preoccupation with policy conflicts at the expense of prompt implementation. But when this very necessary reservation has been made, a conflict of values remains.

It is a curious fact, worth pondering, that no profession of specifically *administrative* consultants has emerged, comparable to those serving business. The nearest equivalent is those political scientists whose advice is sometimes sought in the U.S.A., but rarely in Europe, for help over complex organisational issues. A possible explanation is that the criteria of efficiency in public administration are so broad, and tasks are so various, that no adequate general prescriptions or methods of analysis can be developed. It is true that business consultants are frequently brought in to advise about administrative problems, especially by right-wing governments, but their presence probably owes more to political faith in the supposed efficiency of business methods than to demonstrations of satis-factory results. However, in both public and business administration, increasing use is made of specialised problem-solvers who rely upon a pragmatic use of techniques rather than theories or pre-scriptions. These techniques can be extended to cover broad policy issues, so long as relevant values can be adequately specified (a crucial and often disabling proviso).

The history of the study of public administration has progressed from disenchantment with the formalism of legal studies to a con-centration upon management issues followed by a return to policy issues. This development can be traced in the thought of such a founder-figure of modern administrative studies as Leonard D. White.[18] Legal studies of administration have logically been largely superseded by policy studies, because in most countries government policies and organisation can no longer be adequately defined or discussed in terms of law. The rapid growth of policy studies shows a return to the realm of ends from that of means into which the scientific management school had deposited the study of adminis-tration.

A full treatment of these issues is beyond the bounds of this book. In these last two sections, our aim is to consider two basic questions raised by the list of administrative dilemmas. First, and closely related to the concept of responsibility, comes the place of administration within modern theories of democracy. Secondly, and crucially related to the idea of effectiveness, is the meaning and cultivation of professionalism within a democratic political context.

There is no *single* theory of democracy, and Western democratic practices reflect a variety of theories or regulative ideals, partly in conflict and none fully realised. Administrators need a view of democratic theory, not only as citizens but in their official capacity. As a simplified exercise, three regulative ideals of democracy will be briefly summarised and their administrative implications discussed.[19]

1 *Representative democracy.* This, the most basic and still dominant general theory of democracy, assigns policy-making to the elected representatives of the people. The basic popular control is provided by periodic elections, and representatives have considerable, though arguable, freedom to make policies on the electorate's behalf. In modern democracies, the policy-making function is exercised more through political parties than individual representatives, but democratic theory is not clear as to how far elected leaders should be bound, either positively or negatively, by party programmes as opposed to the exercise of their own discretion. (In practice, the influence of programmes is limited.) Government is entrusted to the leaders of the successful majority party, or in a Presidential system, to a candidate usually chosen by that party; but the system is not crudely majoritarian because of the moderating influence of organised opposition parties bidding for marginal votes and ready to form an alternative government.

2 *Pluralist democracy.* This view of democracy is based on the right of groups to organise so as to press their interests or viewpoints. In a pluralist system, a very large number of organised groups with overlapping memberships can be expected to exist. These groups typically work through the formal machinery of representative democracy, pressing their claims upon elected legislators and upon the elected heads of government or their officials. Pluralist theory accepts that it is reasonable for organised groups to exercise what influence they can upon legislative and executive decisions, subject to qualifications about the use of constitutional methods and 'rules of the game', and perhaps to implicit assumptions about the need for compromise and fair play. It consequently accepts that parties may be largely turned into coalitions of group interests, and that ministers or Presidents may function mainly as arbitrators between contending group interests.

Pluralist concepts can be institutionalised through the creation of legislative or even executive bodies that are chosen from or by organised groups, the effect being to solidify the structure of groups, thereby weakening the basic freedom of group organisation. Alternatively, pluralism can be liberalised through recognising the value of 'potential groups' which are not yet organised, but the interests of such groups can only be expressed politically through the ordinary machinery of representative democracy, where they impinge through the device of politicians gaining latent support from the votes of an unorganised interest or by championing this interest altruistically. Pluralism as a normative theory of democracy can therefore only be plausibly supported as a supplement or corrective to other theories. (As a sociological theory, pluralism runs into other difficulties, for example the definition of group and the structure of power relations, which cannot be pursued here.)

3 *Populist democracy.* This theory holds that all public policy decisions should be made as far as is practicable by the people themselves, for example by members of a concerned public. Populist theories are split, however, between those which seek to ascertain the 'public will' through enlarging the role of the general electorate, and those which seek to interpolate or ascertain the wishes of those individuals who are closely affected by particular public services or decisions. The first approach (classic populism) seeks to shift key decisions from elected representatives to the general electorate, for example by referenda, and to control the acts of representatives – who in theory become delegates – through such devices as frequent elections, powers of recall and possibly mandated instructions. The second type of populism has some analogy with economic theories of consumers' sovereignty and the market system. Political man can be conceived as a 'consumer' of public services and decisions, who should be free to deploy his voting power (that is spending power) according to his tastes and interests.

These versions of populism differ between a collectivist and individualist view of public participation, and between reliance upon general electoral machinery or upon specialised and differentiated consultative devices. However, all populist theories flounder on the problem of the enormous differences of interest, knowledge and concern between members of the public on policy issues. Classic populism can claim advantages for referenda upon issues of basic national importance (where the equal interest of citizens can be plausibly assumed, and general concern and interest can at least be hypothesised as highly desirable); but in other matters, the

282

vesting of greater power in the electorate tends to produce the substitution of demogogic leadership (for example the opinions of the controllers of mass media) for the discretion of representatives, or else the insertion of organised local interests.

The 'consumer' version of populism also cannot solve the problem of how to value the respective interests of individuals in public decisions that concern them. The construction of a voting system that can fairly resolve differences of interest is a difficult task even in relation to such a simple case as provision of roads for a group of farmers who must themselves pay for the facility.[20] Insoluble problems arise over the design of specialised voting systems when beneficiaries and contributors are split and numerous individuals are involved in diverse ways.*

Despite these difficulties, populist theories of democracy have great and increasing appeal. Essentially, they offer a counterpoise to what is regarded as either the excessive power of elected leaders (classic populism) or that of organised groups (consumer populism). While these notions cannot be translated into any viable or satisfactory voting systems, save perhaps for a selective use of referenda, the theories underlie attempts at popular consultation and participation, and the direct investigation of affected interests, which increasingly figure among the suggested practices of modern democracy.[21]

This brief analysis suggests that *pluralist* and *populist* theories are best regarded as additions to, rather than substitutes for, more traditional concepts of representative democracy. Career officials normally accept or even emphasise their subordination to formal political authority as established through electoral procedures, such authority only being questioned in principle when its location is split (as in the U.S.A.) between competing elective institutions. Moreover, it would be reasonable to contend that pluralist or populist forms of participation in government are acceptable only to the extent that they commend themselves to the elected heads of government or members of the legislature.

* However, the device of giving every voter a fixed quantum of votes which he could distribute as he chooses among a limited range of referenda (say twelve a year) raises interesting issues. The citizen could then reserve his votes for those matters which deeply interested or concerned him, and some such matters should occur annually. The drawback would of course be the concentration of strongly partisan votes on particular issues. The device could not establish a reasonable relationship between voting power and particular issues, but would be a device (perhaps a rather desperate one) for stimulating public participation and overcoming apathy on a basis which recognised the democratic case for equal voting rights.

The difficulty is that the growth of specialised policy fields, and the accompanying increase of administrative discretion, has reduced the decision-making capacity of elected political leadership to the point where traditional theory is no longer adequate. For example, until recently British administrators insisted that the will of ministers was a sufficient explanation and justification for all their acts, but the notion has become hollow even to administrators themselves. Whilst the desirability of ultimate political control or review is nowhere questioned within genuine democracies, administration needs the help of theories which can supplement and adapt the guidance provided by general-purpose political leadership.

A critical element for such theories is the treatment of organised groups. Pluralist theories often assume that group interest has a hardness and objectivity which must be denied to the concept of general interest. The notion is false because interest is always a normative concept whose interpretation is endlessly debatable. A consideration of the interests of farmers, for example, raises similar issues in principle to those which concern the interests of the whole community; it raises problems of equity – how far should special help be given to small farmers or farmers on poor soil?; problems of perspective – how far should farmers accept immediate sacrifices for a better future?; and problems of co-operation – how far should farmers concentrate simply on their own prosperity or work for a more prosperous economy which would also benefit them?

The political answers to these issues which a farmers' union articulates reflect debates among its members which will necessarily try to articulate 'farmers' interest' in relationship to both narrower and broader concepts of interest (for example to the interests of some section of farmers at one extreme and to those of the nation or even world at the other), and in relationship also to shorter or longer time perspectives. There is no 'objective' farmers' interest which can confidently be asserted without regard to such considerations, and even the narrowest sectional view-point (for example one which ignores all values save the achievement of certain defined gains for a specified group) must take account of the political and ethical reactions of non-members and also of those members who deny that *their* interest can be so narrowly construed.

'Public interest' is a complex and elusive notion, partly because the range of relevant values which it must encompass is so much broader than those which affect (say) a farmers' union that is primarily concerned with prices and marketing. Still the essential problems of defining interest are not so dissimilar. Just as with the farmers' interest, public or general interest comprises both distribu-

tive and substantive elements.* The distributive element requires
successive balancing and reconciliation of sectional interests – for
example, of wheat producers with livestock producers, of farmers
generally with farm workers, of all agriculturists with consumers
and taxpayers, and so on. The substantive element requires the
determination of an agricultural policy which serves as well as may
be the interests of the whole society.[22]

According to utilitarian theories at least, a fully worked out
distributive version of public interest should be the same as the
substantive version. The interests of the community are identical
with the aggregation of sectional interests, the only and very basic
policy problem being how this aggregation should be performed.
(National policy can also be adjusted to international considerations
through giving appropriate weighting to the interests of outsiders.)
Conversely, according to collectivist or organic theories, community
interest is somehow different from any summation of its parts.

This clash of political theories has had and still has much
importance for the role of administrators. Thus the administrator's
claim to interpret the public interest seems to have been based
historically upon organic theoretical assumptions which are now
widely challenged or disbelieved. But without entering into this
theoretical or ideological disputation, it should be noted that the
administrator's interpretative function in relation to public interest
can survive translation into utilitarian terms. As a tolerably
impartial but informed referee, he can assume some of the onerous
task of identifying, balancing and aggregating interests, but he can
also be pictured as at least a moderate protagonist for certain
interests which have perhaps implicitly been entrusted to him for
reinforcement, for example national economic solvency or the protection of natural resources. Of course, the administrator's claim
to superior wisdom on any policy issue is open to challenge, but
a sophisticated utilitarian theory of the policy process could still
hold that certain 'inputs' of interest into the final decisional equations are best provided by administrators themselves, within a
framework of general political authorisation and guidance.

Whether or not the distributive and substantive elements of
public interest should be equated in some final analysis, in practice

* *Public* interest often stands for predicated rules or standards of distributive justice, and *general* interest for the assumed collective requirements
of the whole community. This difference of terminology is related to the
conflict between utilitarian and organic views of public interest discussed
below. A narrow pluralist view of public interest confines the notion simply
to acceptable *rules*, but rules imply standards of comparison unless justice
is defined purely pragmatically.

these factors have a differentiated impact upon the administrative process. Administrators have to pick their way between the interpretation of substantive policies, representing the general interest as defined by political leaders, and the sifting and weighing of sectional demands as conveyed upwards through the administrative process. Decisions are continually being made and policies revised according to this interchange of view-points, and an adequate theory of public interest needs to specify the type of contribution which should be made to this process by administrators themselves.

What is the relationship between the administrative interpretation of public interest and the treatment of organised groups? The tendency for some correspondence to exist between the structure and procedures of the public bureaucracy and those of organised groups has often been noted. The same search for a broad consensus of opinion and the same disparagement of sectional rivalries which can be found in British administration, supported by the traditional role of the administrative class, is replicated also in the structure and behaviour of interest groups. In the U.S.A., structural fragmentation and competition within the bureaucracy is paralleled by similar behaviour among interest groups.

It is unclear as to how far the behaviour of both public agencies and groups is the product of the same political culture, and how far (as some contend) the bureaucracy imposes its requirements and style upon interest group behaviour. Both causes are doubtless at work, and since interest groups are formed to press sectional demands upon a given governmental system, it is to be expected that their organisation and behaviour will mirror to some extent those of the system in question.

The fact that in some systems (for example Britain) the important groups tend to be few, large and comprehensive is no proof that the total influence of interest groups upon government is greater than in a fragmented system. The concentration of power within interest groups may balance similar concentrations within the machinery of government. A state of balance between these elements cannot of course be assumed. In poorer countries, there are usually few influential interest groups, although those that exist may completely dominate a weak government (for example 'banana republics'); but in developed countries, the variety and pervasiveness of interest groups, and the well-organised and often routinised nature of their relations with administrative agencies, leads easily to the pragmatic assumption that a fair balance of power exists.

However, the pattern of relationships remains important for the administrator's interpretation of public interest. In systems which stress consensus-building upon a broad basis, administrative recognition and encouragement strengthen the position of broad-based organisations which in return will help to synthesise the interests of sub-groups and will tend towards moderate and 'statesmanlike' positions. Reciprocal relations of this kind facilitate broad interpretations of the public interest, but tend towards pluralist conservatism ('syndicalism') and deter the articulation of minority or new interests. Conversely, in fragmented systems the articulation of diverse interests is relatively easy, but the public interest also is typically defined within a narrower context of relevant considerations. Administrative view-points, like those of interest groups, become splintered and parochial.

Thus, despite the partial legitimacy of pluralist doctrine in modern democracies, the old notion that the administrator must defend the public interest against sectional interests remains meaningful and has much importance. This defence takes the form partly of protecting public policy positions against powerful interests, and partly of holding the ring fairly among the discernible interests themselves. Administrators cannot escape responsibility for checking the representativeness of organised groups and the accuracy of their claims, particularly of course where the authority of the group has been extended, directly or indirectly, through administrative recognition. Such checks can only be accomplished through the use of more direct methods for ascertaining the wishes or views of a concerned public. Thus theories of populism serve as a necessary corrective to pluralist theories, as well as possessing an intrinsic claim upon administrative attention.

The many ways in which public wishes might be directly ascertained cannot be discussed here but three possible ways of doing so can be briefly summarised.

1 *Formal machinery for direct public consultation or participation in administrative decisions.* The limitation of all such devices is their liability either to ineffectiveness or else to domination by organised interests. To be useful in this context, an advisory committee must contain a diversity of viewpoints, including unorthodox ones, but the selection of members is intrinsically difficult and the committee always likely to be ineffective in comparison with the weight of well-organised interests. The device of entrusting limited administrative powers to specially elected bodies appears democratic but, as American experience shows, tends to create minor bastions of sectional interests. A more idealistic and ambitious form of consultation is the submission of public policies to the tests of

opinion polls, open meetings, and other participatory devices before these policies are finalised. In many countries, this procedure is now being attempted in relation to the preparation of local plans. It is necessary that the public should be presented with a choice of goals or policies that have been fairly clearly defined, but which do not include so much detail as to restrict the open-mindedness of the planners or channel public reactions into specific grievances. Despite its obvious difficulties, community-oriented participation of this kind seems one significant way of broadening the democratic base of administrative action.

2 *Social surveys of popular needs, opinions and attitudes.* Surveys of this kind are the most obvious device for checking the claims of interest groups, although (unless subtly managed) their use is liable to cool relations between administrators and the group in question. The preference for consensus and harmonious relationships therefore causes administrators to make far too little use of this obvious device. Similarly, and with similar practical limitations, surveys are useful in many contexts as a corrective to technocracy. Many free or subsidised public services cater for a captive audience whose needs can consequently be freely interpreted by professional experts. Architects, for example, encounter only weak consumer resistance to the imposition of their ideas upon the tenants of subsidised housing schemes. Social surveys of the tenants' tastes and wants can improve the situation, if the special interests of some officials and contractors can be over-ridden. Social surveys can also be used to provide information on many matters which are not covered at all by the views of interest groups.

3 *Cost-benefit analysis.* In its broad sense, this device stands for the preparation of a balance-sheet indicating how all relevant interests are affected by a decision; while in a more technical sense it implies the valuation of such interests (or as many of them as possible) in monetary terms. The logical advantages of this technique are obvious. The identification of interests can be more comprehensive than is possible through reliance upon interest groups, or upon consultative machinery and social surveys; for it can include unorganised or potential interests which will only be activated at some future date. In theory, too, the interests can be more objectively assessed and balanced than through other devices. The difficulties, however, are also enormous since the definition, structuring and weighting of interests must still depend upon the analyst's or policy-maker's judgements, while conversion

288

of interests into monetary equivalents encounters grave theoretical as well as political objections. Despite these limitations, cost-benefit analysis may still be defended for offering *one* type of independent check upon the claims of interest groups, as well as for introducing relevant factors which other ways of decision-making may overlook. For example, to judge some development proposal (new towns or an airport) in terms of the reactions of concerned publics is to overlook the value of such proposals to future beneficiaries, for example new town residents or air travellers who cannot as yet be specifically identified or represented (although one should remember that their interests are indirectly articulated by such bodies as new town corporations or airport authorities). It may be claimed that any objective attempt to measure the significance of these 'missing' interests, however suspect its details may be, is a useful contribution towards assessing the totality of public requirements.

This brief recital of consultative devices (many of them fairly novel) itself serves to illustrate the expanding democratic basis of administrative action. For example, elective representatives often are not a little jealous of efforts by planners or administrators to ascertain' public wishes directly, as conflicting with their own traditional prerogatives of interpreting those wishes. It is apparent, however, that the actual knowledge of politicians about the requirements of the public is often deficient, and democratic theory no longer seems to hold that the politicians' interpretative right is an exclusive one. Thus the range of public demands which must be considered in administration has undeniably widened, and the administrator has come to play a more central role over their elucidation.

ADMINISTRATIVE PROFESSIONALISM

One hundred years ago Herbert Spencer railed at the accumulation of State interventions, which were throttling (as he saw it) that growth of individual freedom which was the essence of progress. Other, very different Victorians such as Karl Marx and Frederick Engels were prepared to equate progress with the withering of the State. Today, a great expansion of governmental interventions occurs alike in liberal democracies and Communist countries, and Spencer might well suppose that individual freedom had vanished.

Appearances notwithstanding, one might today reverse Herbert Spencer's title[23] and claim that the State is the ineffective contender in a struggle against human behaviour, including also the behaviour

289

of bureaucracies. Technological and industrial developments, population growth and mobility, and the rise of modern egalitarianism and the mass society, have between them led to a most formidable elaboration of the agendas of governments. Major items (not in order of importance) include environmental pollution and the waste of natural resources; the social effects of technological change and unemployment; problems of violence, deprivation and congestion in big cities; the management of massive urban growth; the provision of adequate social services; continued problems of poverty and inequality; international economic competition; and public participation in economic and technological development.

Relations between the public and private sectors have changed radically in all societies. Government must itself provide the greater part of the physical infrastructure and sponsor science and technology on a large scale; it must prevent or correct many unfortunate by-products of private activities; it must police and assist a business sector that is increasingly monopolistic and international; it must manage the economy and the patterns of urban growth; it must combat unemployment and provide a broadening range of labour-intensive social and public services. There is stark contrast between the rapidly rising productivity but falling labour requirements of modern private industry, and the rising resource and labour requirements of government which are expected both to 'clear up the mess' left by financially profitable activities, and to provide the enormous variety of collective or 'unprofitable' services which are socially demanded. How to manage taxation, expenditure, and employment policies so as to cope with this situation becomes an increasingly urgent problem for all governments. Its resolution will require the transformation of many social attitudes about the nature of the economy, the meanings of economic efficiency, and the relations between public and private action. Much more is necessary than methods of resource planning which seek to anticipate and to limit pressures for government expenditure.

The assignment of these formidable tasks to government has sprung from the nature and environment of modern societies. Certainly bureaucratic inflation of assigned tasks often occurs, and many examples can be suggested of particular powers or programmes which have outlived their usefulness or which might be merged with other forms of public action. The forest needs clearance as well as new planting. However, the stronger indictment against modern governments is that they have failed to tackle the agenda of social problems with sufficient vigour and comprehensiveness.

To cope with this formidable agenda calls for increased skills both in policy formation and execution. Reform must be sought as much in political institutions as in administrative systems. New concepts of professional administration are essential but they can only take shape within adequate guidelines of political leadership. We will reconsider briefly the political conditions of administrative professionalism.

A close linkage between policy formation and execution has become essential for effective government. It is hardly practical and probably not desirable that political leaders should be recruited specifically for their administrative capacity, but at least the selection of political leaders ought to place more weight upon specific policy knowledge combined with executive capacity.

A grave defect of British methods of political advancement is their discouragement of policy specialisation even when this requirement is construed, as certainly it should be, in broad terms. By contrast, in the U.S.A., influence and advancement within Congress require excessive specialisation of a sort which undermines the effectiveness of administration through the detailed inquisitions of committees and sub-committees. In neither legislature is there a concept of policy specialisation such that members will be encouraged to become broadly and responsibly informed about the major policy issues which have been listed.

In Britain, the erratic postings and frequent movements of ministers follow and compound the unspecialised character of their parliamentary apprenticeship. The narrow basis of party programmes and the personalisation of electoral politics around party leaders further weaken political contributions towards policy analysis and prescription at executive levels. This diagnosis is confirmed and illustrated by the excessive claims that party leaders make about their contributions to a few issues (particularly the management of the economy) and their amorphous approach to many key subjects on the governmental agenda. It is true that some British ministers, like some French ones, appear primarily to be competent administrators, but in these cases a bureaucratic style seems more to reflect dependence upon their department than a mastery of its policy problems.

Most U.S. Presidents since the war have come from the Senate. The skills needed for large-scale executive management are quite different from those deployed in face-to-face political manœuvres. One result, according to Harold Seidman, has been over-concentration by Presidents upon policy presentation at the expense of execution, and expansion of the President's own staff to the detriment of effective use of normal departmental machinery. The

291

proliferation of special assistants, task forces, co-ordinating committees, and reorganisation plans goes with a failure to develop general organisational strategies.[24]

The American system of political executives in principle corresponds with the need for a suitable blending of qualities in governmental executives. Lack of experience of government is a serious drawback to many political executives, although a considerable number are well-versed in the programmes which they are called on to administer. A more serious defect is the lack of policy cohesion which comes from very diverse backgrounds and largely personalised loyalties. The 'team spirit' shown by the executives is an ephemeral thing, although with its brief moment of glory when a new President has arrived and change is in the air. Still, one has to remember that the vaunted policy cohesion exhibited by Cabinet government is often formalistic and artificial, and that the importation of political executives is in many ways an effective method of policy change and innovation, despite its unco-ordinated character.

Perhaps the gravest criticism of this system is that it fails to overcome the fragmentation of American administration. Often the political executives themselves are chosen because of their acceptability to, or even membership of, some sectional group or interest, particularly in the case of domestic, client-oriented departments and agencies. Moreover, any attempt by political executives to develop broader-based programmes must contend with the different interests and loyalties of the career officials who are technically their subordinates. These officials know that Presidents and their top executives come and go, but the need to live with Congressional committees and interest groups lasts for ever. Gawthrop has demonstrated the weakness of policy direction and organisational loyalties within the executive branch when compared with large private bureaucracies, although he does not ask (as he should) how far the unified direction and conformity found in business firms is appropriate to the vast arena and variegated tasks of executive government.[25]

These defects of political leadership, in terms of their executive and administrative results, have deep roots within political systems. They can therefore have no easy cure. It is necessary for democratic institutions to adapt their workings so as to meet the necessities of modern governmental agendas. Should this fail to occur, democracies may fail to sustain acceptable standards of executive performance, or alternatively, power will seep away to hidden bureaucracies or to some type of 'business government', leaving political institutions increasingly formalistic.

The necessary direction of change can be at least indicated in general terms. The selection of political leaders must place greater weight upon capacities for policy-making within broad but specific fields of governmental action, corresponding to the problem areas of the earlier agenda. Where a collective executive is drawn from and is dependent upon the legislature, the basic requirement is a change in the attitudes of political parties and their leaders, assisted by parliamentary reforms which genuinely encourage policy specialisation. In the U.S.A., effective reform requires a basic shift in the nature of Congressional-Executive relations, coupled with greater recognition of the merits of broad-based governmental experience for the appointment of political executives.

We turn now to the concept of professional administration. This notion is shot through with subtleties and contradictions. Modern administration contains and requires a bewildering kaleidoscope of specialised experts, each claiming and receiving some title to professional authority. In this sense, professionalism is an expression of the specialisation of labour and the advancement of knowledge, but it is frequently also a divisive force. The multiplication of specialised professions supports the Balkanisation of public programmes and policies, unless the expert contributions are firmly harnessed to broader purposes. A specialised profession within government tends to map out its own corner of exclusive expert authority, and to link up with the pressure exerted by interest groups and other forces for the creation of insulated enclaves of organisational activity. Warnings about the creation of a new administrative feudalism are not merely rhetoric.

At the opposite pole from the concept of the specialised expert stands that of the pure administrator. This individual in his archetypal form is a skilled organiser capable of handling a wide variety of tasks without previous knowledge of their contents or of the special skills which each requires. In principle also, the pure administrator can move without much difficulty between the private and the public sector, as political executives do in the U.S.A. and as some outstanding individuals do in all countries.

Looked at more closely, the notion of the pure administrator dissolves into sub-species. One recognisable variant is the large-scale manager of resources who is competent to run a private oil firm or a public railway system or perhaps a national health service. The use of 'perhaps' shows that the range of managerial capacity which one individual can in fact display is open to argument. For example, it may be contended that health service administration, although certainly an exercise in large-scale resource management, also requires qualities of social sensitivity which an organiser of oil or railways is unlikely to possess. But at least it might be agreed that the mobile resource manager is unlikely to perform so well when confronted with the sort of organisational tasks which call also for skills of a 'diplomatic' or 'semi-judicial' kind.

Another type of pure administrator is defined by his capacity to handle any task that falls within a given organisational and political environment, which is the British notion of a general administrator. Such an individual may shift between providing a credit service to exporters, issuing permits for industrial location, managing the school investment programme, and purchasing equipment for government use. These tasks vary greatly in respect of their content of direct resource management, their scale of operation, and their possible tests of efficiency. The assumption is that their one common requirement, namely the correct use of governmental machinery, is critical enough to serve as a basis for administrative competence. If one rejects this criterion, it seems doubtful whether any alternative conception of managerial capacity can provide a plausible basis for proficiency in the multiple tasks of high-level administration.

Another critical question about the general administrator is whence he derives his policies. As an ideal type, and according to some powerful political conventions, he has no policies of his own other than those pragmatic lessons which can be drawn from working experience. These 'lessons' can of course be a potent source of administrative influence. Since in social discourse, policies occupy an intermediate position between general goals and their detailed application (see Chapter 2), it is quite possible for administrators to by-pass policies they dislike (and to promote those they prefer) through drawing inferences about the significance for agreed high-level goals of their own information and experience. The tactics of an opinionated career official like J. Edgar Hoover were not directly to question the policies of his nominal superiors, but to interpret freely the significance of his own experience for the security of the U.S.A., which no one dares question. Without being so dogmatic, most, if not all, career administrators use the same tactic on occasion.

Within any large bureaucracy, the necessity exists for massive information to be sifted, simplified and filtered upwards to the ultimate decision-makers. In government, this sieving process must be particularly drastic because of the scarce time of leaders who may demand that complex issues be summarised on one sheet of paper. The selection and interpretation of information cannot be done without subjective bias of some kind, and there is little real information about the kinds of bias which administrators introduce. In Britain, the training and traditions of administrators stress objectivity and discourage personal bias. But punctiliousness over methods of presentation is naturally no guarantee that the administrator has an adequate substantive grasp of the subjects being reported; and his professional capacity in this respect is bound to be shallow if he ranges widely and quickly.

There is a certain resemblance between the pure administrator's claim as a policy-maker and those of any specialised expert. In each case, there is no logical inference from the individual's technical knowledge to his policy prescriptions; the connection comes about through the leverage for influencing policy decisions which officials acquire, together with widespread acceptance of the reasonableness (without certain limits) of linking special knowledge with policy opinions about its usage. The general administrator falls in the category of 'broad but shallow' experts discussed in Chapter 6. His organisational know-how has some limited relevance to almost all policy issues.

Vis-à-vis political leadership, the pure administrator's policy advice has a low level of legitimacy once it exceeds the intrinsically shallow levels of strictly administrative experience. He may be very influential as a manipulator of information and advice, but this is contrary to the professional ethics implicit in the administrator's function. His personal policy opinions are backed by knowledge which is not highly esoteric or necessarily important, whereas some specialised experts can threaten politicians with dire predictions if their advice is ignored. The respect which politicians nonetheless often accord to the policy opinions of administrators partly stems from relief at finding a fellow generalist in a world of experts.

The intrinsically directionless character of pure administration means that its practitioners will mirror and indeed exaggerate the directions set by political leadership. The pure administrator needs external direction to bring his organising talents into play. The technical efficiency of pure administration is much needed and admired by authoritarian régimes, where it easily becomes ruthless and dehumanised. Nazi Germany was heavily dependent upon the robot-like efficiency of administrators who claimed to have little interest in policies.

On the other hand, in societies like Britain, general administration can be a valuable support of such democratic conventions as the impartial zeal of the civil service. But if the political leadership is itself unequal to establishing specific and adequate policy goals, general administration cannot fill the gap but will only emphasise it. The administrator's task of combining political, social and technical factors into specific judgements will be vitiated by a weakness of authoritative policy guidance. This is indeed the situation, or at least the danger, in Britain.

One basic problem suggested by this analysis is the width of the gap between specialised experts and generalised administrators. Answers have to be sought through the development of more broad-based professional skills, and through application of the capacity for administrative problem-solving and implementation to particular functional fields. There is no royal route to this destination, since it is necessary in each country to build upon the most helpful features of the existing system. But possible lines of development towards more appropriate concepts of professional administration can be briefly indicated.

In the U.S.A., there is no specialist-generalist dichotomy to be overcome, but the problem is to broaden the experience and attitudes of career executives and to alter the narrow and partisan career structures which are protected by the actual workings of the position-classification system. Innovations such as the inter-agency training programme, the executive assignment system, and the Federal Executive Institute represent modest steps in the right direction, but have a long way to go before overcoming the strong roots of administrative parochialism in Congress and the agencies.

It also seems desirable to extend upwards the ladder of the career civil service so as to cover many positions now occupied by political executives. Admittedly, this course means some loss of political adaptability and innovation, but on balance it seems more important to strengthen the effectiveness of the senior civil service than to protect political appointments which have short tenures and rather low effectiveness. The present system reduces the attraction of the Federal service for persons of ability, and nourishes the parochial attitudes of career officials through denying to them too many of the top positions and engendering split loyalties within the top levels of departments.[26]

In Britain, the creation of the senior policy and management group within the civil service appears to foreshadow a more effective integration of the contributions of specialists and generalists, but the reality continues to be otherwise. Methods of recruitment, promotion and especially training continue to sustain the polarisation of careers. In particular, the general administrator has still to find his appropriate place in modern Britain. The idea that he should

become an expert in general management techniques is wholly out
of line with his actual functions which (to repeat the distinctions
by Desmond Keeling quoted in the last section) combine a mixture
of diplomatic, semi-judicial and managerial activities. If he is to
continue with this curious but in many ways valuable blend of
functions, it would now seem essential to harness these skills to
a much deeper knowledge of particular policy fields. Specialisation
by broad policy area rather than by administrative process represents the desirable evolution for general administration.

In France, the notion of the polyvalent administrator whose
training is geared directly to the needs and purposes of government
would seem to approach closest to the ideal under discussion. Still
there are deficiencies and problems also within the French model.
The traditional élite groups are too entrenched and too moulded by
somewhat dogmatic traditions of training. As a consequence, this
system is too little open to permeation by new skills, professions
and ideas. In particular, there is conflict between loyalty to the
corps and to the department, and consequently professional skills
are not geared effectively enough to the requirements of broad
functional fields. Progress seems to depend upon strengthening the
position of the civil administrators, and integrating their contribution more closely with those of the technical corps.

The need for broad-based forms of administrative professionalism, as well as the failure to get it, are illustrated by the
difficulties of government reorganisation plans. As Chapter 2
showed, a common feature of such plans is the attempt to give
more meaning and coherence to broad fields of governmental action
within which existing programmes frequently conflict. An example
is the Department of the Environment, created in Britain in 1970
to combine responsibilities for local government, regional and local
planning, transportation, housing and construction.

A reorganisation of this kind provides a tighter, more hierarchical
structure of political arbitration between conflicting programmes
and policies, but it does not necessarily achieve much harmonisation of the aims and techniques of the various services encased
within the new giant department. Such harmonisation requires an
integration of professional skills and attitudes, associated probably
with a restructuring of the services themselves. At the same time,
the department needs to build up a new 'philosophy' focused upon
full investigation and discussion of governmental policies in the
environmental field. In practice, though, such reforms of machinery
tend to be superficial because the challenges to new thought and
action which they pose are not taken up. Even such an obvious

device as a training course did not figure in the initial programme of the D.O.E.

Attempts to introduce more systematic and rational forms of decision-making point in the same direction. As has been suggested, too much can be claimed for 'techniques' of decision-making. New methods such as P.P.B.S. in the U.S.A., or P.E.S.C. and P.A.R. in Britain, or R.C.B. in France,[27] can easily become pretentious and obsessed with method at the expense of content. The result may be no more than to compress into narrow boxes the sort of policy analysis which is necessarily open-ended, controversial and resistant to Procrustean treatment. Any *generalised* framework of policy analysis, such as modern methods of resource planning seeks to impose, can do violence to the sophistication of particular policy dialogues which did not start with P.P.B.S. and do not depend upon such devices.

But when this important qualification has been made, it is true that more systematic forms of decision-making can be beneficial to administration. They can focus the attention of policy-makers more clearly upon the choices open to them between policies and programmes, and arm them with at least *some* information about likely consequences and cost measurements. Stripped of pretention, this is one way towards the old dream of clarifying the relation between policy and administration. Such methods can assist elected representatives and political leaders to stick more closely to policy issues and to withdraw from the detailed budgetary and administrative controls which are still seen as a political function.

In consequence, professional administrators may hope to win greater discretion over the translation of policies into detailed programmes, and over the execution of these programmes. But a change of this kind can hardly occur, and certainly will not be used to advantage, unless administrators have (and are encouraged to have) the right mixture of specific knowledge and imaginative vision to link policy and execution together.

Admittedly this concept of professional administration is loose and vague. The general ideals here set out could be realised in a variety of ways, and much could be written about the actual directions in which the senior career officials of various countries might develop. Some analysis of this kind was attempted earlier, especially as regards Britain (Chapters 5–7). But here a broad conclusion must suffice.

Finally, the importance of the kind of partnership which exists between politicians and senior career officials cannot be overstressed. This partnership is necessarily a delicate matter. It must guide the continuous process of government at its most vital point where policy and execution meet, and it must achieve unity of action despite intrinsically opposite tendencies of political and bureaucratic behaviour. Politics tends towards flux, bureaucracy towards routinisation. The problem of blending these contributions is illustrated by the difficulties of achieving forward planning in government. Located within the bureaucratic structure, planning units may be well-staffed but usually have little policy impact; but politicised, such units or 'brains trusts' tend to lack weight and continuity.

One obvious but vital element in the relationship between politicians and officials is trust. In many countries, adequate mutual trust is lacking. American politics, for example, is perenially distrustful of bureaucracy, and democracy is viewed more in terms of 'controlling' officials and distributing the favours of government, than of achieving positive programmes in the public interest through the instrument of an efficient bureaucracy. Career officials have to 'play politics' to be professionally effective. In France, there is also political alienation from bureaucracy, in this case caused by the insulation of officials from many of the forces in French politics. Regionalism is much discussed in France as a possible device for healing the breach between bureaucratic government and alienated political groups.

Britain is fortunate in the amount of mutual trust that exists betwen politicians and officials, which is rooted in stable conventions about the legitimate authority of the two groups. Still, stable conventions are no guarantee that government will be responsive to new challenges, and may indeed encase both participants within a resistant shell of mutual admiration. These conventions are more useful for sustaining the integrative than the adaptive values of administration, and it is the capacity of British administration to adapt to challenges, not its consensus-building capacity, that is now in doubt.

That old recipe for democratic government – effective administrative action within the guidelines of coherent political leadership – is in principle as sound as ever. It is the conditions that have changed in terms of the range and character of the socio-political challenges to which government must respond. To meet the new situation, some fundamental changes are necessary in both political and bureaucratic institutions; and among the most necessary of these is a fresh vision of the tasks of the professional administrator.

REFERENCES

1 For a useful introduction to some of these issues, see A. Etzioni, *Modern Organisations* (Englewood Cliffs, Prentice Hall, 1964).
2 See William H. Whyte, *The Organisation Man* (New York, 1956).
3 Talcott Parsons, *The Social System* (London 1964); Robert K. Merton, *Social Theory and Social Structure*, 3rd ed. (New York, 1968).
4 David Silverman, *The Theory of Organisations* (London, 1970). I am indebted to this author for a useful critique of 'system needs' and summary of the social interaction theory of organisation accepted here.
5 A. F. Bentley, *The Process of Government* (Chicago, 1908).
6 Philip Selznick, *T.V.A. and the Grass Roots* (Berkeley, 1949).
7 David Truman, *The Governmental Process* (New York, 1951).
8 John Gaus, *Reflections on Public Administration* (University of Alabama, 1947), Ch. 1.
9 Peter Drucker, *The Practice of Management* (London, 1955) pp. 29–32.
10 Charles L. Schultze, *The Politics and Economics of Public Spending* (Washington, Brookings Institution, 1968), Chaps. 4 and 5.
11 See, for example, Alan T. Peacock, 'Economic Analysis and Government Expenditure Control', in A. T. Peacock and D. J. Robertson (eds), *Public Expenditure: Appraisal and Control* (Edinburgh, 1963).
12 Desmond Keeling, *Management in Government* (London, 1972).
13 M. Dalton, *Men Who Manage* (New York, 1959).
14 E. L. Normanton, *The Accountability and Audit of Governments* (Manchester University Press, 1966).
15 Lord Bridges, *The Treasury* (London, 1964), pp. 205–6.
16 R. G. S. Brown, *The Administrative Process in Britain* (London, 1970), Chap. 14.
17 Harold Seidman, *Politics, Position and Power* (New York, 1970), Chap. 3.
18 Herbert J. Storing, 'Leonard D. White and the Study of Public Administration', *Public Administration Review* (March 1965).
19 For an interesting analysis, see Robert A. Dahl, *A Preface to Democratic Theory* (Chicago, 1956).
20 James M. Buchanan and Gordon Tullock, *The Calculus of Consent* (Ann Arbor, Michigan, 1962).
21 See Buchanan and Tullock, op. cit., and Anthony Downs, *An An Economic Theory of Democracy* (Stanford, 1956).
22 For fuller discussion of the public interest in agriculture, see P. Self and H. Storing, *The State and the Farmer* (London, 1962), Chap. 10.
23 Herbert Spencer, *The Man Versus the State* (London, 1884, republished 1969).
24 Harold Seidman, op. cit., Chaps. 3, 6 and 9.
25 Louis C. Gawthrop, *Bureaucratic Behaviour in the Executive Branch* (London, 1969).
26 Gawthrop, op. cit., pp. 224–7 for career planning, and Chapter 6 for organisational loyalties.
27 For R.C.B., see Philippe Huet, 'The Rationalisation of Budget Choices in France', *Public Administration* (Autumn 1970).

A SHORT NOTE ON FURTHER READING

Full references to sources have been given after each chapter, and the purpose of this Note is to offer a brief guide to some books which are useful for relating theories to practice.

1 *Guide to Subjects*
a) For theories and criticisms of scientific administration, start with L. Gulick and L. F. Urwick, *Papers on the Science of Administration* (New York, 1937); Chester Barnard, *The Functions of the Executive* (Cambridge, Mass., 1964); Herbert Simon, *Administrative Behaviour*, 2nd ed. (New York, 1957).
b) For the sociology of organisation, see P. M. Blau and W. R. Scott, *Formal Organisations* (London, 1963); A. Etzioni, *Modern Organisations* (Englewood Cliffs, New Jersey, 1964) and *Complex Organisations: A Sociological Reader* (New York, 1961); J. C. March and H. A. Simon, *Organisations* (New York, 1958); D. Silverman, *The Theory of Organisations* (London, 1970).
c) For theories of bureaucracy, see P. M. Blau, *Bureaucracy in Modern Society* (New York, 1959); N. P. Mouzelis, *Organisation and Bureaucracy* (London, 1967); A. Downs, *Inside Bureaucracy* (Boston, 1967); Victor A. Thompson, *Modern Organisation* (New York, 1961); Jean Meynaud, *Technocracy* (London, 1968).
d) For general views of organisation, see B. Gross, *Organisations and their Managing* (New York, 1968), and K. Boulding, *The Organisational Revolution* (New York, 1953).
e) For the policy process, see D. Braybrooke and C. E. Lindblom, *A Strategy of Decision* (New York, 1963); Sir G. Vickers, *The Art of Judgement* (London, 1965); Y. Dror, *Public Policymaking Re-Examined* (San Francisco, 1968).
f) For British administration, see W. J. M. Mackenzie and J. W. Grove, *Central Administration in Britain* (London, 1957); D. N. Chester and F. M. G. Willson, *The Organisation of British Central Government* (London, 1957); Sir Richard Clarke, *New Trends in Government* (London, 1971).
g) For American administration, see J. D. Millett, *Government and Public Administration* (New York, 1959); P. Woll, *American Bureaucracy* (New York, 1963); H. Seidman, *Politics, Position and Power* (New York, 1970).
h) For French administration, see F. F. Ridley and J. Blondel, *Public Administration in France* (London, 1964); B. Gournay,

301

Introduction à la Science Administrative (Paris, 1966); M. Anderson, *Government in France* (Oxford, 1970).

i) For comparative studies, see F. M. Marx, *Elements of Public Administration* (New York, 1946); Brian Chapman, *The Profession of Government* (London, 1959); F. Heady, *Public Administration, A Comparative Perspective* (Englewood Cliffs, New Jersey, 1966).

j) For readings on administrative issues, see D. Waldo, *Ideas and Issues in Public Administration* (New York, 1953); D. C. Rowat, *Basic Issues in Public Administration* (New York, 1961); Richard A. Chapman and A. Dunsire (eds), *Style in Administration: Readings in British Public Administration* (London, 1971).

k) For some selections of case studies, see H. Stein, *Public Administration and Policy Development* (New York, 1952); *Administrators in Action*, Vol. 1 edited by F. M. G. Willson and Vol. 2 edited by G. Rhodes (London, 1961 and 1965); B. B. Schaffer and D. C. Corbett, *Decisions* (Melbourne, 1966). The last deals with Australian cases.

2 *Books Meriting Special Mention*

a) P. Meyer, *Administrative Organisations* (Copenhagen, 1957) offers a classification of types of agency and administrative relations.

b) J. D. Millett, *Organisation for the Public Service* (Princeton, New Jersey, 1966) applies theories of organisation to the special circumstances of government; a useful short book.

c) J. W. Fesler, *Area and Administration* (Alabama, 1949) is a good example of the careful analytic treatment of an administrative issue.

d) R. G. S. Brown, *The Administrative Process in Britain* (London, 1970) relates some administrative theories to aspects of British administration.

e) L. C. Gawthrop, *Bureaucratic Behaviour in the Executive Branch* (New York, 1969), relates some general theories of bureaucracy to the operations of the U.S. Federal Government.

f) M. Crozier, *The Bureaucratic Phenomenon* (London, 1964) relates theories of bureaucracy to the cultural conditions of French administration.

g) R. J. S. Baker, *Administrative Theory and Public Administration* (London, 1972) also relates administrative theories to British administration.

h) C. D. Keeling, *Management in Government* (London, 1972) offers an interesting analysis of the tasks of administrators.

i) A. Dunsire, *Administration: the Word and the Science* (London, 1973) gives a useful historical review of the meanings and study of administration.

j) M. J. Hill, *The Sociology of Public Administration* (London, 1972) is a good introduction to this subject, with British examples.

k) B. Schaffer, *The Administrative Factor* (London, 1973) provides fascinating insights into many aspects of public administration.

Index

Administration: and management 180–1, 215–6, 273–6; and politics 149–52; distinguished from planning 31–3

Administrative appraisal 192–3: and economics 209–15; and training 215–21; in France 197–8; in U.K. 195–7; in U.S.A. 198–9; pathologies of 204–9; problems of 200–4

Administrative class: see under General Administrators

Administrative conflict: analysis of 107–9; and policy conflicts 103–5; and use of resources 104–5; over water resources 102; values of 87–92; see also Competition between agencies

Administrative co-ordination: conflict between functional and managerial aspects 81–5, 254–5; methods of 47–8; opposed to 'goal effectiveness' 90–2; relation to work unit 73; use of committees 105–6; see also Co-ordinating agencies

Administrative efficiency 255, 261–77

Administrative élites 183–4, 237, 241–2, 243–5

Administrative organisation: and functions 77–85; and policy goals 64–76; and organisation theories 248–61; and the social system 256–9; reform of 82–4, 109–19; special features of 73, 251–5; see also Centralisation, Management theories

Administrative politics 152, 154, 255–6

Administrative training 168, 215–21, 239–41

Agency independence: greatest extent of 98–9; influences upon 93–8; political reasons for 96–7; pressures 80–1; values of 90–2

Agency philosophy 92–9, 251, 259

Agriculture, Department of (U.S.A.) 70, 209

Agriculture, Ministry of (U.K.) 62–3

Agriculture, organisation of 62–3, 70

Airport planning 44–8, 202n., 212

Allocation of functions: evolution of 60–1, 63–4; influence of agency philosophy 95–6; influence of work units 72–3; related to political systems 58–60; relation to types of control 61–3; review of principles 55–8

American Federal Government: competition between agencies 100–3, 105–6; co-ordinating (staff) agencies 125–8; defence reorganisation 114–5; financial aid to localities 101, 160–1; interest groups 89–90, 94–5, 155–7, 243; 'substitute administration' 109; see also Civil Service (U.S.A.), Presidency, and titles of agencies

Area principle, 55–6, 79–80, 118

Armstrong, Sir William 174–5

Army Corps of Engineers (U.S.A.) 74–5, 102, 127, 209

Association of First Division Civil Servants (U.K.) 195

Attlee, Clement (Prime Minister) 142

Aviation, organisation of 61

Baker, R. J. S. 51

Banfield, E. 158

Barnard, C. 65

Beer, S. 133, 134, 156

Blau, P. and Scott, W. R. 52

Board of Trade (U.K.) 61, 94, 95, 104

Braybrooke, D. 39–44, 52

Brech, E. 122

Bridges, Lord 32, 134, 179–80, 202, 276

British Broadcasting Corporation 98

British Government:
allocation of functions 58–64
avoidance of duplication 99–100
co-ordinating machinery 106, 128–35, 139–40
creation of giant departments 82–4
defence reorganisation 114–5
health reorganisation 111–3
independent agencies 96–8
methods of delegation 109
see also Civil Service (U.K.) and titles of departments
British Medical Association 111, 112
Brown, R. G. S. 152
Budgeting: in British government 132–5; in U.S.A. government 41–4; results of 265–7; techniques of 133–5, 267–72; theories of 41–4; *see also* Bureau of the Budget, Treasury
Bureau of Reclamation (U.S.A.) 102, 127
Bureaucratic self-regulation 179, 226–7, 233
Bureaucracy: and policy-making 153–8, 184–6; and political control 158–62, 182–4; and political systems 186–90; dysfunctions of 204–9, 224–5, 237–8; motivations in 225–8, 229–30, 234–6; representative 228–9, 230, 242–4
Bureaucratic laws 234–7
Bureaupathology 204–6
Bureau chiefs 172, 181, 198
Bureau of the Budget (U.S.A.) 41–2, 126, 128, 133–4
Buron, R. 176
Business behaviour: 249–50, 262, 264–5, 266–7, 274, 279–80 *see also* Government and business

Cabinet government: comparison with Presidential system 143–4; effects on allocation of work 59–60; methods of co-ordination 128–32
Cabinet Secretariat (U.K.) 21, 130, 131
Career officials: *see under* Civil Service, Politicians and career officials

Central Policy Review Staff (C.P.R.S.) U.K. 132
Centralisation: delegation of powers 108–9; reasons for 135–8, related to airport location 44–8; review of 260–1; Simon's views 35–6
Centre for Administrative Studies (U.K.) 218–19
Chester, D. N. and Willson, F. M. G. 59, 64
Chicago Housing Authority case study 37–8
Chief executives in government: capacity to make decisions 141–5; comparison with business executives 144; use and limits of personal assistance 121–5; *see also* Ministers, Presidency and Prime Minister
Children's Bureau (U.S.A.) 56
Civil Service (France) 166–9, 176–81, 185–6, 188, 197–8, 206, 238–42, 297, 299
Civil Service (U.K.) 163–6, 174–82, 183–4, 195–7, 201–4, 206, 208, 227, 230–3, 238–45, 296–7, 299
Civil Service (U.S.A.) 169–74, 187–90, 198–9, 206, 208–9, 236, 228–32, 242, 296, 299
Civil Service: *see also* Administrative training, Experts, General administrators, Politicians and career officials
Civil Service College 196, 219
Civil Service Commission (U.K.) 164, 233, 240–1, 243
Civil Service Commission (U.S.A.) 126, 171, 229, 233
Civil Service Department (U.K.), 140, 279
Clarke, Sir Richard 84, 140, 272n
Classless civil service 232–3, 241
Client principle 56, 61, 58, 62, 78–80, 82, 89, 94–6, 111, 118
Cohen, H. 224
Commisariat du Plan (France) 157
Committee on Administrative Management (U.S.A.) 20, 125, 126
Competition between agencies: compared with business competition 102; distinguished from conflict

87; influenced by systems and values 87–90; in the U.S.A. 101–3; relation to agency independence 90–92; *see also* Administrative conflict

Concorde, appraisal of 210

Congress (U.S.A.): and budgeting 41–3; and civil servants 169–70, 172, 188, 198, 232; and defence of agencies 100; influence of members 155

Co-ordinating agencies: in British government 139–40; in French government 138–9; in U.S.A. government 121, 125–8; location in different systems 145; purposes 135–8; under Cabinet government 128, 129–30, 132; *see also* Administrative co-ordination

Co-ordinating Ministers 130

'Co-ordination by ideas' 28

Cost-benefit analysis 33–4, 44, 212–13, 268–70, 271, 288–9

Counterpart units 128

Crichel Down case 159

Crozier, M. 224, 237–8

Dale, H. E. 183–4

de Gaulle, Charles (President) 142, 188

Decision-making:
and administrative methods 200–4
and appraisal 192–3
and economics 33–4
and marginal incrementalism 39–41
and planning 31–3
and rationality 34–7
models of 29–31, 34–8
see also Policy-making

Defence, Department of (U.S.A.) 114–5, 228

Defence, Ministry of (U.K.) 40, 114–5

Defence reorganisation 113–5, 118

Democratic theories 281–9

Departmentalism, *see under* Agency independence, Agency philosophy

Downs, A. 87, 234–5, 236

Dror, Y. 38

Ecole Nationale d'Administration (E.N.A.) 168, 218, 219, 238–9, 242

Economic Affairs, Department of (U.K.) 61, 99–100, 103, 140, 251

Economic and Social Council (France) 157

Economic affairs, organisation of 61, 157–8

Economists: as administrative critics 203, as policy advisors 211–5

Education 57, 62, 67–8, 69, 268–9

Environment, Department of (U.K.) 297

Environmental planning:
central supervision of 71
conflicts over industrial location 104
co-ordination with traffic planning 115–6
in London 108, 116
qualification of planners 207
treatment of appeals 175

Esprit de corps 108–9

Executive office of the President (U.S.A.) 126–7, 139

Experts: as controllers 200–1; and policy-making 194, 206–9; conflicts among 209; power of 208–9; relations with generalists 195–9, 204–6, 296–7

Factory Inspectorate (U.K.) 60

Fayol, H. 24, 121, 122, 186

Federal Executive Institute (U.S.A.) 220–1, 296

Field workers: conflicts with controllers 74–5

Finance, Ministry of (France) 139, 177, 178, 211, 237

Forestry Service 208–9

French Government: co-ordinating machinery 128–9, 138–9; economic planning 157–8; public agencies 237–8; *see also* Civil Service (France) and titles of agencies

Fulton Committee, 29, 51, 140, 178, 180, 196, 232–3, 241, 272–3, 279

Functional duplication: in U.K. 99–100; in U.S.A. 100–3
Functional principle 56–8, 82

Gawthrop, L. 14, 189, 292
General administrators:
American proposals for 174, 229
and experts 195–9, 202, 204–6, 296–7
and politicians 163–9, 180–1, 183–6
as policy-makers 294–6
comparisons between France and Britain 168–9, 176–7, 181, 238–42
interpretation of public interest 177–9, 285–7
managerial role 180–2, 293–4
methods of appraisal 201–4
recruitment and promotion 230–1, 232–3, 238–42, 243–5
style of control 134, 174–80, 195–6
unspecialised nature 63, 163–4, 166, 181–2, 196
see also Administrative training, Ministers
General staff (military) 122–3
Giant departments 82–4, 132, 140, 297–8
'Goal effectiveness' 80–1, 90–1, 264, 270
Goals: and administrative conflicts 103; and resources 270–5; as basis for organisation 64–72; meaning of 67, 75–6; see also Policy-making, 'Goal effectiveness'
Government and business compared: their behaviour 249, 250–1; their efficiency 264–7; their inputs and outputs 261–4; their overhead controls 275–6
Government functions: and administrative structure 77–85; described 262–4; growth of 289–91
Grands corps 168, 177, 181, 184, 238, 240, 241
Greater London Council 108, 116, 118

Gulick, L. 19, 21, 50, 55, 58, 121, 122, 123, 124, 130

Haldane Committee Report 20, 55, 56, 64
Health services, organisation of 111–3, 118, 254
Heath, Edward (Prime Minister) 132, 256
Hierarchy: as unrealistic view of government 142–4; and staff and line theories 121, 122–3, 145; conflict with specialisation 22–5, 204–6; defective 121; relation to goal-setting 65–6, 69–72
Home Office (U.K.) 64, 95–6
Hoover Commissions 20, 127, 145, 229, 279
Hoover, J. Edgar. 294
Housing and Local Government, Ministry of (U.K.) 71, 115
Human relations school 48, 50

Imperial Chemical Industries (I.C.I.) 25–6, 27–8
Independent Regulating Commissions (U.S.A.) 97
Institut d'Etudes Politiques (Paris) 168, 218, 240
Integrated hierarchies 196
Interest groups 155–7, 258–9, 281–2, 284–7; see also Client principle
Interior, Department of the (U.S.A.) 57, 68

Johnson, L. B. (President) 106

Keeling, C. D. 273–4

Legislative-executive relations 161, 188–9, 293
Lindblom, C. 39–44, 50, 52
Line managers 274–6
Local government: conflicts 107–9; distribution of central grants to 160–1; reform 39–40, 111–3; role of councillors 149; structure 79–80, 80–1, 84, 254
London planning 108, 116

Machine politics 158–9
Management theories: and adminis-
    trator's role 180–2, 273–6; con-
    flicts with political behaviour
    66–7, 279–80; neglect of politics
    51–2; treatment of administra-
    tive competition 88–9
Mannheim, K. 151–2
Marginal incrementalism 39–41
Meyer, P. 56, 62n, 121
Merton, R. 224, 257
Meynaud, J. 194–5
Millett, J. D. 72–3
Ministerial cabinets (France) 128–9,
    167
Ministers: numbers of 183; partner-
    ship with officials 164–7; rela-
    tions with departments 128–30
Monnet, Jean 167

National Coal Board 26
National Farmers' Union 156
Neustadt, R. 126
New town corporations 272–3

Office of Economic Opportunity
    (U.S.A.) 100–1, 251
Organisation theories and adminis-
    tration, 88–9, 248–61
Organisational loyalties 250–4
Overhead units 74, 135–6, 143, 145

Parliament (U.K.): and budgeting
    270–1; influence of members 155
Partisan mutual adjustment 39–41
P.E.S.C. (public expenditure survey
    committee) 270, 271, 272, 298
Planning: and decision-making 29–
    33; and polycentricity 44–8; in
    conflict with politics 157–8,
    299; see also Airport planning,
    Environmental planning
Plowden Report 203
Policy-making:
    influence of career officials 184–6
    influence of experts 206–9
    influence of interest groups 156–7
    relation to administration 149–52
    relation to goals and tasks 67

role of political parties 153–4, 156
    theories of 38–48
    see also Decision-making
Policy sub-systems 154–5, 156, 189
Political executives (U.S.A.) 169–74,
    184, 292, 293
Political parties 153–4, 156, 281
Political pluralism 89–90, 100–3,
    105–6, 284–7
Politicians: and administrative rules
    158–61; control of civil service
    182–90; methods of policy-
    making 152–5, 155–8, 161–2;
    qualifications of 291–3
Politicians and career officials:
    balance of power between 182–6
    comparison of style 187–90
    convergence of roles 186–7
    in France 166–9
    in U.K. 163–6
    in U.S.A. 169–74
    relations between 152–63
Politics: compared with administra-
    tion 149–52; with management
    180–1
Port of New York Authority 98
P.O.S.D.C.O.R.B. 49–50, 121, 123,
    124, 126, 132, 141
Position classification 229, 231–3,
    296–7
P.P.B.S. (Planning, programming,
    budgeting systems) 44, 114–5,
    271–2, 298
    see also Cost-benefit analysis
Presidency (U.S.A.): effect on ad-
    ministrative organisation 58–9;
    growth of staff assistance 125–7;
    limits of ability to co-ordinate
    127–8; recruitment of executives
    169–74
Prime Minister (France): adminis-
    trative experience of 167; res-
    ponsibilities for co-ordination
    138–9, 143
Prime Minister (U.K.): co-ordinating
    role 143; powers of 130–1; use
    of staff assistance 131–2
Process principle 56, 58, 78–9, 82,
    93–4, 96, 111, 113, 118, 263
Professionalism 255–6, 293, 296–9
Public accountability 22, 275–6,
    277–89

Public finance *see under* Budgeting
Public interest 177–80, 284–7
Public participation 278, 282–3, 287–8

Redcliffe-Maud, Lord 165
Regional planning boards (U.K.) 252–3
Resource efficiency, *see under* Budgeting, Government and business
Robinson, E. A. C. 211
Roads, organisation of 91
Roosevelt, F. D. R. (President) 125–6, 170
Roskill Commission (U.K.) 46–7, 212

Scarce supplies, organisation of 63
Schedule C posts (U.S.A.) 184
Science, organisation of 62
Scientific administrators: influence on reform 19–21, 125–8; theories of organisation 21–9, 48–52; theories of staff and line 121–5, 145; use of military models 22, 122–3
Selznick, P. 224, 258
Simon, H. A. 19, 29, 29–38, 40, 41, 48–9, 51–2, 55, 65
Simon, H., Smithburg D., and Thompson, V. 74, 135, 145
Snow, C. P. (Lord) 208, 216
Social sciences and administration 215–7
Social surveys 288
Span of control 27
Specialisation: and hierarchy 22–5, 204–6; described 23; effects on organisation 78–81; relation to unity of command 23–7
Specialists: *see under* Experts
Staff agencies: *see under* Staff assistance and Co-ordinating agencies
Staff and line theories 121–5
Staff assistance: and needs of executives 121–5, 141–2; for British Ministers 128–32; for French

Ministers 128–9; for U.S.A. Presidency 125–8; personal and institutional aspects of 123–5, 126
State Department (U.S.A.) 235
Storing, H. J. 35n
Systems theories 48–50

Taylor, F. 19, 22, 34
Technocracy 195, 206–9, 217
Technology, Ministry of (U.K.) 58, 62, 99–100
Tennessee Valley Authority 258
Thompson, V. 204–6
Town and Country Planning, Ministry of (U.K.) 140
Trade and Industry, Department of (U.K.) 61, 196
'Traffic in Towns' (Buchanan report) 115, 117
Transport, Ministry of (U.K.) 115, 196
Transportation planning, reform of 115–9
Treasury, the (U.K.) 93, 99, 103, 113, 128, 132–5, 137, 177, 178, 202–3, 211, 276; compared with Bureau of the Budget 133–4; style of control 134–5
Tullock, G. 235, 236

Unity of command: and specialisation 23–7; and staff assistance 122–3, 145
Urwick, L. F. 19, 21, 50, 122–3, 124, 129, 143

Vickers, Sir Geoffrey 110, 115, 193

Walker, N. 227, 239
Weber, Max 194, 224
Wildavsky, A. 41–2
Wilson, Harold (Prime Minister) 131
Wilson, Woodrow 20
Work units 72–3